Computer Literacy
Laboratory Manual

2018-2019 Printing

by

William T. Verts, Ph.D.
University of Massachusetts at Amherst
VERTS@CS.UMASS.EDU
http://www.cs.umass.edu/~verts/

Kendall Hunt
publishing company

Previously titled Computer Literacy Workbook.

Kendall Hunt
publishing company

www.kendallhunt.com
Send all inquiries to:
4050 Westmark Drive
Dubuque, IA 52004-1840

Table of Contents

Table of Contents
(Fine Detail)

Preface (2017)

What a long, strange trip it's been.

I was approached in the early 1990s to write a textbook for my computer literacy class. The first edition of that book came out in time for the start of the 1994-1995 academic year. Every year thereafter I spent most of the months of June and July rewriting the book for the following year. Every update added new material to the old, more through a process of accretion than through serious editing. By the middle of July 2016 the Computer Literacy Workbook was in its 23RD edition, sprawling across three spiral-bound volumes, totaling some 1200 pages, and representing a fair history of the development of personal computing over nearly a quarter-century.

It has become increasingly obvious, however, that the book as originally designed no longer completely serves the purpose for which it was designed, namely to be an introductory text and lab manual for the complete neophyte. Very few students come in to my classes knowing nothing of computers. Most have had some passing familiarity with Web browsing and word processing, and a few have used spreadsheets or designed their own Web pages. It is largely unnecessary today to tell people how to use a keyboard or mouse, and the average freshman tends to know more about social networking than I do. Memes abound of the beloved and bewildered parent or grandparent forced to ask their local teenagers how to "fix" their computers, how to get their email, use The Google, or locate the "any" key, but I don't tend to see folks like this in my classes anymore.

So, the publisher and I agreed this year that the first two volumes of the Workbook (the expository textbook material) could be excised, and the third volume (the homework and laboratory assignments) would be published in a new book called the Computer Literacy Laboratory Manual. Sold alongside my other reference text, the Computer Science Companion, this results in a significant cost-savings for the students and no longer requires them to lug around quite so huge a stack of paper.

I still anticipate spending time every June and July updating this Lab Manual (at least until I retire), but I do not expect that task to be as onerous as updating the whole 1200-page monstrosity the Workbook eventually became. This approach should be easier on all of us.

Preface (2018)

Students seemed to do quite well with just the Computer Literacy Laboratory Manual (and the Computer Science Companion) this year, and didn't miss carrying around a 1200 page textbook. The experiment was largely successful.

For this upcoming year there are few significant changes to the text of the Lab Manual, other than adapting the assignments to the near yearly changes in Microsoft Office for both Microsoft Windows and the Apple Macintosh. The biggest new change is to finally print the manual in color. This change should result in students having less confusion about what they see on screen as they perform the steps of each assignment – the results shown in the book will now more closely match the display on the computer than when the book just contained black text and grayscale images.

In a major break from tradition, I am <u>not</u> updating the Computer Science Companion this year. It isn't perfect, but it is good enough to last for another year or so before I inevitably feel the overwhelming compulsion to add new material.

This year I had over 800 students in six classes (three per semester), bringing my career total to nearly 24,000 students in 28 years of teaching. I have been nominated a number of times over the years for the University Distinguished Teaching Award, which is the only solely student-nominated award on campus. This year I won the award, becoming the very first faculty member in Computer Science at UMass Amherst to win the award. Yay, me!

Chapter 1: Homework Assignments

Introduction

The following pages contain individual homework assignments. If on-line versions of these assignments are available then they are to be submitted electronically and not on paper. Otherwise, you are to photocopy each page, then write your answers on the photocopy to turn in. Please do not rip the pages out of the book: each page has a separate assignment on the front and on the back, which will be assigned at different times. Also, I can't stand the thought of people ripping pages out of books. It's a character flaw, I guess.

It is your responsibility to get assignments in on time. No late homework will be accepted without just cause. We can be lenient if you are ill, but please let us know and have reasonable proof (a doctor's note).

Homework	Due Date	Score
Numbers		
Base Conversions & Binary Addition		
Gates, Patterns, Memory & Kilo		
General Knowledge and the Internet		
Scientific Notation		
MS-DOS		
Fonts and Typefaces		
Spreadsheet Formulas		
Units Conversion		
Databases		
EMail (do immediately after lab #2)		
Web Page (Extra Credit)		

DO NOT write your answers in the book and photocopy the result!
No such homework assignments will be accepted!
It is too easy to cheat that way.
Photocopy the page, then answer!

On-Line Versions of these Homeworks may be made available!
Check your Class Web Site!

At UMass use: `https://people.cs.umass.edu/~verts/coins105/quizzes/quizzes.html`

`http://`

Name		Do not write your answers in the book. If an on-line version of this homework isn't available to you, photocopy the blank page, then write your answers on the copy. Hand in the copy.
Teaching Assistant		

Numbers

<1> (12 Points) For each of the following numbers tell me if it is *integer, rational, irrational*, or *complex*.

A. -15.5

B. ⅔

C. 7+3*i*

D. $\sqrt{-7}$

E. i^2

F. 1

G. π

H. -½

I. $\sqrt{+3}$

J. -6.1234100238283

K. 0.333333… (the threes go on forever)

L. i^3

<2> (4 Points) A hypothetical computer uses 12-bit integer arithmetic.

A. What is the *smallest unsigned integer* that a 12-bit number can represent?

B. What is the *largest unsigned integer* that a 12-bit number can represent?

C. What is the *smallest signed integer* that a 12-bit number can represent?

D. What is the *largest signed integer* that a 12-bit number can represent?

<3> (4 Points) Perform each of the following computations using *complex arithmetic*:

A. 79+7*i* divided by 6-7*i*

B. 2+3*i* plus 6-7*i*

C. 2+3*i* minus 6-7*i*

D. 2+3*i* times 6-7*i*

Name		Do not write your answers in the book. If an on-line version of this homework isn't available to you, photocopy the blank page, then write your answers on the copy. Hand in the copy.
Teaching Assistant		

Base Conversions

<1> (7 Points) Convert the following numbers into decimal (base 10):

Source Number	Result Number (decimal)
1101101011001101_2 (binary)	
111010111_2 (binary)	
21102_3 (trinary)	
73577_8 (octal)	
$2FA3_{16}$ (hexadecimal)	
$2FA4_{16}$ (hexadecimal)	
$1AH_{20}$ (Base 20)	

<2> (24 Points) Convert each decimal (base 10) number into the indicated bases:

Base 10 (decimal)	Base 2 (binary)	Base 3 (trinary)	Base 8 (octal)	Base 16 (hex)
57				
255				
256				
999				
1,066				
1,996				

Binary Addition

<3> (4 Points) Add the following two binary (base 2) numbers together, then convert all three numbers into decimal (base 10) to check your result:

Binary
1 0 0 1 0 0 1 1 1 1 0
+ 1 1 1 1 0 1 1 1 0 1 1
=

➔
➔
➔

Decimal
+
=

Name		Do not write your answers in the book. If an on-line version of this homework isn't available to you, photocopy the blank page, then write your answers on the copy. Hand in the copy.
Teaching Assistant		

Gates

<1> (4 Points) Trace the following gate circuit, and fill in the truth table appropriately:

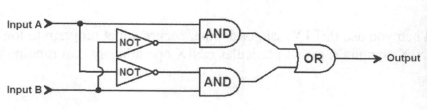

Truth Table		
Inputs		Output
A	B	
0	0	
0	1	
1	0	
1	1	

Patterns

<2> (4 Points) This problem is a base conversion problem masquerading as a "word problem". You are responsible for controlling the stage lights at a small theater. The control box has control switches for 10 separate lights, and each switch can make its corresponding light off, red, green, yellow, or blue. How many different patterns of lighting can you set up? Express your answer as a power, then calculate it out and write that answer down, too.

Memory & Kilo

<3> (7 Points) A "nybble" is often defined as one half of one byte of memory. How many...

    A. _____ Bits are there in a nybble?

    B. _____ Nybbles are there in 5 Kilobytes?

    C. _____ Bytes are there in 5 Kilobytes?

    D. _____ Bytes are there in 5 Kilobits?

    E. _____ Bytes are there in 5 Kilonybbles?

    F. _____ Bits are there in 5 Kilobits?

    G. _____ Bits are there in 5 Kilobytes?

Name		Do not write your answers in the book. If an on-line version of this homework isn't available to you, photocopy the blank page, then write your answers on the copy. Hand in the copy.
Teaching Assistant		

General Knowledge and the Internet

<1> (2 Points) True-or-False: A 3½-inch diskette is a "hard disk"?

<2> (2 Points) Yes-or-No: When you use PuTTY, ssh, or another secure telnet program to log in to an account on a remote UNIX computer, is that particular UNIX operating system running on your computer?

<3> (2 Points) Yes-or-No: Can I run a telnet session, an ftp session, and a Web browser over the same link to the Internet at the same time?

<4> (2 Points) I want to download a large file from the Web. If it is 8:00am where I am located in Massachusetts, should I download the file from a mirror site in California or from Germany?

<5> (4 Points) The following HTML code fragment contains a reference to an image file called frog.gif and with alternate text set to froggy, but the code as written contains a number of errors. Write the HTML line correctly.

```
<IMG SCR=frog.gif ALT=froggy>
```

<6> (4 Points) In a Web page I wish to define a color with the red value equal to 200, the green value equal to 7, and the blue value equal to 254.

    A.   What is the HTML color code (in hexadecimal)?

    B.   Approximately what color will be shown on screen?

<7> (4 Points) Consider the HTML color **"#E9F204"**?

    A.   What are the base-10 values that correspond to the individual hexadecimal red, green, and blue components of this color?

    B.   Approximately what color will be shown on screen?

Name		Do not write your answers in the book. If an on-line version of this homework isn't available to you, photocopy the blank page, then write your answers on the copy. Hand in the copy.
Teaching Assistant		

Scientific Notation

For these problems, N1 represents the number 1.23×10^3 and N2 represents 6.78×10^{-2}.

<1> (2 Points) How do the values of N1 and N2 appear when written out in their full-precision expanded form, and <u>not</u> in scientific notation?

    A.   N1 =

    B.   N2 =

<2> (4 Points) What is the value of N1 × N2…

    A.   …written out in its full-precision expanded form?

    B.   …in scientific notation, with full-precision?

    C.   …in scientific notation, rounded to two decimal places?

    D.   …in scientific notation, rounded to four decimal places?

<3> (4 Points) What is the value of N1 + N2…

    A.   …written out in its full-precision expanded form?

    B.   …in scientific notation, with full-precision?

    C.   …in scientific notation, rounded to two decimal places?

    D.   …in scientific notation, rounded to four decimal places?

Name		Do not write your answers in the book. If an on-line version of
Teaching Assistant		this homework isn't available to you, photocopy the blank page, then write your answers on the copy. Hand in the copy.

MS-DOS

<1> (20 Points) Assume that your prompt is C:\> and that you have a <u>blank</u>, formatted disk in drive A:. Write down the ***single best*** MS-DOS command you must type to accomplish each requested task. Each answer builds on earlier answers. You are NOT expected to actually do this on a computer, but instead keep a mental model of what is happening at each step.

    A.   Without leaving C:\, create a subdirectory at the root of A: called JUNK

    B.   Without leaving C:\, COPY a file called SAMPLE.TXT from the COINS105 subdirectory under the root of drive F: to the JUNK subdirectory of drive A:.

    C.   Make the A: drive the active (default disk drive).

    D.   What is the prompt that you see on screen?

    E.   Change the active subdirectory to the JUNK subdirectory.

    F.   Create a new subdirectory inside JUNK, also called JUNK.

    G.   What is the prompt that you see on screen?

    H.   Change the active subdirectory to the innermost JUNK subdirectory.

    I.   What is the prompt that you see on screen?

    J.   Without leaving the current subdirectory, issue the command to type out the contents of the <u>copy</u> of SAMPLE.TXT that you downloaded a little while ago.

    K.   What is the prompt that you see on screen?

    L.   In one command, change the directory to the root.

    M.   What is the prompt that you see on screen?

    N.   Change the default directory to the innermost JUNK directory.

    O.   What is the prompt that you see on screen?

    P.   Change the default directory up one level from where you are currently.

    Q.   What is the prompt that you see on screen?

Name		Do not write your answers in the book. If an on-line version of
Teaching Assistant		this homework isn't available to you, photocopy the blank page, then write your answers on the copy. Hand in the copy.

Fonts and Typefaces

For the first two problems, consider the following five typeface samples:

A.   Times New Roman

B.   Arial

C.   Lucida Console

D.   **Broadway**

E.   Courier New

<1> (5 Points) Which of the typefaces have serifs, and which are sans serif?

<2> (5 Points) Which of the typefaces are monospaced, and which are proportionally spaced?

<3> (1 Point) If a font is 36 points tall, how far is it in inches from the top of the ascender line to the bottom of the descender line?

<4> (4 Points) In the picture to the right, which pairs of letters can take advantage of kerning?

Name		Do not write your answers in the book. If an on-line version of this homework isn't available to you, photocopy the blank page, then write your answers on the copy. Hand in the copy.
Teaching Assistant		

Spreadsheet Formulas

<1> (4 Points) Cell F32 of your spreadsheet contains the formula:
$$=(B1*1.2-(AX25+B\$6-\$A\$1)+99)$$
If I copy that formula into cell Z60, what will the resulting formula in Z60 be?

<2> (2 Points) Cell FZ9 contains a formula that computes some number, but instead of seeing the number on screen, you see a bunch of ######### (Excel) or ********* (Lotus 1-2-3).

   A.   What is wrong?

   B.   How do you fix it?

<3> (1 Point) Cell G99 contains the formula =G89+1, and cell G89 contains the formula =G99+1. What is this error called?

<4> (8 Points) For the remaining questions, refer to the following spreadsheet model:

	A	B	C	D	E	F	G
1							
2			Jan	Feb	Mar		
3		Sam	2,000	6,500	4,000		
4		Mary	4,000	3,500	5,000		
5		Fred	5,000	5,000	1,000		
6							
7							

   A.   Write formulae in cells G3, G4 and G5 to compute the row incomes.

   B.   Write formulae in cells C7, D7, and E7 to compute the column incomes.

   C.   What is the result of the Excel formula =AVERAGE(C3:E5) or the Lotus 1-2-3 formula @AVG(C3..E5) ?

   D.   What is the result of the Excel formula =MAX(D4:E5) or the Lotus 1-2-3 formula @MAX(D4..E5) ?

Name		Do not write your answers in the book. If an on-line version of this homework isn't available to you, photocopy the blank page, then write your answers on the copy. Hand in the copy.
Teaching Assistant		

Units Conversion/Dimensional Analysis (Spreadsheets)

<1> (20 Points) Using the constants in cells A2:A9, create formulae for cells A12:A15 (surrounded by a dark line) to compute the corresponding "derived" physical constants indicated in cells B12:B15. Then create formulae for cells D18:D23 to compute product prices based on the corresponding input values in A18:A23 and the units in B18:B23. You may use constants from A2:A9 in your formulae, if needed. Write formulae only; do *not* write actual numerical results. For example, if I type any number for grams of Spike Nails into cell A18, then the cost in dollars for that quantity of Spike Nails should automatically appear in cell D18. You write the formula to go in D18 in terms of input cell A18 and the cell addresses of the required conversion constants. Use only cell addresses in your formulae; **do not use actual numbers**.

	A	B	C	D
1	Physical Units		Lumberyard Units	
2	10	mm per cm	$2.50	$/foot Cherry
3	2.54	cm per inch	$0.70	$/foot White Pine
4	12	inches per foot	$1.50	$/foot Red Oak
5	5280	feet per mile	$1.00	$/pound Finish Nails
6	453.5973	grams per pound	$0.75	$/pound Roof Nails
7	2000	pounds per ton	$900.00	$/ton Spike Nails
8	100	cm per meter		
9	1000	meters per km		
10				
11	Your First Set of Answers			
12		inches per mile		
13		cm per mile		
14		mm per mile		
15		grams per ton		Your Second Set
16				of Answers
17	Input	Quantity in Specified Units		Output in Dollars
18	?	grams of Spike Nails		
19	?	tons of Roof Nails		
20	?	grams of Finish Nails		
21	?	meters of Red Oak		
22	?	miles of White Pine		
23	?	kilometers (Km) of Cherry		

Name		Do not write your answers in the book. If an on-line version of this homework isn't available to you, photocopy the blank page, then write your answers on the copy. Hand in the copy.
Teaching Assistant		

Databases

<1> (9 Points) For each field described below, create a <u>reasonable</u> field name, then pick the <u>most appropriate</u> data type for that field. For text types, specify a <u>reasonable</u> maximum field width. For number types, choose the <u>best</u> sub-type. Where appropriate you must also specify <u>reasonable</u> default values and/or validation rules. Indicate which fields are <u>keyed</u> (suitable for an index), if any. Not all fields will have defaults, validation rules, or keys.

- A. The employee's ID number (between 0 and 9999).
- B. The employee's last name.
- C. The employee's first name.
- D. The employee's middle initial.
- E. The employee's salary.
- F. The employee's date of birth.
- G. The employee's number of children.
- H. The employee's marital status (single or married only).
- I. The employee's score on the last performance review (between 0.0 and 100.0).

<2> (11 Points) Examine the following sample database table:

	Part Number	Identifier	Price	Number In Stock
1	1024	Multifrequency Field Coils	$14,774.00	1
2	1132	Polymorphic Transducer Arrays	$2,278.34	12
3	6743	Starboard Power Couplings	$9,703.33	4
4	9999	Noncontinuous Injector Points	$479.12	15
5	5146	Plasma Containment Shields	$47,067.99	0
6	1001	Phased Array Sensor Modules	$31,000.78	3
7	1108	Antimatter Buffer Interfaces	$76,144.00	2
8	2994	Hamburger with a side of Fries	$2.37	2358

- A. How many fields are currently in the table (use both interpretations of "field")?
- B. How many records are currently in the table?
- C. What are the data types of all fields?
- D. What would be the first `Part Number` value if the table was sorted in ascending order on the `Part Number` field?
- E. What would be the first `Part Number` value if the table was sorted in ascending order on the `Price` field?
- F. What would be the last `Part Number` value if the table was sorted in descending order on the `Number In Stock` field?
- G. How many records would be in the result if I executed a query where the `Number In Stock` query box contained the expression `>3` ?

EMail

(10 Points) Do this assignment <u>immediately</u> after you have finished lab #2 (UNIX and the Web). You *must* first log-in to your UNIX account with your username and password. At the UNIX prompt, type the command `pine` to start up the pine email program. If this is the first time that you have run the mailer program you may get a couple of questions asking if you will allow it to create its own subdirectories on your account (answer "Y" for yes), or it may ask you to log-in to the mail program.

> **Your instructor will provide the correct recipient email address to use for this assignment. Write it in this box for future reference.**
>
> At UMass use: `literacy@cs.umass.edu`

Using the mail program compose a short message as described below.

- Type the recipient's email address in the `To:` field.

- Type your own student email address into the `Cc:` (carbon copies) field so that you have a record that you sent the message.

- For the `Subject:` field of the message type `Addresses for` _____ and put your full name in the blank.

- In the body of the message type the following text, <u>exactly</u> as you see it below, filling in the blanks with the correct address information. (The character spacing is not critical, but was done this way to align the corresponding text on successive lines.) Sometimes mail messages get garbled, and only the body of the message gets through, but not the mail headers.   To prevent problems and misunderstandings, for the first message that you ever send to anyone always include your full name and email address as part of the body of the message, as we have you do here:

```
Hello!  My name      is _____,
my email     address is _____,
and my Web address is _____
```

Please use a mixture of upper and lower case (if you compose your message entirely in upper case, people will think you are SHOUTING at them). **Do not add any additional information to this email message.** Send the message when it is complete and checked for errors. In many UNIX-based text editors, the "send" function is labeled on screen as ^X. This notation means [Ctrl]X, or hold down the [Ctrl] key as you strike X.

Web Page (Extra Credit)

(30 Points) This assignment is designed to be performed only after the completion of laboratory assignments #1, #2, and #3. Using the tools you learned in those assignments, create a new Web page from scratch for your site, called `extra_credit.html`, and put it into the `public_html` subdirectory of your UNIX account with the proper permissions.

The Web page that you create *must* include the following items to be considered for grading (if any items from the list below are missing, then don't bother to turn the assignment in; it won't be graded).

Colors: Your Web page must include color definitions for the background color and default text color. This can be accomplished through the `<BODY>` tag or through the use of Cascading Style Sheets (CSS). Similarly, in the body of your page you must also override the default text color in a few places using the `STYLE` attributes of heading and paragraph tags. All colors must be HTML color numbers of *intermediate* shades such as `"#12A5FB"` (i.e., you cannot use color names such as `"red"` or `"green"`, or fully saturated colors such as `"#00FFFF"` or `"#FF00FF"`, although a partially saturated color such as `"#00A5FF"` is allowed). Three-digit short-hex colors are allowed in CSS style definitions. The colors must be chosen so that all text shows up well on the background color, and the text color must be dark enough to show up when printed.

Images: You must include *at least three* artistic images of your *own creation* in your Web page, each one of which must be *at least* 200×200 pixels on a side. This means that you must use something like Windows Paint to create an image, and then save it in `.GIF`, `.JPG`, or `.PNG` format (Windows Paint for all current versions of Microsoft Windows will work fine here, as will the free Paintbrush program downloadable for the Mac). You are also allowed to create an `.SVG` graphic for <u>one</u> of your three images. The images cannot be simple scribbles, but must show some artistic effort on your part, and must be meaningful within the context of the overall Web page. You may include original scanned photographs as *part of one* of these images, so long as there are no copyright or legal violations (i.e., don't swipe somebody else's picture, and no porn!).

Image Map: In addition to the three images above, you must create one more image (of at least 400 pixels wide by 300 pixels tall) to be used as an *image map*, with *at least five* clickable regions on that image, some of which must be circular and some rectangular. You may create polygonal regions if you wish for up to two of the five required regions. These regions are to connect to valid Web sites, such as CNN or Yahoo, or any Web page of your choosing (so long as at least three of the five links are to pages outside of your local Web site). The map must *make sense*, in that using the image map must be intuitive, logical, and appropriate for where it is placed in the overall Web page.

Internal Links: At least one of your hypertext references must be to a point within the current page (an intra-page link). It must be properly labeled, visible, and in a logical place in the Web page.

Tables: There must be at least one table, of at least 4 rows by 4 columns, with at least one usage of `COLSPAN` and/or `ROWSPAN`. Cell contents must include ordinary text, links to other pages, at least one of your images that you designed above (it may be the image map if you so desire).

Lists: There must be at least one list, either ordered or unordered, with at least three list items in the list. List items may be ordinary text or hypertext links. The use of the list must be appropriate, and part of the logical design of the overall page.

General Formats and Guidelines: You must use horizontal rules, line breaks, paragraph breaks, heading tags, boldface, italics, and centering throughout your design. Your name and copyright © must appear in both the visible part of the Web page *and* in comments in the HTML code. Your HTML must be neat, fully commented, and properly indented.

As you should be able to tell, this is not an assignment that can be thrown together at the last minute for a few extra points. Your page must be artistic, and must be well designed and thought out. All of the items listed above must be integrated into a single coherent design. I don't want a bunch of half-assed pages turned in that sort of work and kind of have the right tags in them. I want a thoroughly unique project that you can be proud of. "Slapped together" pages, just to satisfy this assignment, will be rejected with extreme prejudice. Show some style!

You must turn in the following items:

- A printout of the Web page from a browser,

- A printout of the HTML source for the page from within the browser,

- The URL for the page so it can be electronically verified.

If the page cannot be referenced and rendered correctly from any and all Web browsers (Mozilla Firefox, Google Chrome, Apple Safari, Microsoft Internet Explorer , etc.), then no credit will be given. That is, you do not know which browser will be used to view and grade your submission, so it must look correct under all of them. If your submission was created by a Web design program such as Adobe Dreamweaver, Microsoft Expression Studio, etc., it will be rejected and no credit will be given. You must create the code by hand in a text editor.

Chapter 2: Laboratory Assignments

Introduction

This chapter contains a number of assignments to be solved in the laboratory. Various network systems will be configured in different ways, but the assignments can be solved on any system as long as certain software, files, and hardware capabilities are present. Those items are listed in each lab assignment, and are subject to change without notice as the hardware and software in the labs is upgraded. The lab assignments are as follows:

	Title	Date Due	Points Received
1	Web Design: The Personal Computer		
2	Web Design: UNIX		
3	Web Design: Graphics		
4	Word Processing: Words & Graphics		
5	Word Processing: Mail Merge		
6	Spreadsheets: Algonquians in Manhattan		
7	Spreadsheets: Design & Query		
8	Spreadsheets: Road Trip		
9	Databases: Handedness Statistics (Windows only)		
10	Databases: Joining Tables (Windows only)		

Check Lists and Grading Criteria

At the end of each lab assignment is a check list of the things that you are expected to have completed and turned in as part of each report. Also, after each check list you will find a set of criteria that the graders will use in scoring your reports. All reports are considered to be worth 10 points.

Student Responsibilities in the Lab

Most students will perform these assignments at home on their own equipment. If you seek help from the TAs in the laboratory, it is very important that you prepare properly ***before*** going there to work on your assignments. Students who monopolize the attention of the teaching assistants by expecting to be told verbally how to perform each and every instruction wastes the TA's time, pulls the TAs away from students with legitimate problems, and reduces the worth of the lab assignments to mere typing exercises. Even if it doesn't make sense the first couple of times you read it (and it probably won't), it is critical that you:

READ THE ASSIGNMENTS BEFORE GOING TO LAB!

RTFM!

Icons in the Lab Instructions

In several places throughout the lab assignments you will see icons to the left of a group of instructions. These icons are meant to be treated as a "heads up" to you to pay extra close attention to the text of the instruction. A list of the icons is outlined below:

 If you see the "keyboard" icon, you are to type in something special as part of this instruction (rather than using the mouse, or just reading background material). This can be an MS-DOS or UNIX instruction, a spreadsheet formula, or anything requiring you to use the keyboard extensively. Not all keyboard instructions are labeled, but those that are labeled are so important that you can really mess things up if you skip them.

 This "printed page" icon means that you are expected to print out a page or group of pages at the current point. Don't overlook or skip these sections, or you may end up omitting several pages from your final reports!

 The "pointing finger" icon is used to indicate a "tip" that you can follow to speed up or optimize the processes I ask you to perform. In a few cases you can get away with ignoring the tip, but by doing so you may take longer to complete the assignment. It is also used as a "heads-up" for something that requires close attention.

 The "yin-yang" icon is used wherever a set of instructions is different between versions of the same product or between different products with similar functions. You will see this where instructions differ for various versions of Microsoft Office, for different versions of Microsoft Windows, and where tools for Windows differ from tools for the Apple Macintosh. The vertical line to the right of the yin-yang is present to show you the extent of the instructions affected by the different versions.

 Danger, Will Robinson! If you see the "bomb" icon, you are looking at instructions that you must do exactly as you see them or they could cause a lot of trouble for you. Read the instructions very carefully!

 The stop sign is an indication that you can't go on until everything is just right. If you ignore the stop sign and continue on with the instructions blindly, a mistake made now may be extremely difficult to locate and fix later on.

 This symbol is for lab assignments that cannot be performed on certain versions of common software. In particular, neither Microsoft Excel 2010 Starter Edition for Windows nor Microsoft Excel 2008 for the Macintosh support *macros* (but later versions do), and there is no Microsoft Access database for the Mac at this time. If, at some point in the future, you have a version of Microsoft Office for the Mac which does contain Microsoft Access or you have a fully functional version of Microsoft Excel, then you may attempt those "flagged" lab assignments.

Lab #1 – Web Design: The Personal Computer

Introduction & Goals

In this assignment you will be learning the basics of using a computer. This includes techniques for managing disk files, use of a basic text editor to create pages for the World Wide Web, and use of a graphical browser for viewing those pages.

Specifics You Will Learn in This Assignment

You will learn how to run programs that have already been installed on the computer. You will learn how to manage the files on a flash drive or your hard disk, including creating subdirectory folders. One program that you will use is a text editor. In this text editor you will create the basic framework of a home page for the World Wide Web and save that page to a folder on your hard disk or onto a flash drive. Another program that you will use is a graphical browser for the World Wide Web. Examples of browsers include Microsoft Internet Explorer, Mozilla Firefox, Google Chrome, Apple Safari, and others. You will use the browser to access and view the Web page that you yourself created. (You will not make this page visible to the outside world until lab #2.) You will use a printer to print out your work to turn in.

Preparation before Starting Assignment

Read this assignment through in its entirety before doing anything. You may not understand everything on the first pass through the text, but having done so will make the assignment flow that much more smoothly when you actually perform all of the steps.

In the Laboratory

You will need to bring an empty USB flash drive (also known as a memory key, thumb drive, jump drive, etc.). Do not come to lab without a flash drive. Bring this lab assignment.

At Home

You may perform this and all subsequent assignments on a home machine as long as you have a "modern" version of Microsoft Windows. (Older versions of Windows such as 95, 98, ME, NT, or 2000 *may* work for some of the assignments, but nothing will from the Windows 3.1 era of the early 1990s.) An Apple Macintosh with a recent version of macOS or OS X may be used for all laboratory assignments except those that require the Microsoft Access database (labs #9 and #10). The Notepad accessory program is the standard text editor for Windows machines. On the Macintosh the equivalent program is TextEdit. Your system must have a recent Web browser installed such as Mozilla Firefox or Google Chrome (Microsoft Internet Explorer and Apple Safari are not recommended). You will need a working connection to the Web. You will need a working printer in order to turn in your final reports; monochrome is fine, *a color printer is **not** required*. You will need free space on the hard disk or an open USB port for a flash drive.

Data Files

There are no data files provided for this assignment. However, the files that you create in this assignment will be used in labs #2 and #3, so make sure you can find them again when you perform those future assignments.

Starting Up

In the Laboratory

All machines in the lab should be running, and should be configured properly for your use. Follow the screen instructions to log in (what username and password to type). After a few minutes you will see a normal desktop appear.

At Home

Turn on your computer and let it start up normally. If necessary, log-in to your personal profile. Wait until you see the normal desktop appear.

Step-By-Step Procedure

Getting Started: Using the Mouse (Point and Click)

Not that many years ago I had to teach students specifically how to use a mouse. People would roll it off of the pad and keep on going, waving the mouse around in mid-air! They did not know that it was O.K. to move the mouse back to the middle of the pad. If you need practice with a mouse, I suggest that you practice by playing a game such as Solitaire (if it is installed). If you prefer to use a track pad and one is available on your computer, practice with that tool instead of the mouse.

Grab the mouse with your right hand (I encourage even you lefties to use your right hand), rest the index finger of your right hand on the left mouse button, and your middle finger on the right mouse button, if present. Roll the mouse around and watch the actions of the cursor on screen. Make sure that you can quickly move the mouse from any place on screen to any other place on screen; this should become an unconscious act after a while.

 Do not proceed until the desktop is clean (no open windows, only icons on the desktop).

Creating Subdirectory Folders

In this section we will have you create subdirectory folders to be used throughout the semester to hold the various categories of files that you will create. You can create the class folders on the desktop, on the root of your hard drive, or on the root of a removable flash drive. Use a flash drive if you are at a public computer laboratory.

 If you wish to use a <u>flash drive</u>, insert it into the USB port at this time, and let the computer install the appropriate driver as necessary. Otherwise, use the hard disk.

Windows 95-XP: Click on Start-My Computer. In the My Computer window double click on the icon for the appropriate drive letter (use C: for the hard disk; use the correct drive letter for a flash drive). If Windows complains, close any dialogs that get in your way. Click on File, then on New, then on <u>F</u>older.
Windows Vista & 7: Click on Start-Computer. In the Computer window double click on the icon for the appropriate drive letter (use C: for the hard disk; use the correct drive letter for a flash drive). If Windows complains, close any dialogs that get in your way. Click on Organize-New Folder.
Windows 8 (desktop) & 10: Click on the File Explorer icon on the task bar. In the This PC folder double-click on the appropriate drive letter (use C: for the hard disk or another drive letter for a flash drive). Click the Home tab, and in the ribbon click New Folder.
Macintosh: Double-click the icon for the appropriate drive on the desktop (use Macintosh HD for the hard disk; a flash drive will appear with its own appropriate name). In the Finder, click on File-New Folder.
Alternate, Recommended: Right-click (Windows) or two-finger click (Mac) on the desktop, and then either pick New and then Folder or New Folder from the pop-up menu.

A new folder icon will appear in the window named New Folder (Windows) or untitled folder (Macintosh) and with a box or colored region around the name. The box indicates that you can rename the folder at this time. Type in Computer Literacy (including the space between Computer and Literacy), and hit the [Enter ←] key. The box around the name will go away and the folder will have its normal appearance.

Double click on the icon for the new Computer Literacy folder to open it.

Inside Computer Literacy, create a folder (Windows users can *right click* on the body of the window, then on New in the pop-up menu, and then on <u>F</u>older). Name this folder Word Processing, including the space between Word and Processing, and hit the [Enter ←] key.

Create a second folder inside Computer Literacy called Spreadsheets.

Create a third folder inside Computer Literacy called Databases.

Create a fourth folder inside Computer Literacy called Internet.

Create a fifth folder inside Computer Literacy with *your name* as the name of the folder.

Windows (all versions): *Right-click* the body of the window and select View-Large icons.

Macintosh: In Finder, click View-as Icons.

You will see something that resembles either of the following Windows 7 or Macintosh screens (the folders may appear in a different order from what you see here).

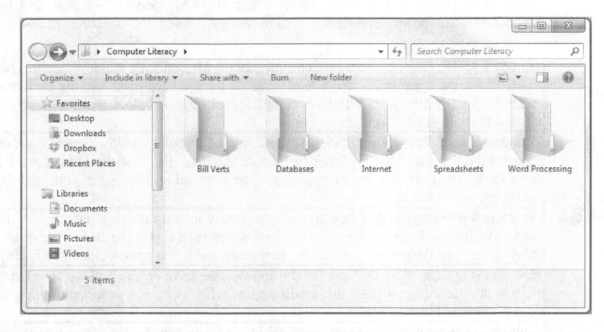

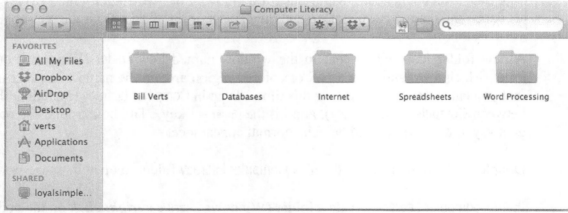

 Correct any mistakes in naming the folders. To rename, click once on the name of the folder, wait a second or two, and then click once again on the name. In Windows you can *right click* on the folder and then select Rename from the pop-up menu. In either case you will get the box around the name allowing you to type in new characters.

 Do not proceed until all five folders have the correct names, as you see in the image (with your name on the fifth folder, not mine!).

Verify that the Folders were Created

There are several methods that we might use to print out the directory information. The method below should work on any private home machine. Ask your instructor or TA what to do if there is an issue with using a computer in a campus laboratory.

Windows (all versions): Press the PrtScr key. This copies the screen to the clipboard. Click on Start-Windows Accessories-Paint or Start-(All)Programs-Accessories-Paint. Inside Windows Paint, click Edit-Paste to put the screen capture into the program. Click File-Print in Windows Paint (the screen capture may come out on more than one page).

Macintosh: Press ⌘⇧Shift3 on the keyboard. This creates a .PNG image file on the desktop containing the screen capture. Double-click the image file to bring it into the Macintosh Preview program. Click File-Print in Preview to print the file. When the file is printed, you may drag the image file to the trash.

Save the printout of your screen-shot for submission with the rest of your assignment.

Printing a Banner Page for your Lab Assignment

Now we will use a simple text editor to print out a banner for the assignment. Text editors allow you to enter raw text, without formatting (so you don't get boldface or italics for anything less than the entire document, or paragraph justification, and you have to hit the Enter↵ key at the end of each line). They are good tools for simple tasks, such as creating memos, notes, and short Web pages.

Windows: Click on Start-Windows Accessories-Notepad or Start-All Programs-Accessories-Notepad to start running the Notepad program. In **Windows 8** click on the Notepad tile in the Apps or Start screens. Maximize the window to full screen. Click on Format, and then verify that Word Wrap has <u>no</u> check mark. If Word Wrap has a check mark beside it, click it to turn it off. Click on Format, and then on Font.... In the dialog box pick **Courier New** for the Font, **Bold** for the Font Style, and **16** for the Size entries. Click on OK to close the dialog box. (Older versions of Notepad will have Word Wrap under Edit. In the oldest versions the Format-Font menu entry does not exist. Do the right thing.)

Macintosh: Open a Finder window, click Applications, and finally double-click on TextEdit. Click TextEdit-Preferences in the menu.

In the New Document page of the preferences dialog set the Format radio button to Plain text, <u>check</u> ☑ the Wrap to page check box, and <u>un-check</u> ☐ the Smart quotes, the Smart dashes and the Smart links check boxes. In the Font section click the change button for Plain text font, and in the new dialog set Family to **Courier New**, Typeface to **Bold**, and Size to **16**.

In the Open and Save page check ☑ either the Ignore rich text commands in HTML files check box or the Display HTML files as HTML code instead of formatted text check box (depending on which version of OS X you are using), and make sure the Saving Files and HTML Encoding drop-downs are both set to **UTF-8**. Close all dialog boxes. These settings do <u>not</u> apply to the current window, but only to new ones. <u>Close all editor windows.</u>

Create a new window with File-New. Type the following text into the text editor (most people will work at home):

If you have a formal lab time, type in:	If you work at home, type in:
Your name LAB ASSIGNMENT #1 WORK AT LAB *The current date*	*Your name* LAB ASSIGNMENT #1 WORK AT HOME *The current date*

The window should look as follows for Notepad and for TextEdit, but with your name instead of mine and the current date entered correctly (however, the file name will not be present on the title bar until after you save the file in the next step). Make sure that the font is set to **16-point Courier New, Boldface**:

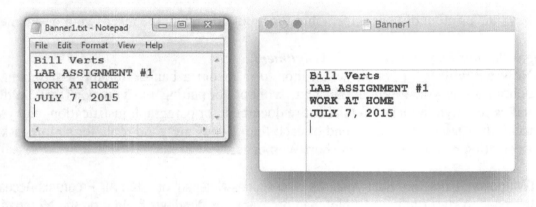

Windows: Click on File-Save As..., and in the dialog box make certain that the Encoding: drop-down list is set to <u>ANSI</u>. Navigate to your files and save the file as **Banner1.txt** in your Computer Literacy folder.

Click on File-Page Setup..., <u>remove all text</u> from both the Header: <u>and</u> Footer: edit boxes, verify that the Orientation is set to Portrait, and then click OK to close the dialog. Doing all this prevents the file name or page number from appearing on the printout.

Click on File-Print, and save the resulting sheet to hand in with the rest of your assignment. The sheet <u>must not</u> contain the `Banner1` file name or the page number.

Macintosh: Click on File-Save..., and in the dialog box make certain the Plain Text Encoding: is set to <u>Unicode UTF-8</u> (not UTF-16). Navigate to your files and save the file as **Banner1.txt** in your Computer Literacy folder.

Click on File-Page Setup..., verify that the Orientation is set to portrait and Scale is set to 100%, and then click OK to close the dialog.

Click on File-Print, make certain that the Print header and footer check box is <u>not</u> checked, print the document, and save the resulting sheet to hand in with the rest of your assignment. The sheet <u>must not</u> contain the `Banner1` file name or the page number.

Creating and Saving HTML pages

Windows: Start running a new copy of Windows Notepad.

Maximize the Notepad window to full screen. Click on Format, and then on Font.... In the dialog box pick **Courier New** for the Font, **Bold** for the Font Style, and <u>12</u> for the Size entries. Click on OK to close the dialog box.

Macintosh: Make sure that TextEdit is running. If not, launch it as you did before.

Click TextEdit-Preferences in the menu, and in the New Document page of the preferences dialog box verify that the Format radio button is set to Plain text, the Wrap to page check box <u>is checked</u> ☑, and the Smart quotes, Smart dashes, and Smart links check boxes are <u>all un-checked</u> ☐.

In the Font section click the change button for Plain text font, and in the new dialog set Family to **Courier New**, Typeface to **Bold**, and Size to <u>12</u>.

Verify in the Open and Save page that either the Ignore rich text commands in HTML files check box or the Display HTML files as HTML code instead of formatted text check box <u>is</u> checked ☑ (depending on which version of OS X you have). This is important! Forgetting to do this means that loading an HTML file into the editor at a later time will show the page as a Web page, instead of the HTML code that you want.

Close all dialog boxes. These settings apply only to new windows, so close all editor windows.

Create a new editor window with File-New. You may see a gray margin around all four sides of the page; this is O.K. (a side effect of the Wrap to page setting).

Type in the HTML code as shown on the next page.

- *Indent exactly 4 spaces per level.* Do <u>not</u> use ⟨Tab⟩ characters for indentation.
- *Capitalize the text exactly as you see it presented here.*
- *Hit* ⟨Enter⟩ *at the end of each line of text that you enter.*
- *Substitute your full name for mine* and *insert the correct date appropriately.*
- *Do not use any Web addresses other than those shown*, except that you may use your favorite news organization instead of CNN, such as NPR, BBC, etc.

You *cannot* show underlining in the text editor, nor can you show indentation lines; they are present only to show you what portions must be changed and where things are supposed to go. All of the <, >, and / must be entered correctly as shown. There are *two* <H2> ... </H2> pairs in the code; this is <u>not</u> a mistake.

```
<!DOCTYPE html>

<HTML>
    <HEAD>
        <TITLE>Bill Verts' Wonderful Web Page</TITLE>

        <STYLE TYPE="text/css">
            BODY  {background-color:#FF8000}
            H1,H2 {text-align:center}
            P     {text-align:justify;
                   font-family:'Arial';
                   font-size:16;
                   width:50%}
            HR    {width:50%}
            TABLE,TD,TH {border:3px solid black;
                   background-color:yellow;
                   text-align:center}
        </STYLE>
    </HEAD>

    <BODY>
        <H1>Welcome to Bill Verts' First Web Page!</H1>
        <H2>Last changed on July 18, 2017</H2>
        <H2>Copyright &copy; Bill Verts</H2>

        <CENTER>
            <P>
            This is my <B>first</B> web page for my computer
            literacy class, and I hope you like it.  It will
            be changing over the next few weeks, so keep checking
            back often!
            </P>

            <TABLE>
                <TR>
                    <TH COLSPAN="3">
                        My Favorite Links
                    </TH>
                </TR>

                <TR>
                    <TD>
                        <A HREF="https://www.yahoo.com/">Yahoo</A>
                    </TD>

                    <TD>
                        <A HREF="http://www.cnn.com/">CNN</A>
                    </TD>

                    <TD>
                        <A HREF="http://people.cs.umass.edu/~verts/">Dr. Bill</A>
                    </TD>
                </TR>

                <TR>
                    <TD COLSPAN="3">
                        <A HREF="http://people.cs.umass.edu/~verts/coins105/coins105.html">
                            COMPSCI 105 Home Page
                        </A>
                    </TD>
                </TR>
            </TABLE>
        </CENTER>
    </BODY>
</HTML>
```

Saving the HTML File

When you have completely typed in the text into the editor, click in the menu on File, then on Save.... Find the group of subdirectories that you created earlier (in the Computer Literacy folder of your hard disk or flash drive), and open the Internet folder.

Windows: In the Save as type drop-down list, choose All Files. In the File name edit box, type in `index.html` (all lower case, and replace any name that is already there), then click the Save button. Your file will be saved.

Macintosh: In the Save dialog box, type in `index.html` as the file name. Verify that the Plain Text Encoding: is set to UTF-8. If the Mac asks if you wish to use `.html` instead of `.txt` as the file extension, do so.

☞ Leave the editor open on the desktop, but <u>do not</u> print the `index.html` file at this time. You will print it out later, after you have verified in the Web browser that it is correct. You may need to come back to the editor to fix errors in your HTML.

Browsing and Correcting your own HTML file

In this section we will have you use a Web browser to view and print your Web page. Most Web browser programs should have icons visible on the desktop. Start your favorite, or whichever is there, by ***double clicking*** on its icon; when it loads it will show either a default Web page or a blank Web page. You may use Microsoft Internet Explorer, Mozilla Firefox, Google Chrome, or Apple Safari, as you see fit (Firefox and Chrome are preferred). Link to the file you just created, which should be on your hard disk in the Internet folder.

Microsoft Internet Explorer: To open a file, either type the file path into the location edit box, or click File-Open..., or key in Ctrl O, then in the pop-up click the Browse button, and use the dialog box to find your file.

Mozilla Firefox/Google Chrome/Apple Safari: Click on File-Open File... or File-Open, as appropriate, and then use the Open dialog box to find your file. The Windows shortcut is Ctrl O and the Mac shortcut is ⌘O.

☞ You should see your Web page appear on screen. To correct any errors, activate the text editor, make your changes, click File-Save, activate the browser, and then click its Reload or Refresh button. Your changes will appear in the browser window.

Repeat this process as often as necessary until your page is correct. When your page is correct, it should look like the image on the following page (but with your name instead of mine, and with the current date in the header). The view in your browser may differ from what you see here depending on the width of the browser window on screen. Word-wrap may cause line breaks to occur in different places in the text in the main body of the page; this is O.K.

What you should see (remember that line breaks will differ from what you see here due to the width of the browser window):

 Do not proceed until your page is correct! If any boxes are missing from the table, or are the wrong size or shape, then carefully re-check the HTML. HINT: In Firefox and Chrome, **right-click** the browser window and select View Page Source from the pop-up. The color-coded text will give you clues as to the locations of your errors. If the main body text is too large, look for errors in the <H1> or <H2> tags. Look for missing < or > or " symbols in the tags. If the links do not work, fix them.

Final Printing (Web Page)

 When you are convinced that the Web page appears correctly on screen in the browser, click on File-Print. Make sure that the printout will contain the date, name of the file, and the URL (the setup dialog for Firefox is shown on the left; Safari on the right). Print the page in **portrait mode**. **Do not print the orange background color! Don't waste ink!**

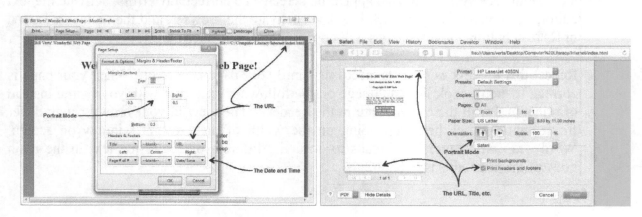

Final Printing (HTML Code)

Activate the text editor window (no changes should have been made since the last time it was saved). The format should still be **12-point, Courier New, Bold**. If not, take steps to make certain that it is.

On the Macintosh, the preferences should include Wrap to page. You can toggle between Wrap to Window and Wrap to page in the Format menu; make certain this is set to Wrap to page before printing. (When correct, you should see a set of light gray margins around the text on the screen.)

Click on File-Page Setup... and in the dialog box that pops up set the orientation to **landscape** (this will print your document "sideways" on the printer so long lines don't wrap around very badly). In Windows Notepad, remove all text from both the Header: and Footer: edit boxes to prevent the file name or page number from appearing on the printout.

Click the OK button to close the dialog box, and then click on File-Print to print out your HTML code. Your text may take a couple of pages to print, and there may still be a couple of wrapped lines. Do not worry about either issue; the file is what it is.

Shutting Down

Close both the editor window and the browser window.

Windows: If you are using a flash drive, click on the Safely Remove Hardware icon in the tray, and then select the flash drive. Wait for Windows to confirm that it is safe to remove the flash drive before pulling it out. *Never* just pull the drive out of the USB port without first informing Windows!

Macintosh: If you are using a flash drive, drag the icon for the flash drive to the trash. Remove the flash drive when all activity has ceased.

In the Laboratory

In laboratory settings, you may be required to "log off" rather than "shut down". This allows the next user to log in quickly without having to wait for the computer to start up. Take whatever action is required by your laboratory administrators.

At Home

Either shut your machine down normally or leave it running, your choice!

What to do if Something Goes Wrong

Sometimes things don't go as expected. Printers may not print, networks fail, etc. Don't panic! Most problems can be repaired without requiring you to do the whole assignment over from scratch. Here are some common problems, and hints on fixing them.

▪ If the Web page does not appear correctly on-screen, carefully check your HTML code. Remember to right-click and View Page Source in Firefox or Chrome to get clues to any syntax errors that may be present. One mistake early on can cause the entire page to vanish. On the Mac, Smart quotes (" and " instead of ") will cause the page to fail.

▪ If your banner did not print, or printed with the wrong font or point size, or was printed with header/footer lines, load up the text editor, open your `Banner1.txt` file from the disk, make any needed changes to the font settings, and print it again.

▪ If the HTML code did not print, or was printed in portrait mode or in the wrong font or point size, open your `index.html` file again in the editor, make any needed changes to the settings, and print it again in landscape mode. If it appears as a Web page instead of as text in Mac TextEdit, go into the preferences dialog, click the Open and Save page, check ☑ the check box labeled either Ignore rich text commands in HTML files or Display HTML files as HTML code instead of formatted text, and load the file again.

▪ When you click File-Open in Windows Notepad and guide the dialog box to where your file is stored, you will *not* see `index.html` listed as one of the files because Notepad by default is looking for `.txt` files instead of `.html` files; click on the Files of <u>t</u>ype: drop down list button (▼) and select All Files (*.*). The `index.html` file will appear in the file list.

▪ If the printout of your own Web page is missing, or is not in portrait mode, start up the browser, load in your Web page, and attempt to print it again. If the page prints but the URL is not on the printout, make the appropriate changes in the setup dialog.

What to Turn In

You will need to turn in the following items, <u>in the following order</u>, stapled together:

☐ Printout of the `Banner1.txt` page, in <u>portrait mode</u>, <u>16 point</u>, <u>Courier New</u>, <u>boldface</u>.
☐ Printout of the screen-capture containing a picture of the folder directory listing.
☐ Printout of your Web page from the Web browser (with your name in it) in <u>portrait mode</u>.
☐ Printout of the HTML code from `index.html`, in <u>landscape mode</u>, <u>12-point</u>, <u>Courier New</u>, <u>boldface</u> (with your name and current date in the text of the Web page).

Grading Policy

Lab assignments are worth 10 points each. Teaching assistants will observe the following criteria for evaluating and scoring the Lab #1 assignments that they receive.

- 1 Point - Report must be stapled together. Remove the full point if the report is paper-clipped together or is submitted loose (even with folded corners). Remove the full point if the pages are not in the order listed here (banner, folders, browser printout of `index.html`, HTML source of the `index.html` file).

- 1 Point - Printout of `Banner1.txt` must be present and must be the <u>first page</u> of the report. Remove the full point if the banner page is missing. Remove ½ point total if any required portion of the banner page is incorrect, or if it is not in 16-point, Courier New, boldface, or if it is not in portrait mode, or if header and footer lines were printed.

- 1 Point - The printout of the folder listing must be present and must be the <u>second page</u> of the report. Remove ½ point if any of the five subdirectory folders are missing or misspelled.

- 3 Points - Printout of the <u>Web</u> version of `index.html` must be present, in <u>portrait mode</u>. Give full credit if the page is obviously the same as the HTML page, 1 point if the two versions are related but different, 0 points otherwise. Remove 1 point if the printout is not in portrait mode.

- 4 Points - Printout of the <u>text</u> of the HTML code of `index.html` must be present, in <u>12-point</u>, <u>Courier New</u>, <u>boldface</u>, <u>landscape</u> mode. Make sure that the page contains all of the parts from the text box listed earlier in this assignment. Up to the maximum of 4 points, remove points as follows:

  Remove 1 point for stylistic problems such as poor indentation or for different upper/lower case in the tags. Remove 1 point if they added new HTML code or changed the color of the page. Remove 1 point if their name does not appear in both the <TITLE> section and the centered heading. Remove 1 point if any part of the <A> links is missing or wrong. Remove 1 point if any portion of the <TABLE> structure is wrong. Remove 1 point if there is any large section missing. Remove 1 point if an opening tag is not closed properly (for example, if it is obvious that the entire page has been formatted with the <H1> heading type, then it is likely that there is a problem with the </H1> closing tag). Remove 1 point if the printout is not in landscape mode. Remove 1 point if the printout is not in 12-point Courier New boldface.

Lab #2 – Web Design: UNIX

Introduction & Goals

This is an involved assignment in that it contains a lot of small pieces. No single piece is particularly difficult, but you need to perform all of them successfully in order to finish the assignment. In lab #1 you created a simple home page for the World Wide Web. Here you will move that page to its permanent location and make that page visible to the outside world.

Specifics You Will Learn in this Assignment

You will learn how to use the following tools and programs in this assignment:

- **Remote UNIX Server** – A server is a computer that you can "talk to" over the Internet. Physically, it may be located nearby, or half-way around the planet. You should be provided with an account on a server running the UNIX operating system. Your instructor will provide you with the host address of that server, as well as your username and default password.

- **Telnet / Encrypted Telnet** – You will learn how to use your personal computer as a "dumb terminal" to connect to the remote UNIX computer system.

- **UNIX** – Once you tie in to the remote computer, you need to know how to navigate. UNIX is the command line interface operating system that runs on many minicomputers, as well as the underlying layer of the modern Apple Macintosh. MS-DOS borrows a lot from UNIX, so if you are already familiar with MS-DOS much of UNIX will look familiar.

- **FTP / Encrypted FTP** – FTP stands for "File Transfer Protocol", and is a means of moving files from one computer to another. There is a UNIX version (which is text only) used for moving files between (primarily) UNIX computers, and both Windows and Macintosh versions that are used to move files between the local computer and remote UNIX systems. You will learn to use both techniques, some in this assignment and some in the assignment after this one.

In the next assignment we will also learn to use a UNIX-based text editor called emacs. Knowing how to use these tools means that all you *ever* need to have available to keep your Web page up to date (or even send and receive email) is some form of text-only connection to your UNIX account. This can be from a modern PC running Microsoft Windows, an Apple Macintosh, a dumb terminal connected directly to a UNIX computer, a dumb terminal and a dial-up modem, or an ancient PC of any vintage running as a dumb terminal.

Preparation before Starting Assignment

Read this assignment through in its entirety before doing anything. There are several Internet addresses that you must know for this assignment. **Write them into the boxes below.** Ask for help and updates from your instructor or TA, as necessary.

You will be provided with a user account (username and password) on a computer that runs the UNIX operating system. This computer is accessible over the Internet; you do not need to know exactly where the computer is physically located. This computer will act as the "server" for your personal Web pages.

For UMass Amherst Students

At UMass, every student has a default campus email address. For example, hypothetical student Fred Smith, with ID number 12345678, might have a campus address of the form `fsmith@umass.edu`, where just the `fsmith` part is his username. For this class, Fred would be assigned a new account on the server, related to but not exactly the same as the default campus address. The server for this class is a computer with `elsrv3.cs.umass.edu` as its host name, located somewhere in the bowels of the Computer Science building. I've seen it only once. The UNIX account provided for Fred would be `fsmith@elsrv3.cs.umass.edu`, with the same username but on the new host. Initial passwords follow the pattern `ELxxxaaa`, where `xxx` are the last three digits of the ID number and `aaa` are the first three letters of the username. Fred's initial password would be `EL678fsm` under these rules (upper and lower case do matter). Fred must change his password after he logs in for the first time. Fred's Web address would be `http://elsrv3.cs.umass.edu/~fsmith` (notice there is no `www`). In the table below fill in your own username into the blanks.

🖥️	**The Host Name for Telnet, FTP**	At UMass: elsrv3.cs.umass.edu
🖱️	**Your own Web address**	At UMass: http://elsrv3.cs.umass.edu/~_____
🖱️	**The Class Web address**	At UMass: http://people.cs.umass.edu/~verts/coins105/coins105.html
📫	**Your own email address**	At UMass: _____@elsrv3.cs.umass.edu
📫	**The Class email address**	At UMass: literacy@cs.umass.edu

In the Laboratory

Bring your flash drive containing the folders and the `index.html` you created in lab #1. Do not come to lab without this material. If you lost your flash drive, you will need to recreate the folders described in lab #1 on a new flash drive, and type in the HTML code for `index.html` once again. Bring this lab assignment.

At Home

Your home machine must satisfy all of the requirements of lab #1, but your home connection to the Web must be working, and additional software is required. The basic telnet and ftp programs that come with Windows and the Mac will <u>not</u> work with many remote sites these days because they use unencrypted communications protocols. Windows users must download and install an *encrypted* telnet program such as PuTTY (recommended) or SecureCRT, and an encrypted ftp program such as WinSCP. Macintosh users should use the built-in ssh program in place of telnet (from the Terminal application), but they need to download and install a graphical ftp program such as Fugu or a similar program. Your instructor may have detailed instructions on how to obtain them locally, as well as how to install them. Make sure you can locate the Computer Literacy folder on your hard disk or your flash drive.

Data Files

There are no data files provided for this assignment. You will use the `index.html` file that you created in the previous assignment.

At the end of this assignment you will have <u>two</u> copies of the `index.html` file: one on your local computer (hard disk or flash drive) and one on your account on the server. If you change one, the other will <u>not</u> automatically change as well.

Step-By-Step Procedure

Start or log in to your computer as you would normally.

Telnet / Encrypted Telnet

Encrypted telnet programs first negotiate an encryption key with the remote computer. If, at any time, any encrypted telnet program asks you any questions about the security of your particular connection, answer that the connection is valid and should proceed.

Windows: Locate the icon for the appropriate encrypted telnet program such as PuTTY (the free PuTTY program may be downloaded directly from its home site at `http://www.chiark.greenend.org.uk/~sgtatham/putty/`; download it directly to your desktop) and run it from there. PuTTY will ask you for the host name of the machine to connect to. Get this from the "Host Name for Telnet" box on the previous page (at UMass it will be `elsrv3.cs.umass.edu`). Make sure that the connection type is set to **ssh** (secure shell). When the connection has been established the remote computer will ask you for your username with a `login:` prompt (this is the UNIX computer talking to you via the PC). Type in your UNIX account username and hit (Enter ←). Fred Smith would type in just `fsmith` here.

Macintosh: Open a Finder window, and then click Applications-Utilities-Terminal to open UNIX Terminal. At the command prompt, type `ssh`, a space, and then your username at the remote computer from the "Host Name for Telnet" box on the previous page. Use your own username and the correct machine address. Here is what Fred Smith would type at UMass:

```
ssh fsmith@elsrv3.cs.umass.edu
```

The UNIX computer will give you a `password:` prompt next.

Type in your password and hit (Enter ←). The password will <u>not echo</u> back on screen (for security purposes). This means that as you type <u>nothing will appear</u> on screen. When correctly logged in you will get a UNIX prompt ending in a % or a > character.

You will get an error message if you did not enter your username and/or password correctly. Think carefully about what you typed in before making another attempt. More than four or five failures in a row will cause the server to block any more attempts from your IP address for several days (it will think you are hacking). Figure out what you are doing wrong (ask your instructor), then move to a different computer or move your laptop to a different wireless access point to get a new IP address. Messages such as `connection reset by peer` or `ssh-exchange-identification: connection closed by remote host` indicate that the server is blocking you.

On a Mac, do <u>not</u> type UNIX commands directly into Terminal without being connected.

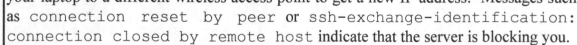

<u>Do not proceed</u> until you can successfully log in to a <u>remote</u> UNIX computer.

Changing your Password

Once logged in, you will be able to type in commands to the remote UNIX operating system and have it execute them. Remember that UNIX is completely command-based, and we will not be using the mouse. Your personal computer is merely passing your typed commands over the Internet to the remote computer running UNIX, and displaying its responses on your screen.

The <u>first time</u> you use your UNIX account you may be forced to immediately change your password. Often, new accounts are established by the system administrators with default passwords that are easily guessable or crackable. If this is the case, you must change your password <u>now</u>. After that, use your new password. Do not forget it, because nobody but you knows what it is. Your instructor may be able to *set* a new password for you if you forget, but he or she *will not know* your password after you change it.

Follow the guidelines on screen for changing your password. The system will ask for your <u>first</u> password again (the one you just used to log in), followed by a <u>new</u> password, followed by the <u>new</u> password again, none of which will echo to the screen.

For passwords it is a good idea to pick something that is not a real word, a string guessable by someone who knows you, or a sequence of letters or digits. Word-pairs might be O.K., but nonsense words or letters with numbers are better. Usually there is a minimum length requirement for passwords, often between six and eight characters. For example, `frog1234` is <u>not</u> a good password as it contains both a dictionary word and a sequence of numbers, but `snArgle9` is probably fine. Use something meaningful to you, that you will remember, and not the sample given here.

Once your password has been changed, the system may log you out automatically. If so, log back in as you did before, but use your new password from now on.

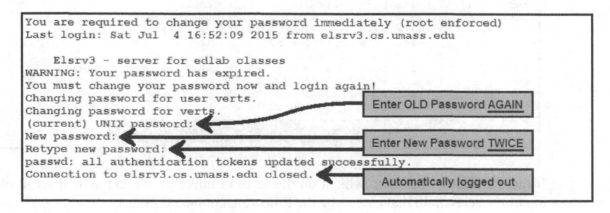

 If you forget your password, your instructor <u>cannot</u> recover it. However, your instructor will be able to reset your password back to its initial default value. Once you have logged in, use the **passwd** command to set the password to something more secure.

Starting up UNIX

Once you get into a UNIX computer system, you may not know quite what to do next because it isn't going to tell you. Both UNIX and MS-DOS are very unfriendly that way. You have to know the list of commands, and their options, in order to get any work done. Even if a command works correctly you will get the next prompt only, but *you get no confirmation* that this command actually did something! This can be very disconcerting if you aren't expecting it. It may not look like anything happened at all.

Whenever you are told to type in UNIX commands, you should assume that you will type ⌨Enter↵ at the end of each command. You will not be told explicitly to hit the ⌨Enter↵ key, but you should always do so.

First, we need to see what files are present already on your account. At the next UNIX prompt, type the following command (do not confuse 1, one, with l, ell; the command below is ell-ess-space-dash-ay-ell):

`ls -al`

Examine the file listing carefully. You should see something like the following:

```
                         The UNIX command you type
                                                        The UNIX permissions codes

elsrv3 ~) > ls -al
total 80
drwxr-xr-x   3 verts grad   4096 Jan 22 10:35 .
drwxr-xr-x 340 root  root  12288 Feb  5 10:02 ..          The "dot" subdirectory
-rwxr--r--   1 verts root    544 Jan 22 10:35 .bash_profile
-rw-r--r--   1 verts root   1640 Jan 22 10:35 .bashrc
drwxr-xr-x   2 verts grad   4096 Jan 22 10:35 bin.linux
-rwxr-xr-x   1 verts root   2614 Jan 22 10:35 .cshrc
-rwxr--r--   1 verts root    679 Jan 22 10:35 .doonce.csh
-rw-r--r--   1 verts grad     23 Jan 22 10:35 .forward
-rwxr-xr-x   1 verts root    256 Jan 22 10:35 .login
-rwxr--r--   1 verts root     76 Jan 22 10:35 .mailrc
-rw-r--r--   1 verts root     46 Jan 22 10:35 .netscape-preferences
-rw-r--r--   1 verts root  15090 Jan 22 10:35 .pinerc
-rwxr--r--   1 verts root    153 Jan 22 10:35 .profile
-rwxr--r--   1 verts root     22 Jan 22 10:35 .project
elsrv3 ~) > ▋
                         The next UNIX prompt you see, and the cursor
```

If there are more files than will fit on the screen (unlikely), the extras will scroll off the top of the screen. In that case, type the following command instead:

`ls -al | more`

Preparing the Nest for your Web Page

We are now going to perform the three "one time only" tasks that allow your account to support a home page on the World Wide Web. These commands are complex, and you have to get them right, but once you get things set up correctly you never need to do them again. The three primary commands are denoted in the instructions by the symbols ①, ②, and ③.

The first file in the listing is a strange file called **.** (dot). This is how UNIX knows where it is right now, and is a pointer to the current directory. Since you are logged into your own account, the **.** subdirectory is a pointer to your very own files.

On the listing (as shown on the previous page), check the permissions for the **.** subdirectory at the left side of the line. It may read something like `drwx------`, where `d` means "directory" and the rest means that you are able to read, write, and execute your own files but nobody else can touch your files at all (generally a good thing!). For people to see your Web pages, however, the permissions need to be set to `drwxr-xr-x`, which means that everybody else can read and execute your Web files, but not write (modify or delete) them.

If the permissions are <u>not</u> correct already, type in the following UNIX command to set your permissions to the appropriate pattern (don't forget the dot at the end):

```
chmod  a+rx,u+w  .
```

The command means change mode (`chmod`) on the **.** subdirectory to add (+) read (`r`) and execute (`x`) permission for all (`a`) people and write (`w`) permission for the user (`u`). Note: as written the instruction uses the <u>symbolic form</u> of `chmod`; you could also have typed `chmod 755 .` to do essentially the same thing using the <u>absolute form</u> of the command. Verify that your permissions are correct by listing your files again:

```
ls  -al
```

It is possible to lock yourself out of your own files with the `chmod` command. For example, if you accidentally typed `chmod a-rx .` with a minus instead of a plus, you would deny yourself the ability to read or write files in your own home directory. You cannot fix this problem by yourself, but must seek help from your instructor. It is likely that your instructor has the sys admin authority to reset your permissions.

 <u>*Do not proceed*</u> until the **.** (dot) subdirectory has `drwxr-xr-x` permissions.

Next, you need to create a special subdirectory for your Web pages. This subdirectory is called `public_html` (all lower case, and you <u>must</u> include the underscore character; it is not a dash and is not a blank). Type in the command:

 ②

`mkdir  public_html`

You will get an error message if the subdirectory already exists. At the next UNIX prompt, make the subdirectory visible to everyone by typing the command:

 ③

`chmod  a+rx  public_html`

Verify that the subdirectory was created and its permissions set correctly by typing the standard command to list your files:

`ls  -al`

You should see something like the following image, with your username instead of `verts`. Don't panic if you don't see everything in your listing that is listed here; the call-out boxes point at the most important items.

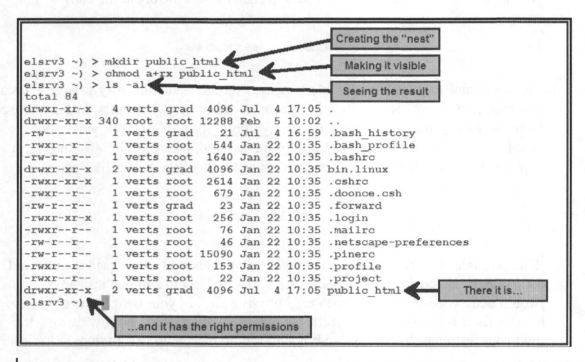

If you get the folder name wrong, such as `public-html` or `Public_html` instead of `public_html`, you can delete the folder by typing the UNIX command **rmdir** (remove directory) followed by the incorrect filename. Once done, go back to step ②.

 Do not proceed until the `public_html` subdirectory exists and has `drwxr-xr-x` permissions, and the . (dot) subdirectory also has `drwxr-xr-x` permissions.

Finally, change into `public_html` with the command:

cd public_html

Now, type the command:

ls -al

If you have done everything correctly up to this point, you should only see the `.` (dot) and `..` (dot-dot) subdirectories in this listing. Verify that you are inside `public_html` by typing the "print working directory" command:

pwd

You should see on screen something like the following image. You will almost certainly see a different starting path from what is shown here, but the path should <u>end</u> with your own username followed by `public_html`.

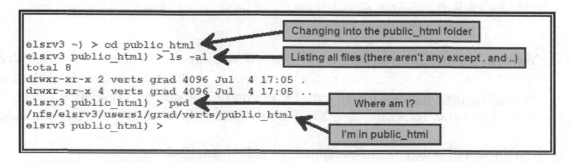

```
elsrv3 ~) > cd public_html                    Changing into the public_html folder
elsrv3 public_html) > ls -al                   Listing all files (there aren't any except . and ..)
total 8
drwxr-xr-x 2 verts grad 4096 Jul  4 17:05 .
drwxr-xr-x 4 verts grad 4096 Jul  4 17:05 ..
elsrv3 public_html) > pwd                       Where am I?
/nfs/elsrv3/users1/grad/verts/public_html
elsrv3 public_html) >                           I'm in public_html
```

 <u>*Do not proceed*</u> until you are certain that the working directory on the UNIX computer is the `public_html` subdirectory of the root of your personal account.

A Note for the Future

From now on, everything that you need on your UNIX account will reside inside the `public_html` folder. That means that nearly any time you log in (whether through PuTTY or through ssh), the very first command that you should type is:

cd public_html

to open up the correct folder. Failure to do so will mean that your actions will happen in the wrong place.

Installing FTP on your local Computer

Leave the encrypted telnet running and minimize its window.

We now need an encrypted graphical ftp program. An ftp (or file transfer protocol) program is used to copy files between two computers over the Internet. In the next assignment we will use ftp under UNIX to move files from a remote UNIX computer to the server hosting your Web pages. In this assignment we will use an ftp program running on your local Windows PC or Macintosh to move your Web page over to your UNIX account on the server.

There are a number of ftp programs available, such as WinSCP on Windows or Fugu on a Macintosh. These programs are <u>not</u> installed on your home computer by default. In either case you will have to download the appropriate package. If you find an ftp program that you like better than the ones listed here, or if WinSCP or Fugu become unavailable for some reason, then feel free to use that other package. For example, Fugu development has been discontinued, but packages such as FileZilla or Cyberduck may be used on the Mac instead. I like Fugu because it is simple to use.

Do not attempt to install software in a public or university computer lab. Such labs will likely already have one of these packages installed, and for security reasons such labs often forbid user software installations.

Windows: WinSCP (secure copy for Windows) is located on the Web at `http://winscp.net/eng/download.php`; make sure to download the current <u>Installation package</u>, not the advertised program. The correct installation package will have a file name like `WinSCP-XXX-Setup.exe`, where XXX is a version number.

Run the install program, and accept all the default suggestions.

Macintosh: Fugu for the Mac is an older package (not updated since 2011) located at `http://rsug.itd.umich.edu/software/fugu/`. There are different versions of Fugu for different versions of OS X; make sure to download the correct one (at least version Fugu-1.2.1pre1 for OS X 10.5 Leopard, OS X 10.7 Lion, or later, which <u>will</u> work under both OS X 10.9 Mavericks and OS X 10.10 Yosemite).

Drag the Fugu program from your Downloads folder to the desktop.

Note that simply double-clicking the Fugu program will generate an error message because of security issues. Your Mac cannot identify where the program came from, and does not trust it. Instead, ***right-click*** (or ***two-finger-click***) the program and select Open from the pop-up menu. You will get a dialog box asking for verification. Clicking Open in the verification dialog will let Fugu run on your Mac from then on.

Running WinSCP (Windows)

Run WinSCP. WinSCP will initially ask for the host name, your user name, and your password in the opening dialog. Enter the **_same host address_** that you used for the telnet session (just the host, not your username), listed at the beginning of this lab, and enter **_your username for the UNIX server_** and **_your new password_** in the appropriate edit boxes.

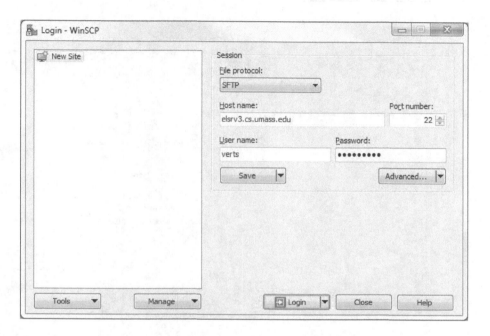

Once logged in, the left pane will show your local Windows computer, and the right pane will show the home folder of your account on the UNIX server. In the local side, navigate to where your `index.html` file is located. You should see something that looks like the following image.

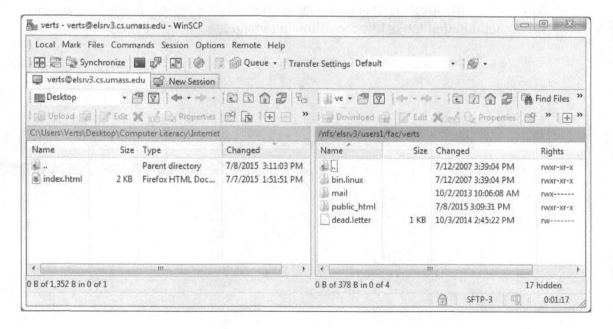

Running Fugu (Macintosh)

Run Fugu. In the Connect to: box, enter the ***same host address*** that you used for the telnet session listed at the beginning of this lab (just the host, but not including your username), and then enter ***your username for the UNIX server*** in the Username edit box (the default username will be for your Mac and is not likely to be correct). Click the Connect button. Type in ***your new password*** when Fugu asks for it in the next dialog box.

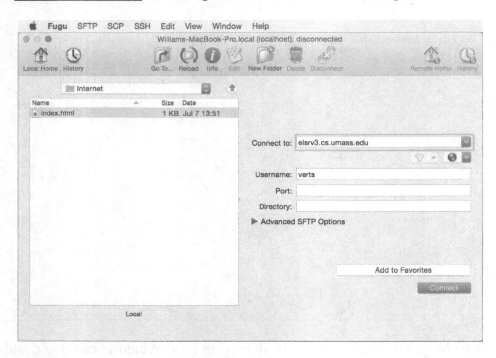

Once logged in, the left pane will show your local Macintosh computer, and the right pane will show the home folder of your account on the UNIX server.

Navigate on the local (left) side to where your `index.html` file is located. You should see something that looks like the following image.

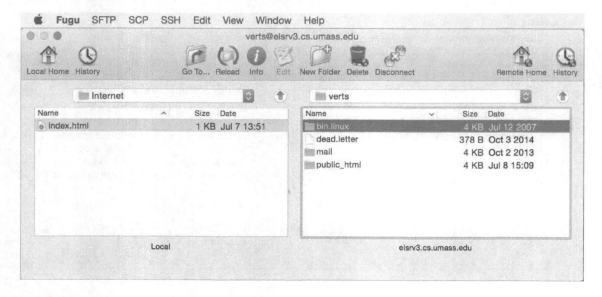

Moving your Web Page into the Nest

In the UNIX window of WinSCP or Fugu (the remote system is on the right side of the split screen), open the `public_html` folder by double-clicking on its folder icon. We are now (almost) ready to move `index.html` into the nest...

Ignore this paragraph if the `public_html` folder on your UNIX account is *empty*. Some people may already have an existing Web page on their UNIX account called `index.html`. **If you already have an existing, older Web page already called `index.html`**, then please rename our Web page to `myindex.html` before performing the following transfer steps. This is so you do not erase your existing work. If you rename the file, all further references in this assignment to `index.html` should be replaced by references to your new file name. **Do not rename** the file if `public_html` is empty.

WinSCP: Click the `index.html` file on the local system, and then hit [F5] to copy it to the remote system. (You may also drag the file from the left pane to the right pane to achieve the same effect.) In the dialog box that pops up select Text in Transfer Settings.

Fugu: Simply drag the file to the UNIX side. Fugu will use the correct transfer mode.

When the process is complete you will see the `index.html` file appear in the remote system's window. This file transfer is complete! These actions may be slightly different if you use another ftp program. Make certain to set the transfer mode to ASCII or Text, depending on the program, before copying the file to the remote computer.

Make sure you use the correct username and password. Messages such as `connection reset by peer` or `ssh-exchange-identification: connection closed by remote host` indicate that the server is blocking you.

Enabling Your Web Page

Bring up the telnet window again by clicking on its task bar or dock button. You should still be inside the `public_html` subdirectory (use `pwd` to find out, and use the `cd` command to change into `public_html` if you are not already there). Type in the following command:

```
ls -al
```

You should see `index.html` listed there. If `index.html` is <u>not</u> present, you may have moved it over to the root of your UNIX account, instead of into the `public_html` subdirectory. If there is a problem, go back and use the ftp program to move the file into the correct folder.

STOP *Do not proceed* until `index.html` is in the `public_html` subdirectory.

Examine the permissions mask on the index.html file in the listing; we want the permissions to be -rw-r--r--, but it is quite likely that they are different. If they are different, you must now explicitly set them to -rw-r--r-- (the leading - is not a permission, *per se*, but instead says that this is an ordinary file, and the remaining nine permission bits indicate you can read and write the file but everybody else can only read it). In the telnet window, use the chmod command to set the permissions appropriately, as in either of the following commands (do one of them, don't do both):

```
chmod  a+r  *.*
chmod  644  *.*
```

The first form of the command says to add (+) read permission (r) for all people (a) to all files with all extensions (*.*). If you choose to use the second form of the chmod command, the permissions pattern -rw-r--r-- corresponds directly to the octal number 644 (as before, the leading - indicates that this is an ordinary file, the permissions rw- mean $110_2 = 6$, and r-- means $100_2 = 4$).

Verify that the permissions have been set correctly by typing the command:

```
ls  -al
```

 Do not proceed until the index.html file is in the public_html subdirectory <u>and</u> has -rw-r--r-- as its final permissions mask.

Testing Your Web Page

Minimize both the telnet window and the ftp window to the task bar or dock, if they are not already minimized. Load up your favorite Web browser (Mozilla Firefox, Google Chrome, etc.).

Click in the location box of the Web browser, then type in your own URL (from the "Addresses" section of this assignment), and hit [Enter↵]. If everything works correctly you should see your Web page appear in the browser window, and it will look exactly like the version you created in lab #1. It *should* look the same: it's the same file!

If you get a message from the browser saying that the page cannot be found or that access is forbidden, one of the following problems is likely:
1. The index.html file is missing (you did not move it over to your UNIX account).
2. The index.html file is in the wrong folder (at the root instead of public_html).
3. The permissions on your account (the dot subdirectory) are wrong.
4. The public_html folder is missing or has the wrong name/capitalization.
5. There are multiple, nested public_html folders and you are using the wrong one.
6. The permissions on public_html are wrong.
7. The index.html file has the wrong permissions.
8. The index.html file has the wrong file name, such as myindex.html or Index.html or INDEX.HTML or something else.

Go back and review each of the required steps to see if you can find out where you made a mistake. You may need to seek help from your instructor if you have really tangled things up, but it is likely that a simple set of UNIX commands can undo all the damage!

 Do not proceed until you can view your page in a browser with your own URL (not just the version on your disk).

At this point your Web page is visible to **anyone** on the planet who happens to know your Web address! Congratulations! You have now just extended the Internet!

Printing

Launch a copy of Windows Notepad or Macintosh TextEdit, and set the font to **16-point, Courier New, boldface**. In Mac TextEdit remember to set the preferences to Plain text and Wrap to page. In Windows Notepad remember to remove Header and Footer text in the Page Setup dialog. Create a banner page for this assignment just as you did in lab #1, with the text at the top of the page.

If you have a formal lab time, type in:	If you work at home, type in:
Your name LAB ASSIGNMENT #2 WORK AT LAB _The current date_	_Your name_ LAB ASSIGNMENT #2 WORK AT HOME _The current date_

 Save this file with your other files on your hard disk or flash drive as `Banner2.txt`, and then print it in **portrait mode** with no filename or page number in the header or footer (refer back to the instructions in lab #1 if you do not remember how to do these steps). Close the text editor. This page will be the _top_ page of the report you turn in.

As you did in lab #1, print out your Web page in **portrait mode** with the File-Print menu commands. Make sure that the printout will contain the date, name of the file, and the URL (go back to lab #1 to see how to do this if you have forgotten). **Do not print the orange background color! Don't waste ink!**

Using the browser, capture and view the <u>source</u> of your HTML document as follows:

Microsoft Internet Explorer: Click on View-Source. Your HTML document will automatically appear in a Notepad window. Print in **landscape mode**.
Mozilla Firefox/Google Chrome: Click on View-Page Source, or *right-click* the window and pick View Page Source from the popup menu. The window that appears is <u>not</u> in Notepad, but you can pretend that it is. Print in **landscape mode**.
Apple Safari: New versions of Safari no longer have the View menu and cannot print HTML source directly. Mozilla Firefox and Google Chrome are browsers for both Windows <u>and</u> the Mac that can be downloaded and installed quickly, and both <u>can</u> print HTML source correctly. The printed text is a bit small, but the printouts have both the source and the URL. Please use one of these other browsers instead of Safari. Print in **landscape mode**. If you <u>must</u> use Safari, click Safari-Preferences, Advanced, and check ☑ Show Develop menu in menu bar. Then, click Develop-Show Page Source. In the title bar for the middle pane at the bottom of the screen, select Source Code instead of DOM tree. Select all the text (⌘A), copy it to the clipboard (⌘C), paste it into a new TextEdit window, and print from there (the URL will not print). Print in **landscape mode**.

Shutting Down

Type **logout** and [Enter←] at the UNIX prompt.

Windows: In PuTTY, <u>do not</u> hit the ☒ or other close button to close its window; it will close automatically when you log out.
Mac: You will need to type **logout** in Terminal as well to close the local session. <u>Now</u> you may close the Terminal window.

Close down the ftp program if it is still running.
Close down the browser.
Close down any text editor windows that are still open.
Close down your computer as needed.

What to Turn In

You will need to turn in the following items, in the following order:

☐ Printout in **portrait mode** of the `Banner2.txt` file in **16-point, Courier New, boldface**, with no header or footer information (title or page number).

☐ Printout in **portrait mode** of your page from the Web browser, showing your name and the address of the page on the printout.

☐ Printout from within the browser of the corresponding HTML code. **Landscape mode** is required, and the printout <u>must</u> contain the URL of your site. If you were forced to use Safari and TextEdit, the URL will not be printed as part of the document you turn in. In this case write **SAFARI** on the top of the TextEdit printout and no credit will be removed.

Grading Policy

Lab assignments are worth 10 points each. Teaching assistants will observe the following criteria for evaluating and scoring the Lab #2 assignments that they receive. The printout of the Web page should be identical to the one that was turned in for lab #1, except that now the Web printout shows the true Web address URL instead of a file folder as its location. The printout of the HTML source must match the browser version.

- 1 Point - Report must be stapled together. Remove the full point if the report is paper-clipped together or is submitted loose (even with folded corners). Remove the full point if the pages are not in the order listed here
  1. Banner,
  2. browser printout of Web page showing the URL,
  3. HTML source.

- 1 Point - Printout of `Banner2.txt` must be present and must be the <u>first page</u> of the report. Remove the full point if it is missing; remove ½ point if any required portion of the banner page is missing or incorrect, has the file name or page number in the header or footer, or if it is not in <u>portrait mode, 16-point, Courier New, boldface</u>.

- 4 Points – Remove all 4 points if the printout from the browser window is missing *or* if the student's name is missing *or* if the printout is present but there is <u>no printed URL</u> of the student's Web address *or* if the printed URL points to a <u>disk file</u> instead of to the Web. (Writing it in by hand does <u>not</u> count.) TAs must check the printed URL to make certain that it is a correct server address and not a file address. Remove 1 point if the printout is not in portrait mode.

- 4 Points – Remove all 4 points if the printout of the source HTML is missing *or* if the HTML version does not match the version from the browser *or* if the student's name is missing from the HTML. Remove 1 point if the printout is not in landscape mode. Remove 2 points if the HTML printout does not contain the same URL as the browser printout, <u>unless</u> the student has written **SAFARI** on the top of the printout (no penalty in this case).

Oh, By the Way... One Final Task

☞ Now that this lab has been completed, go look on page 13 in the **Homeworks** chapter at the beginning of this book for the **EMail Assignment** to send a message containing your name, email address, and Web address to the <u>class account</u>. That email assignment is <u>not</u> part of this lab, and is scored separately. The correct address to use should be in the table at the beginning of this assignment; if not get it from your instructor.

Lab #3 – Web Design: Graphics

Introduction & Goals

In lab #1 you created a simple home page for the World Wide Web. In lab #2 you moved it into its UNIX nest and made it visible on the Web. Here you will add some graphics to the page. You will learn how to edit files directly on the UNIX computer where they reside.

Specifics You Will Learn in this Assignment

You will learn how to use the following tools and programs in this assignment:

- **FTP / Encrypted FTP** – FTP stands for "File Transfer Protocol", and is a means of moving files from one computer to another. We will now use the UNIX version (which is text only) used for moving a graphic image from a remote site into the nest with our Web page.

- **Emacs** – This is a text editor for UNIX. It has far more capabilities than either Notepad or Text Edit, but it is considerably harder to use.

- **Scalable Vector Graphics** – While SVG files are most often created by a graphical design program, we will build one the hard way, by hand.

Now you have all the basic tools you will *ever* need to keep your Web page up to date!

Preparation before Starting Assignment

Read this assignment through in its entirety before doing anything. Refer to the appropriate addresses at the beginning of lab #2 for making telnet and ftp connections, as before.

In the Laboratory

Bring this lab assignment.

At Home

Your home machine must satisfy all of the requirements of lab #1 and lab #2, and your home connection to the Web must be working.

Data Files

There are no data files provided for this assignment. You will be using the `index.html` file that you created in lab #1 and installed on the server in lab #2. At the end of this assignment your UNIX account will contain a number of new files.

Step-By-Step Procedure

Start or log in to your computer as you would normally.

Log back in to your UNIX account with the appropriate encrypted telnet program (PuTTY on a Windows PC or `ssh` from within Terminal on an Apple Macintosh). If this seems unfamiliar, please review the appropriate steps in lab #2.

Change into the `public_html` directory with the UNIX command:

$$\textbf{cd} \quad \textbf{public\_html}$$

Type the `ls -al` command to verify that you are in the appropriate folder where `index.html` is currently residing.

Do not proceed until you are in the `public_html` subdirectory of your UNIX account, and `index.html` is visible.

Using Ftp (UNIX side) to find Image Files at a Remote Site

Now we want to visit remote sites across the Internet looking for graphics image files to include in our Web page (those with extensions of `.gif`, `.jpg`, or `.png`). Pulling images from any site on the Internet is often OK if you intend to use the images privately, but it is your responsibility to make sure that images you make public on your Web page are free from copyright problems. When you get some images, please do not use any that already have copyright notices or company logos embedded in the actual picture, inappropriate content, or material that can be easily identified (such as Sports Illustrated swimsuit images).

This portion of the assignment requires that we use the UNIX version of the File Transfer Protocol program. At the next UNIX prompt, type:

$$\textbf{ftp}$$

The prompt will change to `ftp>` instead of the normal UNIX prompt. You are now running the UNIX version of the ftp program (note that your instructor may have you run `sftp` instead). This is a text-only program, and is somewhat harder to use than the graphical version, but it allows us to transfer files from a remote UNIX site into our local UNIX account (something that the graphical versions of ftp cannot do).

Many sites that once supported ftp no longer exist, but as of 2018 working sites include:

`nssdcftp.gsfc.nasa.gov`	(United States),
`nic.funet.fi`	(Finland).

Type `open` followed by the name of the desired site:

open _____

This will establish a connection to the remote site. (If none of these work, your instructor will give you the address of an ftp site to use.) When the remote system asks for your username type `anonymous`, and when it asks for your password type in your own email address (it will <u>not echo</u> when you are typing it in). If the remote system *does not* accept your log-in, type `close` at the next ftp prompt and try to open another site.

Do not proceed until you have successfully logged in to a remote ftp site.

Once the remote system accepts your log-in, it will give you some introductory information. It may or may not be valuable; read it over quickly.

Afterwards, you will be left staring at an ftp prompt. Because this ftp program is text-only, we tell it what to do by typing in text commands instead of using the mouse. Here are the most common commands you will use (some should be familiar):

- Type **dir** to find out what is in the current subdirectory (this should be essentially every other command),

- Type **cd** _____ to change into (open) a subdirectory from the current directory listing by putting its name in the slot,

- Type **cd ..** to close the current subdirectory and return to the enclosing directory, and

- Type **pwd** to find out what subdirectory you are currently in.

EXPLORE! I don't know what you will find, where, or in what directory! Use **dir**, **cd** _____, **cd ..**, and **pwd** to navigate up and down through the subdirectories to look for `.gif`, `.jpg`, or `.png` files of **between 10,000 and 250,000 bytes** in size (the first candidate directory to try with `cd` is often called `pub`).

Do not proceed until you have found acceptable files to download from a remote ftp site.

Once you have found a suitable list of files, you need to fetch one to your local UNIX account. To make certain that the file is transferred cleanly, type the following command at the next ftp prompt:

binary

Now, <u>fetch the file</u> you want by typing the following command (fill in the complete file name of the candidate file into the slot after the `get` command below):

get _____

Repeat the `get` command for any other image files you wish to fetch.

Note that you do not have any information about what is in an image file except from its file name. Sometimes file names are clear and unambiguous (`doggy.gif` for example) and sometimes they are not (`P000067.jpg` for example). You are taking a risk that the image is inappropriate in some way; if this occurs, just download something else.

At this point you have moved files from the remote archive into your private UNIX account. Drop the connection to the remote site by typing at the next ftp prompt:

close

At this point you can open an ftp connection to another site with the `open` command.

When you are done browsing ftp sites, get out of ftp and back to UNIX by typing:

quit

The prompt will change back to the normal UNIX command prompt.

Did you do Everything Correctly?

Now that you are out of ftp and back to a UNIX prompt, <u>verify</u> that the files are in your UNIX account, by typing the command:

```
ls  -al
```

You may have to repeat the ftp session if any of the expected files are missing. If you did everything correctly, the image files should be residing in the `public_html` subdirectory of your UNIX account. One possible mistake could be to have copied the image files into the root (home) directory of your UNIX account instead of into the `public_html` subdirectory as expected. If so, you will have to move them into the `public_html` subdirectory by typing the commands from the following script:

<table>
<tr><td colspan="2"><u>Don't do this</u> unless you accidentally put your image files
at the root (home) directory of your account:</td></tr>
<tr><td><code>cd ~</code></td><td>(change into your home directory)</td></tr>
<tr><td><code>ls -al</code></td><td>(see if there are any image files here,
if not then skip all the mv commands)</td></tr>
<tr><td><code>mv filename1 public_html</code></td><td>(move first file)</td></tr>
<tr><td><code>mv filename2 public_html</code>
...</td><td>(move second file)</td></tr>
<tr><td><code>mv filenameN public_html</code></td><td>(move last file)</td></tr>
<tr><td><code>cd public_html</code></td><td>(change back into the Web folder)</td></tr>
<tr><td><code>ls -al</code></td><td>(verify that the images are present)</td></tr>
</table>

Set the Permissions on the Image Files

Still in `public_html`, set the permissions on the file you downloaded to `rw-r--r--` with the `chmod` command:

```
chmod 644 filename
```

<u>Test the image file.</u> Do this by appending the file name to your own web address:

```
http://hostname/~username/filename
```

The image should appear by itself. If it does not, then you need to check to see if the file was downloaded into the correct place and has the correct permissions.

 Do not proceed until you have downloaded at least one `.gif`, `.jpg`, or `.png` file from a remote ftp site and set its permissions correctly.

Creating an SVG File

Activate the telnet window if necessary (click on its task bar button). You should still see a UNIX prompt, and you should still be inside the `public_html` subdirectory. Verify this with the `pwd` command. We will now create a file called `Desert.svg` in the emacs text editor. Type the following command:

emacs Desert.svg

You will see a blank window, with a status bar at the bottom. The next step is to type in the SVG code to draw a picture of a simple desert scene, with a sun in the sky above a desert floor, with mountains in the background. Type in all of the text of the `.SVG` file, *exactly* as you see it here, but put in ***your name*** in the two underlined places where indicated (the underlining will not show up on screen).

```
<?xml version="1.0" encoding="UTF-8" standalone="no"?>
<!-- your name goes here -->
<svg
    xmlns:svg="http://www.w3.org/2000/svg"
    xmlns="http://www.w3.org/2000/svg"
    version="1.1"
    x="0px"
    y="0px"
    width="320px"
    height="240px">

    <style type="text/css">
        <![CDATA[
        polygon {stroke-linejoin:miter;stroke-width:3;stroke:black;}
        circle,line {stroke-width:2;stroke:green;}
        ]]>
    </style>

    <rect x="0" y="140" width="320" height="100" fill="#FF8000"/>
    <rect x="0" y="0" width="320" height="140" fill="#00FFFF"/>

    <polygon points="250,100 190,160 310,160 250,100" fill="#000080"/>
    <polygon points="250,100 230,120 270,120 250,100" fill="#FFFFFF"/>
    <polygon points="210,130 160,160 250,160 210,130" fill="#004040"/>
    <polygon points="270,140 220,170 310,170 270,140" fill="#008080"/>
    <polygon points="180,130 140,170 240,170 180,130" fill="#00C000"/>
    <polygon points="250,140 290,180 190,180 250,140" fill="#00FF00"/>

    <circle cx="50" cy="40" r="20" fill="yellow" style="stroke:red"/>

    <text x="5" y="135"
        font-family="Arial, sans-serif"
        font-size="10pt"
        font-weight="bold"
        fill="blue">
      your name goes here
    </text>
</svg>
```

Pay particular attention to indentation, spacing, and capitalization. Every line must be perfect; while some mistakes can be made without harming the file, many capitalization errors will be fatal. Some lines are likely to be longer than the emacs window is wide, so they may word-wrap as you type them in. This is fine, let them word-wrap.

 Type [Ctrl]x [Ctrl]c to **exit emacs and save the file**. Answer y when emacs asks you to confirm that you will be saving the file.

Now that the image files are residing in the public_html subdirectory, along with your index.html Web page file, you must make them visible to the outside world by typing the command:

```
chmod  a+r  *.*
```

As before, this adds "read permission" for everybody to all files with any extension. If you skip this step your files will not be visible on the Web.

Verify that all files in the public_html subdirectory have the correct permission mask -rw-r--r-- by typing the command:

```
ls  -al
```

Test the SVG file.
Append the Desert.svg file name to your own personal web address:

http://*hostname*/~*username*/Desert.svg

The image should appear by itself, and should look as follows (with your name instead of mine):

Fixing SVG errors

If the SVG file does not appear at all, check to see if the file was created correctly, is in the correct folder, and has the correct permissions.

You may have made a number of mistakes in creating the SVG file itself. If that happens, you will need to load the SVG file in emacs (`emacs Desert.svg`), make your changes, save the file, then test it again. Repeat the process until all errors have been eliminated.

In the following example, the SVG file appears in the browser, but the floor of the desert is the wrong color. Look at the text of the file in the editor, find the `<rect .../>` command for the desert floor (it's the first one), and then look at the `fill` attribute. The error is there.

This next example shows a case where the colors are all correct, but one point in a polygon has an incorrect coordinate value. You'll need to determine which polygon is in error and edit its coordinate. Because this is the white polygon, it will be the one where the `fill` color is `#FFFFFF` (the second one in the listing).

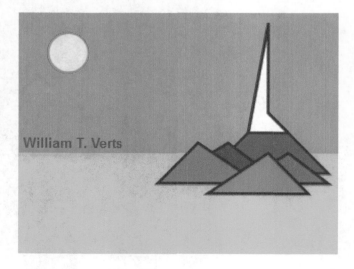

Sometimes it is not easy to fix problems because of a syntax error that prevents the SVG file from appearing at all. In the following example, the browser has identified the exact place where the error occurred. On line 19, at column 12, it found a character that it was not expecting, namely a " instead of an = sign. The = sign is missing. Going into the editor, counting down to line 19 and column 12, then putting in an = sign at that point fixes the problem.

```
XML Parsing Error: not well-formed
Location: http://elsrv3.cs.umass.edu/~verts/Desert.svg
Line Number 19, Column 12:

    <rect x"0" y="140" width="320" height="100" fill="#FF8000"/>
 ----------^
```

Here is an error that is not so easy to find. In the following example, line 12 is actually fine; there is nothing wrong with it at all. However, it is the first place where an *earlier* error was finally noticed. It turns out that there was a > symbol missing from the end of the previous line; the browser kept looking for the > symbol, but only realized that it was missing when it finally hit the < on line 12.

```
XML Parsing Error: not well-formed
Location: http://elsrv3.cs.umass.edu/~verts/Desert.svg
Line Number 12, Column 5:

    <style type="text/css">
----^
```

When you get a syntax error, start with the indicated line. If you cannot determine the error there, start scanning *backwards* through the text until you do find the mistake.

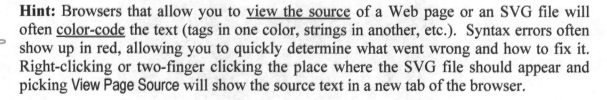

Hint: Browsers that allow you to view the source of a Web page or an SVG file will often color-code the text (tags in one color, strings in another, etc.). Syntax errors often show up in red, allowing you to quickly determine what went wrong and how to fix it. Right-clicking or two-finger clicking the place where the SVG file should appear and picking View Page Source will show the source text in a new tab of the browser.

Do not proceed until there is at least one `.gif`, `.jpg`, or `.png` file in your `public_html` subdirectory, along with `Desert.svg`, the file permissions have been set to `-rw-r--r--` on *every* file in that subdirectory, and all images are viewable in your browser.

Extra Credit

For **TWO POINTS EXTRA CREDIT**: Add the following lines to the SVG file <u>between</u> the two rectangle `<rect .../>` commands. This adds a perspective grid to the floor of the desert. **Test the new version** of the SVG file.

```
<line x1="0" y1="140" x2="320" y2="140"/>
<line x1="0" y1="143" x2="320" y2="143"/>
<line x1="0" y1="148" x2="320" y2="148"/>
<line x1="0" y1="155" x2="320" y2="155"/>
<line x1="0" y1="164" x2="320" y2="164"/>
<line x1="0" y1="175" x2="320" y2="175"/>
<line x1="0" y1="188" x2="320" y2="188"/>
<line x1="0" y1="203" x2="320" y2="203"/>
<line x1="0" y1="220" x2="320" y2="220"/>
<line x1="0" y1="239" x2="320" y2="239"/>

<line x1="-560" y1="240" x2="160" y2="120"/>
<line x1="-480" y1="240" x2="160" y2="120"/>
<line x1="-400" y1="240" x2="160" y2="120"/>
<line x1="-320" y1="240" x2="160" y2="120"/>
<line x1="-240" y1="240" x2="160" y2="120"/>
<line x1="-160" y1="240" x2="160" y2="120"/>
<line x1="-80"  y1="240" x2="160" y2="120"/>
<line x1="0"    y1="240" x2="160" y2="120"/>
<line x1="80"   y1="240" x2="160" y2="120"/>
<line x1="160"  y1="240" x2="160" y2="120"/>
<line x1="240"  y1="240" x2="160" y2="120"/>
<line x1="320"  y1="240" x2="160" y2="120"/>
<line x1="400"  y1="240" x2="160" y2="120"/>
<line x1="480"  y1="240" x2="160" y2="120"/>
<line x1="560"  y1="240" x2="160" y2="120"/>
<line x1="640"  y1="240" x2="160" y2="120"/>
<line x1="720"  y1="240" x2="160" y2="120"/>
<line x1="800"  y1="240" x2="160" y2="120"/>
```

The graphic should now look like this when you test it (with your name instead of mine):

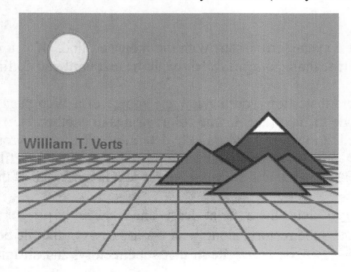

Changing your Page with Emacs

You should still see a UNIX prompt, and you should <u>still</u> be inside the `public_html` subdirectory. Verify this with the `pwd` command.

To activate emacs on the `index.html` file, type the following command at the prompt:

`emacs    index.html`

If you see a <u>blank</u> window, you did something wrong. Either you typed the command in incorrectly, or you were in the wrong subdirectory (likely), or the `index.html` file never got transferred correctly to the UNIX account. To exit emacs, hit the sequence `Ctrl`x `Ctrl`c, and then ask your instructor or TA for help.

<u>*Do not proceed*</u> until emacs has been loaded successfully, with `index.html` visible on the screen.

Once in your `index.html` file, **<u>change the date line</u>** to show the correct date for the current grading cycle.

In the HTML body (<u>not</u> in the `<STYLE>`...`</STYLE>` block, but in the main `<BODY>`...`</BODY>` section), open up a blank line between the `<CENTER>` tag and the first `<P>` tag. In this blank line, type in the following HTML commands (properly indented to match the indentation in the rest of the `index.html` document):

```
<IFRAME  SRC="Desert.svg"
         WIDTH="320"
         HEIGHT="240"
         FRAMEBORDER="NO"></IFRAME>
<BR>
<IMG  SRC="_____"            (Filename goes here)
      ALT="_____"            (Description goes here)
      TITLE="_____"          (Description goes here)
      WIDTH="320">
<BR>
```

The first command "embeds" the `Desert.svg` file into the document as an in-line frame (`IFRAME`).

Insert the name of your image file that you downloaded with ftp into the first underlined area of the `IMG` tag, and type the <u>same</u> short description of that file into <u>both</u> the second and third underlined areas.

The `<IMG SRC="...">` command inserts an "in-line image" (IMG) into the Web page. The source (`SRC`) of the image is the name of a local UNIX file (one of the `.gif`, `.jpg`, or `.png` files you found with ftp), and the alternate (`ALT`) text is descriptive text for people who view your page with a text-only browser and cannot see the image. All modern browsers support the title (`TITLE`) attribute to show fly-over text when floating the mouse over the picture, but older browsers only use the `ALT` attribute. Many of the images on the Web are very large, so the `WIDTH="320"` attribute scales the width to 320 pixels wide (and the height correspondingly) to easily fit the page.

The name of the file must be spelled correctly, and must match upper and lower case with the file on UNIX. For example, if I had a file called `verts.gif`, I would create the corresponding HTML phrase as:

```
<IMG SRC="verts.gif"
     ALT="My Ugly Mug"
     TITLE="My Ugly Mug"
     WIDTH="320">
```

 Type Ctrl x Ctrl c to **exit emacs and save the file**. Answer y when emacs asks you to confirm that you will be saving the file.

Activate the Web browser and point it at your Web page. It may be necessary for you to hit the Reload or Refresh button.

You should see your Web page appear containing the graphic images, with the desert scene on top of the image you downloaded through ftp. The color of the "desert" in the SVG file matches the background color of the Web page, so it looks like the image is part of the background.

 Note: Only the most recent versions of Microsoft Internet Explorer can display SVG files; if you have version 8 or earlier you <u>must</u> use another browser such as Mozilla Firefox, Apple Safari, or Google Chrome to view the desert scene.

What can go Wrong

If you do not see the images, first make sure that the file permissions have been set correctly. All permissions should be `-rw-r--r--` (read access for everyone, write access reserved for you alone).

In `index.html` you may have typed in the `IFRAME` or the `IMG` commands incorrectly, spelled the file names incorrectly, or used the wrong letter case in the file names.

In `Desert.svg` you may still have a number of mistakes that prevent the desert scene from showing up correctly.

To fix problems in the files themselves, reload emacs (either `emacs Desert.svg` or `emacs index.html`, as appropriate) and check the code carefully. Save any changes, and test your page again. Repeat the cycle as long as necessary.

The Edit Cycle

To update any portion of your Web page (such as adding content, including other graphics images, etc.), always follow these same instructions:

- Connect to the server and log in to your UNIX account.
- Change into the `public_html` folder (`cd public_html`).
- Load the editor (`emacs index.html` or `emacs Desert.svg`).
- Edit the text of the document.
- Save the new version of the Web page and exit `emacs` with Ctrl x Ctrl c
- Refresh the page in the Web browser to view the changes.
- Repeat the Load-Edit-Save-Refresh cycle as necessary.
- Log out when you are done.

If everything has gone well, at this time you should have a working Web page, visible from anywhere on the Internet, which contains a pair of images, one an SVG and the other a bitmapped graphic of some sort. The presence and visibility of this page is proof that you have performed all of the steps correctly.

 Do not proceed until your Web page has a working SVG file and an in-line image, and has the new date.

Printing

Launch a copy of Windows Notepad or Macintosh TextEdit, and set the font to **16-point, Courier New, boldface**. In Mac TextEdit remember to set the preferences to Plain text and Wrap to page. In Windows Notepad remember to remove Header and Footer text in the Page Setup dialog. Create a banner page for this assignment just as you did in lab #1 and lab #2, with the text at the top of the page.

If you have a formal lab time, type in:	If you work at home, type in:
Your name LAB ASSIGNMENT #3 WORK AT LAB *The current date*	*Your name* LAB ASSIGNMENT #3 WORK AT HOME *The current date*

Save this file with your other files on your hard disk or flash drive as `Banner3.txt`, and then print it in **portrait mode** with <u>no filename or page number</u> in the header or footer (refer back to the instructions in lab #1 if you do not remember how to do these steps). Close the text editor. This page will be the *top* page of the report you turn in.

Activate the Web browser window. As you did in lab #1 and lab #2, print out your Web page in **portrait mode** (now containing the graphic images) with the File-Print menu commands. Make sure that the printout will contain the date, name of the file, and the URL (go back to lab #1 to see how to do this if you have forgotten). **Do not print the ORANGE background color, so that the SVG file will stand out on the white paper!**

Using the browser, capture and view the <u>source</u> of your HTML document as follows:

Microsoft Internet Explorer: Click on View-Source. Your HTML document will automatically appear in a Notepad window. Print in **landscape mode**.

Mozilla Firefox/Google Chrome: Click on View-Page Source, or *right-click* the window and pick View Page Source from the popup menu. The window that appears is <u>not</u> in Notepad, but you can pretend that it is. Print in **landscape mode**.

Apple Safari: New versions of Safari no longer have the View menu and cannot print HTML source directly. Mozilla Firefox and Google Chrome are browsers for both Windows <u>and</u> the Mac that can be downloaded and installed quickly, and both can print HTML source correctly. The printed text is a bit small, but the printouts have both the source and the URL. Please use one of these other browsers instead of Safari. Print in **landscape mode**.

If you <u>must</u> use Safari, click Safari-Preferences, Advanced, and check ☑ Show Develop menu in menu bar. Then, click Develop-Show Page Source. In the title bar for the middle pane at the bottom of the screen, select Source Code instead of DOM tree. Select all the text (⌘A), copy it to the clipboard (⌘C), paste it into a new TextEdit window, and print from there (the URL will not print). Print in **landscape mode**.

Explicitly load the `Desert.svg` file by itself into the browser. As you did earlier, do this by appending the file name to your own personal web address:

$$\texttt{http://}\underline{\textit{hostname}}\texttt{/~}\underline{\textit{username}}\texttt{/Desert.svg}$$

The desert scene should appear by itself in the browser window.

As you did above, view the <u>source</u> of this document (you will see the code you typed into emacs), and print it in **<u>landscape mode</u>**.

Shutting Down

Log out of UNIX and close the telnet window.
Close the browser.
Close any text editor windows that are still open.
Close down your computer normally.

What to Turn In

You will need to turn in the following items, in the following order:

☐ Printout in **<u>portrait mode</u>** of the `Banner3.txt` file in **16-point, Courier New, boldface**, with no header or footer information (title or page number).

☐ Printout of your page from the Web browser, in **<u>portrait mode</u>**, showing your name, the **new date**, `Desert.svg`, and one graphic image acquired through ftp.

☐ Printout from within the browser of the corresponding HTML code in **<u>landscape mode</u>**. If you were forced to use Safari and TextEdit, the URL will not be printed as part of the document you turn in. In this case write **SAFARI** on the top of the TextEdit printout and no credit will be removed.

☐ Printout from within the browser of the `Desert.svg` code in **<u>landscape mode</u>**. If you were forced to use Safari and TextEdit, the URL will not be printed as part of the document you turn in. In this case write **SAFARI** on the top of the TextEdit printout and no credit will be removed.

Grading Policy

Lab assignments are worth 10 points each. Teaching assistants will observe the following criteria for evaluating and scoring the Lab #3 assignments that they receive. The printout of the Web page should be effectively identical to the one that was turned in for lab #2, except for the presence of two graphic images and a new date.

- 1 Point – Report must be stapled together. Remove the full point if the report is paper-clipped together or is submitted loose (even with folded corners). Remove the full point if the pages are not in the order listed here (banner, browser printout, HTML source, and then SVG source).

- 1 Point – Printout of `Banner3.txt` must be present and must be the <u>first page</u> of the report. Remove the full point if it is missing; remove ½ point if any required portion of the banner page is missing or incorrect, if it contains the file name or page number in the header or footer, or if it is not in <u>portrait mode, 16-point, Courier New, boldface</u>.

- 3 Points – Remove all 3 points if the printout from the browser window is missing *or* if the printout is present but the student's name is missing *or* if the printout is present but there is <u>no printed URL</u> of the student's Web address *or* if the printed URL points to a <u>disk file</u> instead of to the Web. (Writing it in by hand does not count.) TAs must check the printed URL to make certain that it is not a file address. Assuming that the browser printout is present, contains the student's name, and is visible on the Web, score it as follows (but do not remove more than 3 points total):

  - Remove 2 points if the browser version does not contain the `Desert.svg` file or if a "broken image" appears instead of the graphic.

  - Remove 2 points if the browser version does not contain at least one graphic from an ftp site or if a "broken image" appears instead of the graphic.

  - Remove 1 point if the SVG file contains data errors (lines or polygons with the wrong coordinates or colors).

  - Remove 1 point if the graphic from the ftp site is obviously "small" (fewer than 10,000 bytes), scaled to 320 pixels wide. Examples include tiny graphic symbols such as plus sign icons, and are not pictures of recognizable natural objects.

  - Remove 1 point if the browser version is not in <u>portrait mode</u>,

  - Remove 1 point if the date on the Web page has not been changed to the appropriate grading cycle.

- 3 Points – Remove all 3 points if the printout of the source HTML is missing *or* if the printout is present but the student's name is missing *or* if the HTML version does not match the version from the browser *or* if the student turned in the lab #1 or lab #2 printout for lab #3 without the addition of the IFRAME and/or IMG tags.

  Assuming that the HTML printout is present, contains the student's name, and corresponds to the browser printout, score it as follows (but do not remove more than 3 points total):

  - Remove 1 point if the ALT section is missing from the image tag.

  - Remove 1 point if the TITLE section is missing from the image tag.

  - Remove 1 point if the WIDTH="320" section is missing from the image tag.

  - Remove 1 point if the HTML printout does not contain the same URL as the browser printout, <u>unless</u> the student has written **SAFARI** on the top of the printout (no penalty in this case).

- 2 Points – Remove 2 points if the printout of the SVG source is missing *or* if the student's name is missing, either from the comment or the image.

  - Remove 1 point if the SVG source printout does not contain the same URL as the browser printout, <u>unless</u> the student has written **SAFARI** on the top of the printout (no penalty in this case).

Extra Credit Grading Policy

Assuming that the SVG file is present and visible, carefully look for any perspective lines on the desert floor. If the perspective floor lines are not present, then no extra credit is to be added. Otherwise, add extra credit as follows:

- +1 Point – Add one point extra credit if all horizontal perspective lines are present and are in the correct places on the desert floor of the image. Add only ½ point if some horizontal lines are present or if some are visibly in incorrect places.

- +1 Point – Add one point extra credit if all angled perspective lines are present and are directed towards the correct vanishing point (which is slightly above the horizon line). Add only ½ point if some angled lines are present or if some are visibly in incorrect places.

Lab #4 – Word Processing: Words & Graphics

Introduction & Goals

In this assignment you will learn the basics of word processing (editing a document, cut and paste, saving and printing). You will also learn to use a number of the tools associated with word processing that will make your documents more than simply words on a page. The tasks you will perform include using the clipboard to insert into your text "special" characters from different fonts and the result from the calculator utility. You will also learn to use a paintbrush program to create a graphic image that you can insert into your document as well.

Specifics You Will Learn in this Assignment

You will learn how to use the following tools in this assignment.

- **Microsoft Word** – This is the word processing program. It is large and will take a long time to learn to use well, but as you will see in this assignment you will be able to produce results almost immediately. While Word for the Macintosh generates files compatible with later versions of Word for Windows, its menu commands are very similar to those for the old Word 2003 for Windows.

- **Calculator** – Found in Start-(All)Programs-Accessories in Windows 7 and earlier, in the Start menu in Windows 10, and in Finder-Applications on the Mac. Rather than calculate numeric answers by hand, or with a pocket calculator, and then transcribe the results into your document manually, you will see how to transfer numbers quickly and accurately through the clipboard.

- **Character Map** – Found in Start-(All)Programs-Accessories-System Tools in Windows 7 and earlier, or in Start-Windows Accessories in Windows 10. On the Macintosh a similar tool is available through Finder-Edit-Special Characters. These tools provide quick and easy access to all of the typefaces and characters available to your computer, including special symbols and foreign language characters.

- **Paint** – Found in Start-(All)Programs-Accessories in Windows 7 and earlier, and in Start-Windows Accessories in Windows 10. There is no equivalent program that comes with the Mac, but freeware tools similar to Windows Paint can be downloaded from the Internet. One place to look is http://sourceforge.net/projects/paintbrush/ for a Mac program called Paintbrush. With a paint program you can create graphic images and save those images to disk files. These files may be copied and pasted through the clipboard, or loaded in from the disk.

Preparation before Starting Assignment

Read this assignment through in its entirety before doing anything. This lab does not depend on any earlier data files, but you will store new files in the directories created in lab #1.

In the Laboratory

Bring your flash drive containing the folders created in lab #1 and this lab assignment. Do not come to lab without these items.

At Home

Your home machine must have a working Web connection so that you can download the data file. You must have Microsoft Word available. If not then you must come into the laboratory to complete this assignment. You must be able to find the Computer Literacy folder and the five subfolders that you created in lab #1, either on your hard disk or on a flash drive. Mac users should locate, download, and install a free paint program.

Data Files

There are two data files for this assignment, called Top and Bottom, provided to you on the class Web site in a single compressed .zip archive. These files contain the top and bottom halves of an article about a former mayor of Portland, Oregon. You must download the archive and unpack it into your Word Processing folder.

Step-By-Step Procedure

Sit down at a machine in the lab (or your machine at home), and start it up normally.

Starting Up

Start up a Web browser, and point it at the class page where all of the data files are located (your instructor will give you the appropriate URL to use). Find the link for the data file and click on it.

Windows: The browser may bring up a dialog box asking you what to do with the file. Save the file into the Word Processing folder you created in lab #1. If the browser downloads files to some default folder, find and open that folder and drag the file from there into your Word Processing folder. Double-click the .zip icon to open the archive, then copy the two files contained inside and paste them into the Word Processing folder.

Mac: Macs automatically unpack the archive into a regular folder in the downloads area. Open it, then copy the two files inside and paste them into your Word Processing folder.

Do not proceed until the Word Processing folder contains the unpacked versions of Top.doc and Bottom.doc (Word 2003 and earlier for Windows) or Top.docx and Bottom.docx (later versions for Windows and for the Mac).

Starting Up Word

Find the Microsoft Word program and run it (it may take several seconds to start up).

Word for Mac: Click Word document, then click Choose.
Word 2007-2016 for Windows: Click Blank document.

On Windows, maximize the window by clicking its □ button in the upper right corner, as necessary. On the Macintosh, manually resize the window to a large size, as necessary, or click the green button in the upper left corner to maximize the window.

Word 2003 / Word for Mac: Find the tiny buttons in the <u>lower left</u> corner of Word.
Word 2007-2016 for Windows: Find the tiny buttons in the <u>lower right</u> corner of Word.

There will be three or more of these tiny buttons, one will be pushed in. As you float the mouse over each one, you will see their functions pop up. Move to the button where the message box says Print Layout or Print Layout View (this is called Page Layout View in Word 97) and click it if it is not already depressed. Do this <u>each time</u> you load Microsoft Word.

Word 2003 and Word 2008-2011 (Mac): Click on the View menu entry, and then on the Toolbars submenu entry. Since the Toolbars entry contains an arrow (▶), another menu will pop up to its right. In this menu, make sure that ***both*** the Standard and Formatting entries have a check mark (✔), but no other entries in the menu do. Check or uncheck the entries in this list appropriately.

Click on the View menu entry, wait for the menu to expand if Ruler is not visible (Word 2000), and then make sure that the Ruler menu entry has a check mark to its left. If it is not already checked, then click on the Ruler entry to make rulers appear to the top and left of the document.

In the top line of tool buttons, just under the menu line, you will see a drop down list containing a percentage. This is called the "Zoom" control. Click the drop down button (▾) and select Page Width from the list. You will see just the top part of the document, but large enough that you could read any text that you might type. The Zoom control box will now contain a number such as 88% or 114% or 144%, depending on your screen resolution, but the actual number does not matter.

Word 2007-2016: Click on the View tab in the ribbon. Make sure there is a check mark (✔) in the box next to Ruler in the Show/Hide or Show panel, and that no other entries in that panel are checked.

Still in the View tab, click on the Zoom button in the Zoom panel, and select Page width from the pop-up dialog box. The Zoom percent setting will contain a number such as 88%, 114%, or 144%, but the actual number does not matter. Alternatively, you could click the Page Width shortcut button visible in the Zoom panel. Click OK to finish.

 <u>*Do not proceed*</u> until you see the rulers on screen.

Setting Margins

The image below shows a view of the ruler with its control buttons labeled. Set a 1½ inch left margin and a 1½ inch right margin, with no indentation. Set the left margin first, and then set the right margin once the left margin is correct.

Be careful when you set the left and right margins to put the mouse on the very tiny area between the indent buttons, where the mouse cursor turns into a small double headed arrow; it is easy to hit one of the indent buttons by mistake. (Tip: if you hold down the Alt or Option key as you click-drag each item on the ruler, the ruler will show its absolute position measurements in inches.) Your ruler settings should look something like this:

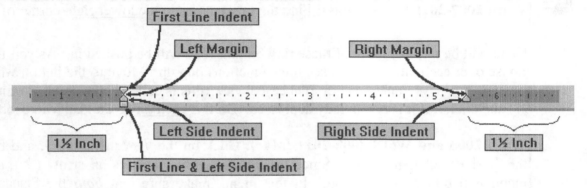

 Word 2003 / Word 2008-2011 (Mac): In the Zoom box drop down list, select Whole Page from the list.

Word 2007-2016: In the View tab of the ribbon click the Zoom button then in the pop-up dialog select Whole page from the list, and then click OK to close the dialog. Alternatively, you could click the One Page button in the Zoom panel.

You will see the entire page of the document appear on screen, but any text that you type in this view will be too small to read. Set the top and bottom margins to approximately 1½ inch each by click dragging on the ruler at the **_left side_** of the window (this is not the best way of setting the margins, but we will have you do it a better way in a future assignment).

 Do not proceed until you have a 1½ inch margin around the entire document (at the top, bottom, left, and right sides). Make sure that all three indent buttons are flush with their respective margins.

Restore the Zoom setting to Page Width.

The First (Banner) Page

In the empty document window that appears, type:

- Your name [Enter ⏎],
- the phrase LAB ASSIGNMENT #4 [Enter ⏎],
- either WORK AT LAB or WORK AT HOME [Enter ⏎], and
- the current date [Enter ⏎]

Each line is a single-line paragraph.

Select these four lines (entirely cover all four single-line paragraphs), then:

- Set the typeface to Times New Roman.
- Change the size to 20 points.

Bring up the Paragraph dialog box as follows:

Word 2003 / Word 2008-2011 (Mac): Click on Format-Paragraph...

Word 2007-2016: go to the Home tab and click on the tiny arrow at the bottom right corner of the Paragraph panel

- In the Indents and Spacing tab, click on the Alignment: drop down list and select Centered.
- In the Line spacing: drop down list select Single.
- Set any Before: or After: values to <u>zero</u>.
- Click OK.

Click the mouse in the window <u>below</u> the line containing the date. The selection (which was covering all four lines of text) will collapse down to a blinking insertion point. The four lines of text should now be in 20-point Times New Roman, centered on the screen, and single-spaced, with the cursor below the last line.

Word 2003-2016: Hold down the [Ctrl] key with one hand and strike the [Enter ⏎] key with the other. This action inserts a page break into the text.

Word 2008-2011 (Mac): Click in the menu on Insert-Break-Page Break. This action inserts a page break into the text.

Do not proceed until you have the four banner lines on page 1, set to 20-point Times New Roman with no extra white space between the lines, and a blank page 2.

Saving

Save your document to the Word Processing folder that you created in lab #1.

Word 2003: Click on the File-Save <u>A</u>s... menu. In the Save As... dialog box make sure that the Save in: control points at your Word Processing folder. Save the document as **LAB4.DOC** in your Word Processing folder.

Word 2007: Click on the Office Button-Save As-Word Document menu. In the Save As dialog box make sure that it points at your Word Processing folder. Save the document as **LAB4.DOCX** in your Word Processing folder.

Word 2010-2016: Click on the File tab in the ribbon, then click Save As from the menu. In **Word 2013/2016** click the Browse button next. Point the Save As dialog box at your Word Processing folder. Save the document as **LAB4.DOCX** in your Word Processing folder.

Word 2008-2011 (Mac): Click on the File-Save <u>A</u>s... menu. In the Save As... dialog box make sure that the Save in: or folder control points at your Word Processing folder. Save the document as **LAB4.DOCX** in your Word Processing folder.

Hint: Once the file has been successfully saved to your Word Processing folder, the easiest way to save any subsequent changes is to hit Ctrl S in Windows or ⌘S on the Macintosh. You should do this frequently.

The Document Pieces

Now we need to load in the two documents that you downloaded from the class Web site.

Word 2003 / Word 2008-2011 (Mac): Click on the F̲ile-O̲pen... menu, then load in the `Top` document from your Word Processing folder. Your `LAB4` document will temporarily disappear. Repeat the steps to load in `Bottom` as well. At this point, Word will have `LAB4`, `Top`, and `Bottom` all loaded into individual windows. Use the W̲indow menu entry to practice switching between the three loaded documents (at the bottom of the W̲indow drop down menu you will see the names of the three documents with a number in front of each; the *active* document will have a check mark).

Word 2007: Click on Office Button-Open, then load in `Top.docx` from your Word Processing folder. Your `LAB4.docx` document will temporarily disappear. Repeat the steps to load in `Bottom.docx` as well. At this point, you will have `LAB4.docx`, `Top.docx`, and `Bottom.docx` all loaded into what looks like individual copies of Word, each with its own button on the task bar.

Word 2010-2016: Click on the File tab in the ribbon, and then on Open. In **Word 2013** click Computer. In **Word 2013/2016** click the Browse button. Load in `Top.docx` from your Word Processing folder. Your `LAB4.docx` document will temporarily disappear. If you get a message warning that the file originated from an Internet location, click the Enable Editing button. Repeat the steps to load in `Bottom.docx` as well. At this point, you will have `LAB4.docx`, `Top.docx`, and `Bottom.docx` all loaded into what looks like individual copies of Word, each with its own button or preview icon on the task bar.

Set the window size (zoom) of the window containing the `Top` document to Page Width.

Set the `Bottom` document size to Page Width as well.

Do not proceed until all three windows (`LAB4`, `Top`, and `Bottom`) are loaded into Word and have been sized appropriately.

Stitching the Pieces Together

Word 2003 / Word 2008-2011 (Mac): Make the Top document active. In the menu click on Edit-Select All, then on Edit-Copy to copy the entire document to the clipboard. Switch back to the LAB4 document, click at the bottom of the document (which will be on page 2, after the page break that we inserted), then click Edit-Paste to paste the clipboard contents into the current document. The text from Top will appear at the top of page 2 (remember that page 1 of LAB4 contains the banner information).

Word 2007-2016: Make the Top document active. In the Home tab of the ribbon, go to the Editing panel and click on Select-Select All, then in the Clipboard panel click on Copy to copy the entire document to the clipboard. Switch back to the LAB4 document, click at the bottom of the document (which will be on page 2, after the page break that we inserted), then in the Home tab of the ribbon click Paste in the Clipboard panel to paste the clipboard contents into the current document. The text from Top will appear at the top of page 2 (remember that page 1 of LAB4 contains the banner information).

Switch to the window containing the Bottom document.

Repeat the copy and paste process to copy the entire contents of Bottom onto the <u>bottom</u> of the LAB4 document <u>after</u> the section we pasted earlier.

<u>Delete any blank lines</u> that appear <u>between</u> the two pieces of the document.

Switch to the window containing the Top document.

Word 2003 / Word 2008-2011 (Mac): Click on File-Close to close the window.

Word 2007: Click on Office Button-Close to close the window.

Word 2010-2016: Click on the File tab, and then click Close to close the window.

If Word asks if you wish to save any changes to Top, answer "No" (it should not ask if you have done everything correctly).

Close the Bottom document window as well. Do not save any changes to this window if asked.

You should now be somewhere in the LAB4 document window (it will be the only Word window left). Browse and read the completed document.

Save your LAB4 document now.

Do not proceed until LAB4 contains the banner page and the contents of both source documents, in the correct order and with no extra blank lines in the body of the text.

The Calculator

Windows: Click Start-All Programs-Accessories-Calculator (Windows 7 or earlier) or Start-Calculator or Start-Windows Accessories-Calculator (Windows 10) to start the calculator program. In Windows 8 click the Calculator tile from the Apps screen. Depending on your version of Windows, the View menu will contain modes called Standard, Scientific, Programmer, or Statistics. Check out each mode, then select View (if there is a menu) or click the mode button (the Windows 10 version) and select Standard before proceeding.

Macintosh: Click Finder-Applications-Calculator to start the calculator program. The View menu will contain modes called Basic, Scientific, and Programmer. Check out each mode, then select View-Basic before proceeding.

Here you see examples of calculators from various operating systems:

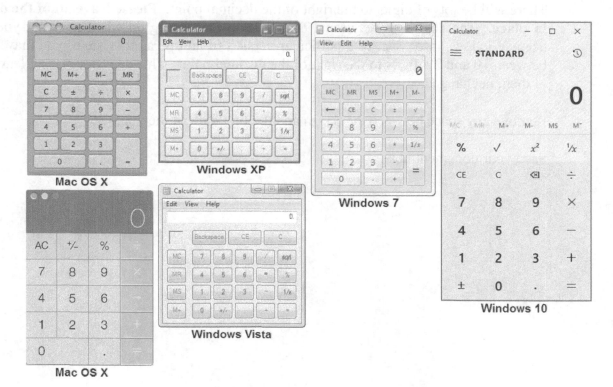

Mac OS X   Windows XP   Windows 7   Windows 10

Mac OS X   Windows Vista

As you read the article about the mayor, notice that he still owed $71,000 from his campaign with a year to go in office. In the calculator, divide 71000 by 365 to get the number of dollars the mayor would have to pay back each day to clear his debt by the time he left office. Once you get the answer, use Edit-Copy in the Calculator window to copy the number into the clipboard (in the Windows 10 version, right-click the display, then select Copy from the pop-up).

Minimize the calculator (do not close it).

Switch back to the LAB4 document, and scroll to the <u>bottom</u> of the text.

Click with the mouse to set the insertion point at the <u>end of the final sentence</u>.

Insert a new paragraph (a new line) saying:

> Mayor Clark needs to pay back $ per day.

The new text may not appear at the same point size as the surrounding text. Do not worry about it now; we will set the typeface and point size for the entire document later.

Click the mouse just to the right of the $ sign to move the text insertion point, and then *paste* the answer from the calculator.

There will be <u>lots</u> of digits to the right of the decimal point. **Please leave all of the digits in place.** The answer is between 194 and 195. Depending on whether or not you are using Windows or a Mac, or a particular version of an operating system, you may have between 10 and 29 digits to the right of the decimal point. This does not matter; leave all of them unchanged.

Remove any space between the $ sign and the first digit of the number.

Save your document now.

Paint a Dollar Bill

Since the Mayor needed dollars, we will draw a cartoon of a dollar bill to include in the document. Don't even think about doing it for real! Some very humorless people will come visit you!

Windows: Click on Start-All Programs-Accessories-Paint (Windows 7 or earlier) or in Start-Windows Accessories-Paint (Windows 10) to start the paintbrush program. In Windows 8 click on the Paint tile in the Apps screen. Maximize its window if it is not already maximized.

Macintosh: There is no free equivalent to Paint that comes with the Mac. You have several options for completing this part of the assignment. You can (1) download, install, and use a free paint tool from the Internet such as Paintbrush, available from `http://sourceforge.net/projects/paintbrush/`, (2) if you have a legal copy of Adobe PhotoShop you may use that, or (3) you can use Windows Paint on a Windows PC with the instructions here and then copy your final file to the Word Processing folder of your flash drive. Be prepared to translate the instructions here into the equivalent form for the program you end up using.

Set the width of the image to 800 pixels and the height to 340 pixels (the approximate dimensions of a real dollar bill). If necessary in Windows Paint, select color mode instead of black-and-white in the Colors radio button group.

Use the Flood-Fill tool to initialize the image to a medium green color, and then employ the entire drawing area in creating your design. In your graphic, you must use:

- At least two different text strings, one of which must be your name,
- At least two different filled rectangles,
- At least two different ellipses,
- At least two different lines with different widths,
- At least two different colors,
- At least two different Bézier curves (it must be obvious these are Béziers),
- At least two uses of the Airbrush (the spray can).

Have fun! I've seen some wonderful cartoon dollar bills, and some that would embarrass a first grader. Show a little artistry!

Hint: those of you printing out your dollar bill on a monochrome printer must choose adjacent colors that are high contrast. Drawing a red next to a green will cause identical shades of gray to be printed, and you won't be able to distinguish where one stops and the next one starts. However, if you place a dark color next to a light color the boundary will show up when both colors are converted to gray shades.

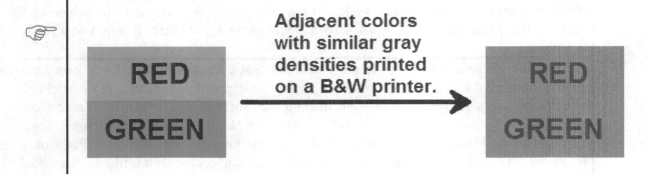

Adjacent colors with similar gray densities printed on a B&W printer.

Here is a "dollar bill" that satisfies the requirements of this part of the assignment. Try to pick out the places where I used each tool. (Surely you can do a better job than I can!)

Click on File-Save As... and save the drawing in your Word Processing folder as **DOLLAR.PNG**. You may save the image as DOLLAR.GIF if that format is available, but remember that the .gif format is limited to a maximum of 256 colors. Do not use the .JPG format unless the image contains more than 256 distinct colors.

Minimize the window for the painting program.

Loading the Image into the Document

Activate the Microsoft Word document LAB4. Use the mouse to position the insertion point just <u>below the banner lines on page 1</u> containing your name, lab time, date, etc.

Open up a couple of blank lines below all of the banner information (by hitting the Enter↵ key), and make sure that the insertion point is in the bottom blank line.

Word 2003 / Word 2008-2011 (Mac): Click on Insert-Picture-From File... (2008) or Insert-Photo-Picture From File... (2011)

Word 2007-2016: In the Insert tab of the ribbon, click in the Illustrations panel on Picture or Pictures.

Find your DOLLAR image on your disk and load it in (click on its file name in the Insert Picture dialog box, then click the Insert button). You should see your dollar appear below the banner information. Make certain that the dollar bill **appears on the front page below your banner**, and that the first text of the article appears on the second page.

Center the image between the margins. Since the dollar bill image is fairly large, there may not be any visible effect when you center the image.

Save your document now.

Final Formats

Find the article title at the start of page 2. Select all five of the title and header lines and the blank line(s) in between.

Word 2003 / Word 2008-2011 (Mac): Click on Format-Paragraph... in the menu.

Word 2007-2016: In the Home tab of the ribbon click the tiny arrow in the lower right corner of the Paragraph panel.

In the dialog box that pops up:

- Set Alignment to Centered.
- Set Line Spacing to Single.
- Set both Before and After spacing is set to zero.

Click OK to close the dialog.

Select just the <u>two</u> title lines, and then set these two lines to Times New Roman, Bold, and **20 points**.

Select the next three lines (the by-line down through the date of the article). Set these three lines to **12-point** Times New Roman (but <u>not</u> bold).

Starting with the first complete sentences <u>below the header lines</u> of the article, click drag downwards to select the ***rest*** of the document (everything from the first sentence to the bottom of the document). Set these lines to **16-point**, Times New Roman (but <u>not</u> bold).

The text should still be selected. If not, make it so. Don't hit anything on the keyboard, as any keys you type will replace the selected text (you would need to undo the edits to restore the document).

Word 2003 / Word 2008-2011 (Mac): Click on Format-Paragraph... in the menu.

Word 2007-2016: In the Home tab of the ribbon click the tiny arrow in the lower right corner of the Paragraph panel.

In the dialog box that pops up enter these settings in the Indents and Spacing notebook page (look at the tab at the top of the dialog box):

- In the Indentation group, click on Special:, then select First Line. Make sure the By: box is set to 0.5" to set a ½ inch indent on the first line of every selected paragraph.
- In the Spacing box, set Line Spacing: to 1.5 lines.
- Set Before: to 12 pt. and set After: to 0 pt.
- Set Alignment: to Justified.

Finally, click on the OK button to apply these formats to the selected paragraphs.

Save your document now.

Inserting Special Symbols

Set the insertion point in LAB4 to the start of the one-sentence paragraph you just typed in about how much the mayor must pay back per day

Word 2008 (Mac): Click Insert-Symbol...

Word 2011 (Mac): Click Insert-Symbol-Advanced Symbol...

Word 2010-2016: Click on the Insert tab, and then click Symbol-More Symbols... in the Symbols panel.

This will bring up a dialog box called Symbol, which will provide access to all the installed fonts and characters on the computer.

In the Symbols tab of the Symbol dialog box, set the Font to Wingdings.

Find and select the ☺ smiley face character.

Click the Insert button to insert it into the document.

Close the Symbol dialog box.

The final sentence should now look like the following image (most or all of the x-characters shown below will be numeric digits).

> ☺Mayor Clark needs to pay back $194.xxxxxxxxxxxxxxxxxxxxxxxxxxxxxx per day.

Note: in Microsoft Windows there is a special, separate program called Character Map which can do the same task for any Windows program. To activate it in Windows 7 or earlier, click on Start-Programs-Accessories-(System Tools)-Character Map, but in Windows 8 you need to click on the Character Map tile from the Apps screen. In Windows 10 it is in Start-Windows Accessories.

Make certain that the line still has **full justification**, and then save your document.

Note that the length of the number's fraction may cause the full paragraph justification for this line to insert a lot of extra white space. The line will look really odd as a result. This is O.K. Ignore it.

Page Numbers

Word 2003 / Word 2008-2011 (Mac): Click on Insert-Page Numbers... in the menu. In the dialog box that pops up, set the Position: of the page numbers to Bottom of Page (Footer), set the Alignment: to Center, and make sure that the Show number on first page check box ***does not*** contain a check mark.

Still in the Page Numbers dialog box, click on the Format... button. In the Page Number Format dialog box that pops up, click the Start at: radio button (in the Page numbering group), and set the number in the corresponding spin edit box to 0 (zero).

Click on the OK button when all of these settings are correct.

Click on the OK button in the Page Numbers dialog box.

Word 2007-2016: Click on the Insert tab of the ribbon, then in the Header & Footer panel click on Footer and select Blank from the pop-up list of footers (the panel may be in View instead of Insert in some variations).

Click again on the Insert tab of the ribbon, then in the Header & Footer panel click on Page Number-Bottom of Page-Plain Number 1.

Double-click in the footer and select the paragraph containing the page number, then on the Home tab of the ribbon, then in the Paragraph panel on the button to center the text.

In the Design tab of the ribbon for Header & Footer click in the Options panel on Different First Page.

Still in the Design tab, click in the Header & Footer panel and select Page Number-Format Page Numbers.... In the dialog click the Start at: radio button and enter 0 (zero) into the spin edit box. Click on the OK button.

Word 2007 WARNING: Problems are occasionally reported with this step in Word 2007 because the galleries of options in the headers and footers, page numbers, etc., were missing. If this is the case, there are help pages at the Microsoft Web site that can help fix the problem.

By starting the page numbering at zero, but not printing the page number on the first page of the document, we have just created a header page without page numbers, and the first page of text will be labeled as page number 1. On screen you will see the page numbers appear at the bottom of the document in a light gray color.

Save your document now.

Putting Your Name in the Footer

Word 2003: Click on View-Header and Footer in the menu. Two regions will appear, one (the header) at the top of the page, and the other (the footer) at the bottom of the page. Also, a Header and Footer tool box window will appear.

In File-Page Setup, click the Layout notebook tab, and then set the Footer: spin edit value to 1".

Make sure that the Apply to: drop down list contains Whole Document. Click the OK button to close the dialog box.

Another button on the Header and Footer tool box will be labeled Switch Between Header and Footer when you float the mouse over it. Click this button until the insertion point is in the footer region, along with the page number.

Word 2007-2016: If the footer is not already selected, double-click in the footer next to (to the right of) the page number.

In the Design tab of the ribbon, click in the Position panel on the spin edit control for Footer from Bottom to set this value to 1".

Word 2008-2011 (Mac): Click on View-Header and Footer in the menu.

Click on Format-Document, and in the Margins tab set the From Edge-Footer value to 1".

Make sure that the Apply to: drop down list contains Whole Document. Click the OK button to close the dialog box.

Set the insertion point in the footer region, to the right of the page number.

You have expanded the footer region vertically to just below the bottom of the text; we now have enough space to print the page number and your name (entered below) on any printer.

Hit Enter⏎ to open up a blank line, then type in your name. Center the paragraph containing your name if not already set that way. Your name should appear centered below the page number.

Select all the text in the footer and change it to **12-point Times New Roman**.

Close the header and footer region and return to the main document (by double clicking somewhere in the body of the document).

Your name and the page number should appear in gray at the bottom of every page of the document *except* the banner page.

Save your document now.

Printing

Word 2003 / Word 2008-2011 (Mac): Click on File-Print or the File-Print Preview menu entry to see how your document will look on the printer.

Word 2007: Click on the Office Button-Print-Print Preview menu entry to see how your document will look on the printer.

Word 2010-2016: Click on the File tab and then select the Print menu entry to see how your document will look on the printer.

Use the tools in the dialog to step through each of the pages of your document. If possible, practice zooming in on the page numbers in the footer, the Wingding at the bottom of the document, and the dollar bill on the first page. If necessary, exit the dialog, correct any mistakes and preview the document once again.

Word 2003 / Word 2008-2011 (Mac): Use the File-Print menu commands to print out your completed document.

Word 2007: Use the Office Button-Print-Print menu commands to print out your completed document.

Word 2010-2016: Use the File tab and then select the Print-Print All Pages menu commands to print out your completed document.

Verification

Check your document now. The first page (and the stack) should look like the following diagram, with your dollar bill design in place of mine. Make any corrections and reprint it as necessary.

Shutting Down

Close all programs. If Microsoft Word asks you if you want to save any changes, you generally should answer "yes". Close down your computer normally.

What to Turn In

You will need to turn in the printout of your document, which will be several pages long, containing the following items (check off the items in the list below):

Page #1 (the banner page) must contain, all **single spaced**:
- ☐ Your name (centered, 20 points),
- ☐ LAB ASSIGNMENT #4 (centered, 20 points),
- ☐ WORK AT LAB or WORK AT HOME (centered, 20 points),
- ☐ Current date (centered, 20 points),
- ☐ Dollar bill graphic image (centered) containing <u>at least two</u> of each object:
  - ☐ text (one of which must be student's name),
  - ☐ filled rectangles,
  - ☐ ellipses,
  - ☐ lines with different widths,
  - ☐ different colors (will appear as shades of gray on non-color printers),
  - ☐ Bézier curves (these must be obviously Bézier, and not simple lines),
  - ☐ Airbrush (the spray can),
- ☐ but the banner page must **_not_** have a page number or your name in the footer.

All Remaining Text Pages must contain:
- ☐ 1½ inch margin around all four sides,
- ☐ Document text (containing both `Top` and `Bottom`, in that order) with:
  - ☐ <u>All</u> text must be in Times New Roman (except one Wingding),
  - ☐ 20 point title lines (top two lines), all centered, boldface, single space,
  - ☐ 12 point by-line, publisher line, and date line, all centered, single space,
  - ☐ 16 point text (all remaining sentences below date line),
  - ☐ first line of each paragraph indented ½ inch,
  - ☐ 1½ line spacing,
  - ☐ 12 point blank line above each paragraph,
  - ☐ fully justified paragraphs,
- ☐ Sentence with Wingding ☺ saying: "☺Mayor Clark needs to pay back…",
- ☐ Calculator result (full precision),
- ☐ Footer, with:
  - ☐ page numbers at bottom of page,
  - ☐ page numbers centered,
  - ☐ page numbers starting on first page of text (not banner page),
  - ☐ first page number = 1,
  - ☐ your name in the footer, below the page number, on every text page,
  - ☐ all footer text must be 12-point Times New Roman.

Important Note: Putting your name in the footer region, as described on the previous page, is critical to your grade. If your name is not typed <u>by Word</u> on every page, then professors are forced to assume that the pages are copies of someone else's work. Your printout will be rejected out of hand if your name is missing. If you do the assignment correctly and your name still does not appear in the footer, please seek help from your instructors immediately.

Grading Policy

Lab assignments are worth 10 points each. Teaching assistants will observe the following criteria for evaluating and scoring the Lab #4 assignments that they receive.

- Any report that does not have the student's name *typed* on *all* pages (centered at the top of the banner page, and in the footer region of all remaining text pages) will be *rejected*, and if submitted will receive a *zero*. If any student writes their name in by hand instead of typing it then the report must be rejected. Signing their name in addition to typing it is O.K.

- 1 Point - Report must be stapled together. Remove the full point if the report is paper-clipped together or is submitted loose (even with folded corners). Remove the full point if the pages are not in the correct order listed here (banner page, followed by the Word document in the correct page-number order).

- 1 Point - Printout of the banner page must be present and must contain the appropriate lines of banner information. Remove ½ point if any banner line is missing or incorrect (for example, remove the ½ point if any line is not centered, not single spaced, or if the font size is not set to 20 points). Remove the full point if most or all lines of text are missing.

- 4 Points - The banner page must also contain the dollar bill image, containing the aforementioned graphic objects. Remove all 4 points if no dollar bill image is present. Score the dollar bill as follows.

  Remove ½ point (up to 2 points) for each of the following items that are missing or incorrect. Each category must occur at least twice:
  - text,
  - filled rectangles,
  - ellipses,
  - lines with different widths,
  - different colors,
  - Bézier curves, and
  - airbrush.

  Remove 1 point if the dollar bill image appears in the wrong place (either in the wrong place on the banner page, or on the wrong page altogether).

  Remove 1 point if student's name is missing from the image.

▪ 4 Points - The main body of the document must be present and in the correct numerical page order. Score the text as follows.

Remove 1 full point for any errors in the basic text layout (both `Top` and `Bottom` must be present in the correct order with no extra or missing pieces of text).

Remove ½ point <u>for each error</u> in formatting (up to 1 full point), including errors in:

> document margins,
> line spacing,
> font size,
> indentation, and
> paragraph justification (including centering and spacing the title and header lines).
>
> Margins are supposed to be 1½ inches all around – remove the credit if they are less than 1" or greater than 2" (it may be difficult for students to hit 1½ exactly by using the ruler).

Remove ½ point for each error in the final sentence (up to 1 full point), including errors in the required new text ("Mayor Clark needs…"), the smiley face ☺ Wingding, and the calculator result.

Remove 1 point for errors in the footer region, including any errors in the page numbering or centering the student's name.

Lab #5 – Word Processing: Mail Merge

Introduction & Goals

In this assignment you will learn how to perform mail merge to create personalized letters to a large number of people. To accomplish this, you will need to create a "boilerplate" letter that contains the general information that will be received by everybody and placeholders to receive the specific information and a data file containing the true information to plug into the placeholders.

Specifics You Will Learn in this Assignment

You will learn how to perform the following tasks in this assignment.

- **Create a Master Document** – This is the document containing the general information. There should be nothing in this document specific to any one recipient; i.e., everyone will receive this text.

- **Create a Data Document** – This is the document that contains the data to merge into the master document. It has a special format, and special tools for editing it. Data may be added or deleted as necessary.

- **Merge the two documents to the Printer** – You can merge the two documents and create a third file, which you could then modify, or you can merge the result directly to the printer. All of the placeholders in the master document will be replaced by records from the data file, and you will get as many copies of the updated master document as you have records of data.

Preparation before Starting Assignment

Read this assignment through in its entirety before doing anything. This lab does not depend on the data files you created in any earlier assignment, but you will store new files in the directories created in lab #1.

In the Laboratory

Bring your flash drive containing the folders created in lab #1 and this lab assignment. Do not come to lab without these items.

At Home

Your home machine must have a working version of Microsoft Word and a working printer, as usual. You must be able to locate the folders you created in lab #1.

Data Files

There are no data files provided for this assignment.

Step-By-Step Procedure

Starting Up

Start your machine normally. Find the Microsoft Word program, start it running, and open a new blank document. If the window is not already maximized, maximize it by clicking its □ button, or expand the window until it mostly fills the screen. Configure Word normally, as you did in the previous assignment. I recommend setting the "view" to Page Width.

In the previous assignment, we had you set the margins by click-dragging on the ruler bars. This time, we will have you set the margins precisely using a dialog box.

Word 2003: Click on File-Page Setup... in the menu.
Word 2007: Click on Office Button-Print-Print Preview. In the print preview, click in the Page Setup panel on Margins, then click Custom Margins...
Word 2010-2016: Click on the File tab, then Print, and then on the drop-down list having to do with margins (it may say Normal Margins or it may say something else). From the drop-down list click Custom Margins...
Word 2008-2011 (Mac): Click on Format-Document in the menu.

A tabbed notebook dialog box will pop up, as you see here for Word 2010/2013/2016 for Windows and Word 2008/2011 for the Mac. The dialog for other versions of Word will be similar, but not necessarily identical.

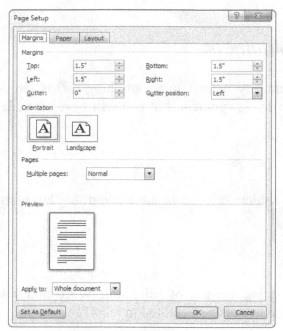
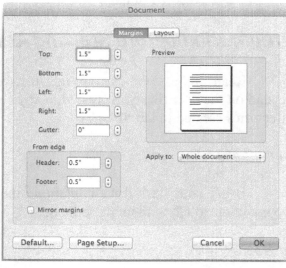

In the Margins tab, set all four margins (Top:, Bottom:, Left:, and Right:) to 1.5" (1½ inches). Make sure that the Apply to: drop down list is set to Whole document, and then click the OK button to close the dialog box.

Word 2007: Close Print Preview, and then, if necessary, click on the Home tab in the ribbon.

Word 2010: Click on the Home tab in the ribbon.

Word 2013/2016: Hit [Esc] to close the Print dialog. Click on the Home tab in the ribbon.

Creating the Banner page

In the document window type four lines containing:

- your name,
- the phrase LAB ASSIGNMENT #5,
- either WORK AT LAB or WORK AT HOME, and
- the current date,

hitting [Enter ←] after each line. Select these four lines with the mouse. **Center** them and change the size to **20 points**, set the Font to **Times New Roman**, and make the lines **single-spaced** with *no extra spacing above, below, or between* the paragraphs:

William T. Verts
LAB ASSIGNMENT #5
WORK AT HOME
October 25, 2013

As you did in the previous assignment, save this document in your Word Processing folder, but this time save it as **LAB5.DOCX** (or **LAB5.DOC** if using an older version of Word).

Print the page. **Put this page aside to turn in with the rest of your report.**

Creating the Master Document

Word 2003-2016: Click on the File-New menu entry. Select <u>Blank document</u>.

Word 2008-2011 (Mac): Click on the File-New Blank Document menu entry.

A new document will appear, and LAB5 will be hidden.

The new document will probably <u>not</u> have the same settings that you established for the LAB5 banner page. Using any method you have learned, set the margins to 1.5" (1½ inches) on <u>all four sides</u> of this new document.

Note: The mail merge process is one that has undergone a lot of changes over the years. Every version of Word seems to take a slightly different approach to the structure of menus and dialog boxes; there is NO guarantee that the instructions here will work with any newer version of Word.

Word 2003: Click on the Tools-Letters and Mailings-Mail Merge Wizard... entry in the menu. A panel on the right side of the screen will appear, with the title **Mail Merge** at the top and the message **Step 1 of 6** at the bottom. Select the Letters radio button (it may already be selected), then click the <u>Next: Starting Document</u> message.

In the **Step 2 of 6** panel select the Use the current document radio button (it may already be selected), then click the <u>Next: Select recipients</u> message.

Word 2007-2013: Click on the Mailings tab in the ribbon, then on the Start Mail Merge button in the Start Mail Merge panel. Select Step-by-Step Mail Merge Wizard from the drop-down menu. A panel on the right side of the screen will appear, with the title **Mail Merge** at the top and the message **Step 1 of 6** at the bottom. Select the Letters radio button (it may already be selected), then click the <u>Next: Starting Document</u> message.

In the **Step 2 of 6** panel select the Use the current document radio button (it may already be selected), then click the <u>Next: Select recipients</u> message.

Word 2016: Click on the Mailings tab in the ribbon, then on the Start Mail Merge button in the Start Mail Merge panel. Select Letters from the drop-down menu.

Word 2008-2011 (Mac): Click on Tools-Mail Merge Manager in the menu. A dialog will appear containing six items, with the title **Mail Merge Manager** at the top. In **step 1** (Select Document Type) click Create New and pick Form Letters.

Creating the Data Document

Word 2003-2013: In **Step 3 of 6** click the radio button labeled Type a new list from the **Select Recipients** section. As soon as you select this option, the panel will change to include a section titled **Type a new list**. In that section click on the Create... message.

The New Address List dialog box will appear. Click the Customize... (or Customize Columns...) button. The Customize Address List dialog box will pop up on top of the previous dialog box, containing all of the available fields.

Word 2016: Still in the Mailings tab, click Select Recipients, and then choose Create a new list... in the dropdown menu. This will open a form to edit the fields.

Word 2008-2011 (Mac): In **step 2** of the Mail Merge Manager (Select Recipients List) click Get List, then pick New Data Source. A Create Data Source dialog will appear.

The desired field names must be just:
  Title,
  First Name,
  Last Name,
  either Address Line 1 or Address 1,
  City,
  State,
  ZIP Code,
  Country or Region, and
  Prize.

The default items in this step will include some but not all of these already, and it will have fields that we do not need. Our first task is to delete any unnecessary fields, and to insert the ones that are missing. Use the buttons in the dialog to delete fields or add fields as required. Depending on the version of Word you are using, your final result should look something like the following image. Click OK when complete.

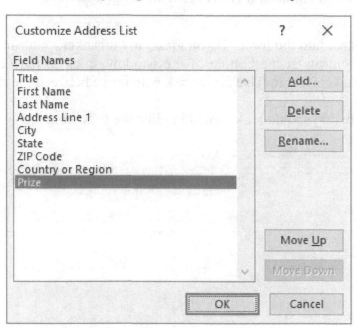

Word 2008-2011 (Mac), Word 2016: At this point Word may ask to save the new structure; if so, save the data file as **My Data.docx** into your Word Processing folder.

The Data to Enter

We now need to create a database for the individuals to whom we will send a customized letter. The database will consist of a set of records, one record per recipient, where each record is composed of fields.

Here are the data you will need to enter:

	Record #1	**Record #2**	**Record #3**	**Record #4**
Title:	Mr.	Mr.	Ms.	Dr.
First Name:	Fred	Sam	Mary	Frieda
Last Name:	Smith	Jones	Baker	Walker
Address 1:	123 Main Street	321 East Street	444 N. 9th Street	1030 Tippecanoe
City:	Amherst	Sunderland	Corvallis	Lafayette
State:	MA	MA	OR	IN
ZIP Code:	01002	01375	97330	47904
Country:	USA	USA	USA	USA
Prize:	car	boat	TV	watch

 Note that the "Address 1" field may be called "Address Line 1", and "Country" may be called "Country or Region" or even "Country/Region". The differences are not critical; use whichever version you see.

 Note to UMass students: the Zip Code for the University of Massachusetts is 01003, but for the town of Amherst it is 01002. This is <u>not</u> a typo.

 Type the data into the form. If you make any mistakes, you can step through the records with the controls at the bottom of the window, click in the field where you made the mistake, and correct it. Use the [Tab] key to move between the slots in the form.

The final dialog should look something like the following image:

Word 2003-2013: Finally, when everything is satisfactory, click the Close or OK button to close the dialog box. You have now successfully created your data document, containing 4 records.

You will get a Save Address List dialog box on screen. Find the Word Processing folder on your disk. (It may already be visible in the dialog box since you just stored the LAB5 document there. Find the folder if it is not visible. You should not have to create it at this time.) In the File name: edit box, type as the new file name **My Data.MDB** and click the Save button.

If you see a Mail Merge Recipients dialog box appear, with all four records checked (if not, then check them). Click on the OK button. (Note that you can come back to the recipients list by clicking on the Edit Recipient List in the Start Mail Merge panel of the Mailings tab in the ribbon.)

In **Step 3 of 6**, click the <u>Next: Write your letter</u> message.

Word 2016: Finally, when everything is satisfactory, click the Close or OK button to close the dialog box. You have now successfully created your data document, containing 4 records. At this point Word may ask to save the new structure; if so, save the data file as **My Data.docx** into your Word Processing folder.

Word 2008-2011 (Mac): Finally, when everything is satisfactory, click the OK button to close the dialog box. You have now successfully created your data document, containing 4 records. At this point Word may ask to save the new structure; if so, save the data file as **My Data.docx** into your Word Processing folder.

Filling in the Master Document

You should now be looking at an empty document on screen (your master document).

> **Word 2003:** Click on File-Save As... and save the master document file with the name **My Letter.DOC** in your Word Processing folder.
>
> There is a new set of tool buttons at the top of the screen. These are for the mail merge process. Float the mouse for a few seconds over each button in turn to familiarize yourself with their pop up labels, such as Insert Merge Field, Insert Word Field, etc.

> **Word 2007:** Click on Office Button-Save As... and save the master document file with the name **My Letter.DOCX** in your Word Processing folder. Find the Insert Merge Field button in the Mailings tab of the ribbon.

> **Word 2010-2016:** Click on the File tab, then click Save As... and save the master document file with the name **My Letter.DOCX** in your Word Processing folder. Find the Insert Merge Field button in the Mailings tab of the ribbon.

> **Word 2008-2011 (Mac):** Click on File-Save As and save the master document with the name **My Letter.DOCX** in your Word Processing folder.

In the master document, type in the letter below, with the placeholder or merge field «tags» as described on the next page. In your letter, **update the year** to next year's number (i.e., if it is 2018 right now change the year to 2019, if it is 2019 right now change it to 2020, and so on). Type in the **current date** where indicated, and type in **your own name** as the sender of the letter.

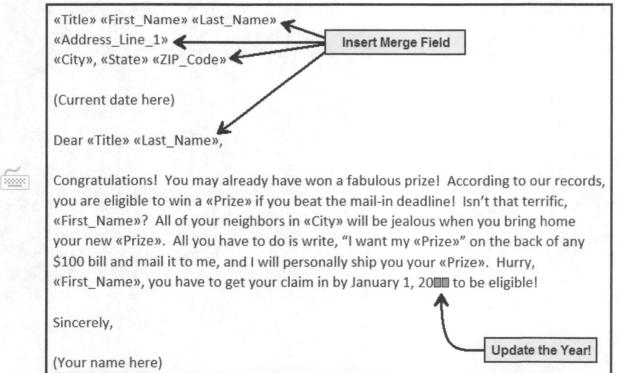

Word 2003-2016: For each of the tags surrounded by double angle brackets «tag», click on the Insert Merge Field button and select the desired field name from the list. The double angle brackets will be automatically inserted.

Word 2008-2011 (Mac): For each of the tags surrounded by double angle brackets «tag», drag the correct placeholders into the document from **step 3** (Insert Placeholders)

Warning: Make certain that you use the proper button or method to enter the placeholders or merge fields into the master document. Do <u>NOT</u> type two less-than << or two greater-than >> symbols! Using the proper method will enter the merge field automatically surrounded by the appropriate «double angle» brackets.

Make sure the punctuation in the header of the letter is correct. This includes inserting spaces and commas where appropriate between tags. Study the example letter carefully. Don't worry if the line breaks aren't exactly at the same positions as shown in the image; we'll get the format straightened out in the next steps.

Formatting the Master Document

- Key in ⌨Ctrl⌨A (Windows) or ⌘A (Mac) to select all of the text. Set the point size of the <u>entire</u> document to **16-point Times New Roman, single-spaced** with *no additional spacing above or below paragraphs*, and then click the mouse anywhere in the document to collapse the selection back to a simple insertion point. Add blank lines where necessary.

- **Right justify** the date line (fill in the <u>current date</u>, whatever it is)

- **Fully justify** the body of the letter.

- **Indent the signature lines** (from "Sincerely" through the end of the letter) to the <u>mid-point</u> of the letter with the indent buttons on the ruler bar. To do this, click drag on the little square button on the ruler where the floating help box says Left Indent. **INDENT BUT DO NOT CENTER THESE LINES.**

When complete, the layout of your document should appear very close to what follows, subject to the current margin settings, with the year changed to the appropriate value (again, do not worry at this time about where word-wrap breaks the lines in the main body of the letter):

«Title» «First_Name» «Last_Name»
«Address_Line_1»
«City», «State» «ZIP_Code»

(Current date here)

Dear «Title» «Last_Name»,

Congratulations! You may already have won a fabulous prize! According to our records, you are eligible to win a «Prize» if you beat the mail-in deadline! Isn't that terrific, «First_Name»? All of your neighbors in «City» will be jealous when you bring home your new «Prize». All you have to do is write, "I want my «Prize»" on the back of any $100 bill and mail it to me, and I will personally ship you your «Prize». Hurry, «First_Name», you have to get your claim in by January 1, 20▓ to be eligible!

Sincerely,

(Your name here)

Save your document now.

Performing the Mail Merge

> **Word 2003:** Click the View Merged Data button just to the right of the Insert Word Field button (pushing it in).
>
> **Word 2007-2016:** In the Mailings tab click on Preview Results in the Preview Results panel.
>
> **Word 2008-2011 (Mac):** Click the View Merged Data button in **step 5** of the Mail Merge Manager (Preview Results).

Use the controls that look like those on a VCR or DVD player to scroll through and view the four data records merged into the context of the letter. It is possible that preview does not show all four letters, but the printing process *should* print all of them.

When done, click the same button again (popping it out) to view the master document without the data.

You may find that you need to make changes, either to the master document or to the data. Changing the master document is fairly easy, since it is already visible on screen.

> **Word 2003-2013:** You should still be in **Step 4 of 6** in the panel on the right side of the screen. Step 5 is Preview your letters, and Step 6 is Complete the merge, but we are performing these steps manually, so <u>stop</u> at step 4 by closing the panel.
>
> **Word 2016:** Nothing to do here.
>
> **Word 2008-2011 (Mac):** Nothing to do here.

 Do not proceed until the merged letters appear correct when you view them.

Printing

 If you do not have a personal printer, I recommend that you "print" to a PDF file instead. That file can be copied onto a flash drive and brought to any computer which does have a printer, and printed there without you needing to perform the mail-merge again.

> **Word 2003:** Find the Merge to Printer button by floating the mouse over each button on the tool bar in turn. Click on the Merge to Printer button, select the <u>A</u>ll radio button, click OK, and then click on OK in the Print dialog box to print your letters.
>
> **Word 2007-2016:** In the Mailings tab of the ribbon, click on Finish & Merge in the Finish panel, select Print Documents from the drop-down menu, and in the Merge to Printer dialog box make certain the Print records radio button is set to All. Finally, click OK to print your letters. It is possible that Word prints fewer than four letters. If this happens, try the process again, but in Print Documents choose Save as PDF instead. The PDF file should contain all four letters, and can be printed separately.
>
> **Word 2008-2011 (Mac):** In **step 6** of the Mail Merge Manager (Complete Merge), click the Merge to Printer button. In the dialog box make sure that the Pages radio button is set to All. Click the Print button to print your letters. Close the Mail Merge Manager.

Final Concerns

If for some reason you do <u>not</u> get all four pages printed out on the printer, you can merge the data with the letters again, select any missing page, and then print that single missing page as a normal document. You may also merge to a new Word file and print that file as a normal document, or print to a PDF file as described earlier. Any or all of these workarounds may be necessary in order to get the final desired result.

One or more printed pages containing the <u>framework</u> of the letter but <u>no data</u> probably means that there are extra blank records at the end of your data document. You may go back and edit the data document to eliminate the extra records, or you may simply discard any extra printed pages.

You may choose to also sign each of the four letters with a pen. This is optional, and will not affect your grade if you do not sign the letters.

Shutting Down

Close Microsoft Word. If it asks you if you want to save any changes to any of the documents, you should click the Yes button. Close down your computer normally.

What to Turn In

You will need to turn in the printout of your document, containing the following items (check off the items in the list below):

Page #1 (the banner page) must contain:
- ☐ Your name (centered),
- ☐ LAB ASSIGNMENT #5 (centered),
- ☐ WORK AT LAB or WORK AT HOME (centered),
- ☐ Current date (centered),
- ☐ No extra spaces between lines.
- ☐ Size must be set to 20 Points.
- ☐ Typeface must be set to Times New Roman.

Four Mail-Merged Letters, one per page, containing:
- ☐ Each letter customized to a different person (Fred, Sam, Mary, Frieda),
- ☐ Date line right justified, with the current date,
- ☐ Body of letter fully justified,
- ☐ Your Name typed as the signature of the letter,
- ☐ Signature lines indented to midpoint of letter,
- ☐ All text set to 16 points in size,
- ☐ All text single-spaced,
- ☐ All text set to Times New Roman.

Grading Policy

Lab assignments are worth 10 points each. Teaching assistants will observe the following criteria for evaluating and scoring the Lab #5 assignments that they receive.

- Any report that does not have the student's name *typed* on *all* pages (centered at the top of the banner page, and as the signature of all remaining pages) will be *rejected*, and if submitted will receive a *zero*. If any student writes their name in by hand, instead of typing it, then the report must be rejected. (Signing their name by hand *in addition* to typing it is O.K., but is not required.)

- 1 Point - Report must be stapled together. Remove the full point if the report is paper-clipped together or is submitted loose (even with folded corners). Remove the full point if the pages are not in the order listed here (banner, letters for Fred Smith, Sam Jones, Mary Baker, and Frieda Walker).

- 1 Point - Printout of the banner page must be present and must contain the appropriate lines of banner information. Remove ½ point if any line of the banner page is missing or incorrect (for example, remove the ½ point if any line is not centered or if the font size is not set to 20 point, Times New Roman). Remove ½ point if the lines are not single spaced. Remove the full point if all banner lines are in error or the entire page is missing.

- 4 Points - Remove 1 point for each missing letter. No extra credit if the students include more than four customized letters.

- 1 Point - Remove the point for using fewer than all nine merge fields (i.e., modifying the text of the letter so that some fields are missing). No extra credit if a student includes more than the nine required data fields.

- 3 Points - The document must be formatted correctly according to the following schedule. Points will be removed for infractions up to but not more than the 3 points available for this section. Remove ½ point for errors in indenting the signature lines (i.e., if the students centered the lines instead of indenting them). Remove ½ point if the date line is not right justified. Remove ½ point for the wrong date. Remove ½ point if the document is not fully justified. Remove ½ point if the lines are not obviously single-spaced. Remove ½ point if the text size has not been set to 16 points. Remove ½ point if the text typeface is not Times New Roman.

Lab #6 – Spreadsheets: Algonquians in Manhattan

Introduction & Goals

This is your first spreadsheet assignment. You will first create a spreadsheet, and then you will run some "what-if" tests on it to look for a particular answer. You will then change the spreadsheet calculations and repeat the "what-if" tests.

According to legend, in 1626 the Dutch colonist Peter Minuit tricked the Native Americans from the Algonquian peoples into giving Manhattan Island to the Dutch settlers in exchange for beads worth about 24 dollars. (The locals thought they were pulling a fast one on the Dutch. They took the beads thinking that the Dutch were silly in believing that they could actually own the land!) If Manhattan Island is worth one hundred billion dollars today ($100,000,000,000, or 1.0×10^{11} in scientific notation), at what interest rate should the Natives have invested their $24 in order to have accumulated this sum by the current year? Assume yearly compounding.

To compute the amount that would have been in the bank for a particular year, take what was in the bank the <u>previous</u> year, and add to it what was in the bank in the previous year times the interest rate, then subtract off the amount of the service charge. Your answer should be the *smallest* interest rate to <u>five</u> decimal places (displayed as a percentage with three decimal places) which yields *at least* one hundred billion dollars; a "1" followed by eleven more digits.

A note about the origins of this project: when I took over teaching the computer literacy course in 1990, this was already a well-used and venerable assignment. I continued to use it because it is a wonderful introduction to spreadsheets; it requires both relative and absolute cell addressing in formulae, cell and column formatting, practice with printing multiple ranges, and a whole bunch of other basic spreadsheet skills. It wasn't until I had been using it for years that I found out who originally came up with the idea of the assignment. My thanks to Professor Robert Moll for permission to include this project here!

Specifics You Will Learn in This Assignment

You will learn the following things in this assignment.

- **Writing Formulae** – This is a very basic spreadsheet, and you will learn techniques for writing mathematical formulae. There are two major formulae to worry about in this assignment, both repeated many times down the spreadsheet. The first formula is used to generate a sequence of years between 1626 and the current year, and each occurrence of the formula simply adds 1 to the year number in the cell just above it. The second formula is used to compute how much money is in the bank for any particular year, based on an interest rate, a service charge, and how much money was in the bank in the previous year.

- **Relative versus Absolute addressing** – One very important exercise in this assignment is to learn the difference between these two cell addressing modes. This issue would not exist if we could not copy formulae, but because we can (and because it is such a useful thing to do) we have to be able to control which parts of a formula change during the copy (the relative part) and which parts do not (the absolute part).

- **Microsoft Excel** – This is the spreadsheet program. It is a very large, very complicated program, but you will see that you can get effective results from it almost immediately. Many of the techniques you learn as part of Excel transfer unchanged to other spreadsheet packages.

- **Numerical Precision** – We will be building a long chain of computations, where each member of the chain depends on the previous result. You will discover that a very small change in the starting number can have *enormous* influence on the values at the other end of the chain. Partly this is just the nature of compound interest, but we must take into consideration the precision of numbers as they are stored on a particular computer. Different spreadsheet programs that use numbers with different precisions will get slightly different answers, even when applied to identical spreadsheet models.

Preparation before Starting Assignment

Read this assignment through in its entirety before doing anything. This lab does not depend on the data files you created in any earlier assignment, but you will store new files in the directories created in lab #1.

In the Laboratory

Bring your flash drive containing the folders created in lab #1 and this lab assignment. Do not come to lab without these items.

At Home

Your home machine must have a working version of Microsoft Excel and a working printer, as usual. Almost any version of Excel will work here from Excel 97 onwards, but the instructions are written for much later versions of Excel for both Microsoft Windows PCs and for the Apple Macintosh. You must be able to locate the folders created in lab #1.

Data Files

There are no data files provided for this assignment.

Step-By-Step Procedure

Sit down at a machine in the lab (or your machine at home), and start it up normally. You should have the Spreadsheets folder that you created in lab #1, inside the Computer Literacy folder, on some disk somewhere. If you do not, please get your TA or instructor to show you how to create it (you really ought to be able to do this by yourself by now).

Starting Up

Find the Microsoft Excel program and start it running (it may take several seconds to start up, so be patient). If necessary, select Excel Workbook or Blank workbook. Once running, if the window is not already maximized, click the window's □ button.

Excel 2003 & Excel 2008-2011 (Mac): Click on the File-Save As... menu.

Excel 2007: Click on the Office Button-Save As...-Excel Workbook menu.

Excel 2010: Click on the File tab, and then on the Save As... menu.

Excel 2013/2016: Click on the File tab, on the Save As... item, and then the Browse button.

In the Save As... dialog box make sure that the Save in: or Where: edit box, file path bar, or path list points at your Spreadsheets folder; if the folder still does not exist at this time, create it using the appropriate button in the tool bar of the dialog box:

Excel 2003: Save the document as **LAB6.XLS** in your Spreadsheets folder. From now on, any instruction to "save your spreadsheet" means that you must either click on File-Save in the menu, click the save icon in the tool bar, or type in [Ctrl]S at the keyboard.

Excel 2007-2016, & Excel 2008-2011 (Mac): Save the document as **LAB6.XLSX** in your Spreadsheets folder. From now on, any instruction to "save your spreadsheet" means that for Windows PCs you must either click on either the Office Button or the File tab and then on Save, or type in [Ctrl]S at the keyboard, and for Macintosh you must either click on File-Save or ⌘S at the keyboard.

Configuring Excel

We need to set up Microsoft Excel in a "standard" configuration. Make sure that Excel is set up this way each time you start it up.

Excel 2003 & Excel 2008-2011 (Mac): Click on the View menu entry, and in the menu that pops up click on Normal (it may already be set that way).

Excel 2007-2016: Click on the View tab in the ribbon, and click Normal in Workbook Views (it may already be set that way).

Excel 2003 & Excel 2008-2011 (Mac): Click again on the View menu entry, and verify that there is a check mark (✔) next to both the Formula Bar and Status Bar entries. Add check marks as needed.

Excel 2007-2016: Still in the View tab of the ribbon, verify that there is a check mark (✔) next to Formula Bar, Headings, and Gridlines. Add check marks as needed.

Excel 2003 & Excel 2008-2011 (Mac): Click on View-Toolbars, and in the submenu that pops up make sure that both Standard and Formatting have check marks present. Add check marks to those two entries as needed, and remove check marks from any other entries that have them present.

Excel 2007-2016: Nothing to do here; all required items are already present in the Home tab of the ribbon.

Type in the Simple Stuff

Examine the following spreadsheet template. Except for shading, this is basically what your spreadsheet will look like when it is complete. The cells just to the right of the RATE and SERVICE cells indicate "input" data that a user of your spreadsheet is allowed to change; all other cells are either unchanging or are automatically calculated by the program. Columns will need to be widened to accommodate large numbers.

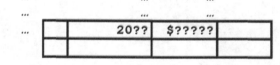

	A	B	C	D	
1		William T. Verts			*(your name as part of the header)*
2		WORK AT HOME			*(WORK AT LAB or WORK AT HOME)*
3		=NOW()			*(the current date/time)*
4					
5		RATE	9.000%		*(starting value of 9%, you will change this later)*
6		SERVICE	$0.00		*($0.00 in part 1, $2.00 in part 2)*
7					
8		CURRENTLY	$?????		*(the answer copied from the current year cell,*
9					*just over $100,000,000,000.00)*
10					
11					
12		YEAR	AMOUNT		*(all cells are right aligned)*
13		1626	$24.00		*(1626 & 24 are constants, 24 formatted as currency)*
14		1627	$26.16		*(these numbers and all following*
...		...	...		*are computed by formulae,*
...		...	...		*lots of lines of calculations go here)*
...		...	...		
...		20??	$?????		*(whatever the current year happens to be, and*
					just over $100,000,000,000.00 in current year)

 Make sure that the very top part of your spreadsheet (cells B1, B2, and B3) contains your name, either <u>WORK AT LAB</u> or <u>WORK AT HOME</u>, and the formula =NOW(), respectively. Type the labels **RATE**, **SERVICE**, **CURRENTLY**, **YEAR** and **AMOUNT** into the appropriate cells. Right justify these five new labels. Make all eight labels boldface.

 Type numeric constants **0.09** and **0** into the cells to the right of the RATE and SERVICE labels, respectively. Do <u>not</u> type anything into the cell to the right of the CURRENTLY label at this time (we will fill this cell in with a formula in a later step).

Excel 2003 & Excel 2008-2011 (Mac): Left click on the cell containing 0.09, then click on Edit-Format-Cells... in the menu (or right-click and select from the pop-up menu).

Excel 2007-2016: Left click on the cell containing 0.09, then click on the Home tab of the ribbon, and finally on the tiny arrow in the right corner of the Number panel.

Windows or Mac: Alternatively, you may <u>right click</u> on the cell containing 0.09, then choose Format Cells... from the pop up menu.

(Any method brings up a dialog box where you change the appearance of selected cells.)

In the Number tab of the Format Cells dialog, select Percentage from the Category: list, and set the Decimal Places: spin box to the value 3. Click on the OK button when these settings are correct. The 0.09 will change to appear on screen as 9.000% (it has the same value as before, just with a different format).

 Do not proceed until the format of this cell is set correctly.

Click on the cell containing the 0 next to SERVICE (to move the spreadsheet cursor), and bring up the Format Cells dialog box as you did before. If necessary, click on the Number tab in the dialog box. Set the format of this cell as follows:

- The Category: list must be set to Currency,
- The Decimal Places: spin box must be set to 2,
- The Symbol: drop down list contains a dollar sign ($), and
- The Negative Numbers: style is set to the last of the four styles, which appears on screen as ($1,234.10) in red.

Click the OK button when all options are correctly set, as shown in the following image, with Excel 2010/2013/2016 for Windows on the left and Excel 2008/2011 for the Mac on the right:

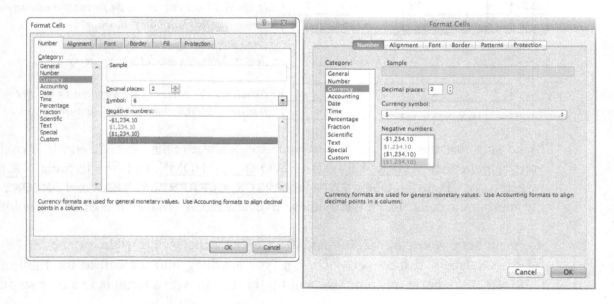

 This cell should now appear as $0.00 on screen. *Do not proceed* until this is so.

 Enter the constant **1626** in the cell below YEAR and the constant **24** in the cell below AMOUNT. Do not format these cells at this time. We will format the cell containing the 24 as currency in a later step.

Save your spreadsheet now.

Mousing around the Spreadsheet

Now that we have typed in the simple stuff, it is time to step back and examine some of the actions that you can perform in Excel using the mouse. This is necessary because there are a number of things you can accomplish just by "grabbing" various regions of the selected cell with the mouse and dragging them to another position on the spreadsheet.

Distinguishing between these actions can only be done by looking at the shape of the mouse cursor as it floats over the various regions of the selected cell(s). There are only a few basic mouse cursor shapes to be aware of. The "white cross" is used to <u>select</u> a region of cells (to establish formats for a lot of cells simultaneously, for example). The "quadruple arrow" in Excel XP-2016 for Windows and "hand" in Excel 2008-2011 for the Mac (or simple "arrow" in versions of Excel for Windows prior to Office XP) is used to <u>move</u> a formula or group of formulae from one place to another. The "black cross" is used to <u>copy</u> formulae from one place to another. The mouse cursor shapes are as follows:

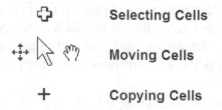

Selecting Cells

Moving Cells

Copying Cells

The mouse cursor is shown as the white cross if it is totally inside (or totally outside) the selected cell. It changes to the arrow or hand shapes for moving cells if it is placed on the edge of the selected cell, and it changes to the black cross for copying cells if it is placed on the tiny square in the lower right corner of the selected cell. These three regions are shown in the following image.

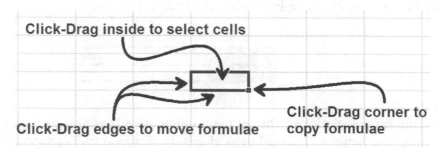

Click-Drag inside to select cells

Click-Drag edges to move formulae

Click-Drag corner to copy formulae

If you click-drag over a region of cells (white cross), the first of the selected cells will show up with a light background and the rest will have a darker background. This large region may be moved (arrow) or copied (black cross) in the same way as before. A single click on a cell will collapse a large selected region down to that newly selected cell. Practice selecting and collapsing groups of cells, floating the mouse over the black edges, and floating the mouse over the lower right corner of the selected regions until you are familiar with all mouse cursor shapes.

Setting Borders and Patterns

Select by click dragging (white cross) over the cells containing your name, WORK AT LAB or WORK AT HOME, and the current date/time at the top of your spreadsheet until all of the text in those three cells is inside the selection box (you may need to select both columns B and C, rows 1 through 3). While the cells are selected, bring up the Format-Cells... dialog box as you did earlier. Select (click on) the Border tab, click on a medium thick solid line from the Style: box, then click on the Outline button. This will draw a border around the selected cells. Next, click on the tab labeled Patterns (in Excel 2003 or Excel 2008 for the Mac) or Fill (in Excel 2007-2016 for Windows and Excel 2011 for the Mac), and then select a light color from the grid of colors (for this book I used the light cyan color, which maps to a medium gray on a black and white laser printer). Finally, click on the OK button to apply the border and pattern styles to the selected cells. Click in an empty cell of the spreadsheet to collapse the selected region and see your changes.

If you did these steps correctly, your name and other header information will be in a lightly colored box with a dark line around it. If you did not do these steps correctly, then go back and reselect the region, bring up the Format Cells dialog box, and try again. If you pick a background color that is too dark, your printout may show up as black on black. If so, reselect the region and pick a lighter background color. Do not pick a background color that is too light to show up on the printer.

Next, select the <u>four</u> cells containing RATE, SERVICE, and their corresponding values. Bring up the Format Cells dialog box, and in the Border tab select the same solid line style you did before, but this time click on **both** the Outline and Inside buttons, then close the dialog box by clicking on the OK button. Select the <u>two</u> cells containing the RATE and SERVICE labels only, bring up the Format Cells dialog box, and in the Patterns or Fill tab pick the same background color you did before. Click on the OK button to close the dialog box, and then click in an empty cell to collapse the selected region. If you did everything correctly, these four cells will look as follows:

RATE	9.000%
SERVICE	$0.00

Using the same techniques, format the remaining cells as you see in the image below (use the same line widths and background colors that you did earlier). Do not change the format of the cells containing 1626 or 24 at this time. Save your spreadsheet.

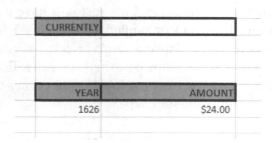

CURRENTLY	
YEAR	AMOUNT
1626	$24.00

Enter the Year Formulae

Now we start the interesting part of this assignment: creating the formulae that do the actual work!

Find the cell containing the number 1626, and click in the empty cell below it. The spreadsheet cursor will move to this empty cell.

In this empty cell, <u>write a formula</u> to calculate the value of the subsequent year (which is 1627, of course). This new formula should reference the *address of the cell* containing the 1626 and the *constant* 1, but should <u>not</u> contain either of the actual constant values 1626 or 1627. Remember that all formulae in Excel start with an equal sign.

Make sure that the spreadsheet cursor (the box with the dark outline) is in the cell that now contains the value 1627. Using the mouse, grab the small dark square in the lower right corner of that cell (the mouse cursor will change from the white cross to the black cross), then click drag the outline of the cursor box down a few cells. When you release the mouse button, the formula that generated the 1627 will be copied to all of the highlighted cells, and you will see a sequence of years (1627, 1628, 1629, ...) appear.

If you do not see this sequence of values appear, then you will need to go back and verify that you typed in the correct formula, then attempt to copy it again. If you see the sequence 1626, 1626, 1626, ..., the sequence 1627, 1627, 1627, ..., or get any message about circular references, then your formulae are in error and you need to reexamine them carefully. Move the spreadsheet cursor to any cells in error and then reenter the correct formulae.

Once you are satisfied that the formula is correct and that you can copy it successfully down a few cells, we are ready to have you copy the formula down to its full extent. Select one of the cells in the sequence of years generated by your year formula (any cell containing a year value from 1627 onwards will do), then copy it by click dragging the small black dot in the lower right corner of the cell (black cross) down some 400 or so cells. The sequence of years will start at 1626 and go some distance past the current year.

Because we intentionally had you go too far, you must erase some of the cells at the bottom of this column. Your position on screen should be at the bottom of the column of years; click on the cell containing the <u>last</u> year in the column to set the spreadsheet cursor to that point. Position your mouse pointer (white cross) inside the selected cell, then click drag *upwards* to select all cells back to and including the cell containing the *first year <u>after</u> the current year* (if it is 2018 right now then select years 2019 and beyond for deletion; if it is 2019 right now then select 2020 and beyond for deletion, and so on). Hit the [Del] key (Windows) or Edit-Clear-All (Mac) to get rid of all of the unneeded cell values; the last year remaining must be the current year. Your cursor will be at the bottom of the block you just erased. Go back to cell A1 at the top of your spreadsheet.

Save your spreadsheet again.

Design the Interest Formulae

What are interest rates and service charges? An interest rate is a percentage applied to how much you have in the bank that the bank pays to you (adds to your account) for the privilege of holding your money. A service charge is the price the bank extracts from you (subtracts from your account) for the business of maintaining your account. With any luck the interest you gain is more than the charge you lose!

For example, assume that we had $100 in the bank last year. With a 5% annual interest rate and a $1 per year service charge, the amount in our bank account this year will be computed as $100 + $100×5% - $1. By the normal order-of-operations of mathematics used in spreadsheets, this reduces to $100 + $5 - $1, or $104 as the final result. The amount in the bank for next year will be $104 + $104×5% - $1, or $108.20, and so on. The formula is essentially the same in all cases: the amount in the bank last year, plus the amount in the bank last year times the interest rate, minus the service charge.

```
(Amount  +  Amount * Interest Rate  -  Service Charge)
```

To write this expression into an Excel formula, you **replace the numbers with the appropriate <u>cell addresses</u>**. You do <u>not</u> write the formula using any numeric constants! Even though the value of the service charge starts out at zero you still <u>must</u> use its cell address in your formula now. We will change its value later.

The tricky part of this formula is that the cell address of the amount is *allowed to change* when the formula is copied, but the addresses to the interest rate and service charge cells *must remain unchanged* no matter how the formula is copied. This is one of the major concepts of this assignment: when do you use relative addressing (no dollar signs, as in X15) and when do you use absolute addressing (with dollar signs, as in $X$15)?

Enter the Interest Formula

In the amount cell next to year 1627 have the spreadsheet calculate the amount in the bank for that year. To do this, <u>write a formula</u> that starts with the value that was in the bank for the *previous* year, and then add to it the amount generated by interest, and finally subtract off the service charge. For 9% interest and $0 service charge, you will see 26.16 appear as the amount for 1627.

Copy this formula down so there is an answer for every year from 1626 to the present.

The resulting numbers you see on screen should visibly **increase**. At this stage the service charge is zero, so with any positive interest value the numbers logically will increase (you get more and more money in the bank each year). Your original formula contains an error if the numbers stay the same for a while or grow wildly, or if you get any error message such as #VALUE!. Check the addressing mode (relative vs. absolute) for the interest rate and service charge cells in your formula. Correct your formula (the one that computes the amount for 1627), then copy the corrected formula down through all years from 1627 to the present.

Final Formats

You may be in the lower section of your spreadsheet at this time. Send the cursor back to cell A1.

Click drag to <u>select</u> (not copy) the entire column of money numbers, from the 24 down to the amount in the bank for the current year, bring up the Format Cells... dialog box, then format the entire column using the same currency styles as before (Currency, 2 decimals, using the last of the four Negative Numbers: styles, and using the $ symbol). The entire column will acquire this format. In some versions of Excel, a few numbers would be so large that they will appear as ########### in the cells; in other versions Excel will automatically widen the column appropriately. We will adjust column widths in a later step, as necessary.

Save your spreadsheet again.

Getting the Final Result

We now need to be able to change the interest rate and service charge cells and see the final result for the current year appear nearby, without jumping back and forth between the top of the spreadsheet (to set the new values) and bottom of the spreadsheet (to see the result in the current year).

In the cell just to the right of the CURRENTLY cell, **write a formula** that picks up and displays the <u>final calculated amount</u> from the <u>cell containing the last year</u> of calculations. It is a surprisingly simple formula, so I'll leave it to you to figure out! Format the cell to appear as currency as you did before.

This cell may appear as ###########, as will many of the calculations farther on down the spreadsheet. This means that the numbers are so large that with the requested formatting they will not fit into the cells. To widen the column, move the mouse up to the column header at the top of the spreadsheet, position it between the column that is too narrow and the one to its right (the mouse cursor will change to a double headed arrow), then click drag the boundary to the right. When you release the mouse button, the column will adjust to the new size. If the column is still not big enough, repeat the process until it is.

Save your spreadsheet.

At this point, you are done with your spreadsheet design. Unless you made mistakes, you will not change any formulae again. What remains is to change the input numbers until we get the desired output, and print the results.

Reality Check

It took a lot of work to get to this point. The Excel 2013/2016 image below shows what you should see on screen at this time. Notice that the cells are all properly formatted, the formulae have been entered, and the final result (for 2018 in this case) appears in cell C8. Make sure that everything is correct before proceeding to the next steps.

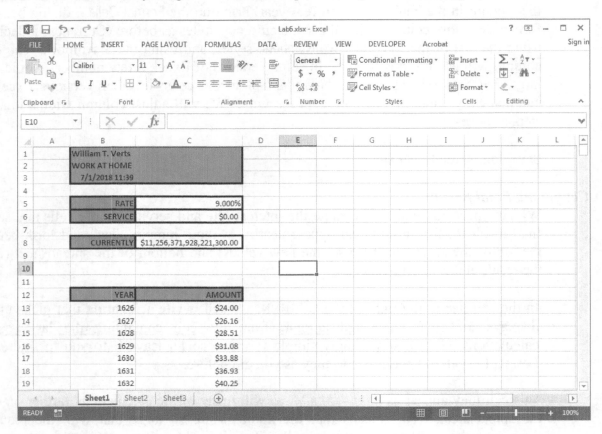

Depending on when you perform this assignment, the final result for the current year may be different from what you see in the image. The table below shows the final results expected for various years, under 9.000% interest and $0 service charge. Note that the amounts you actually get may differ slightly from the numbers shown here if you use a spreadsheet package other than Microsoft Excel (internal variations in how numbers are stored may cause problems with numeric precision).

Current Year	Final Amount for 9.000%
2015	$8,691,984,448,395,600.00
2016	$9,474,263,048,751,200.00
2017	$10,326,946,723,138,800.00
2018	$11,256,371,928,221,300.00
2019	$12,269,445,401,761,200.00
2020	$13,373,695,487,919,700.00
2021	$14,577,328,081,832,500.00

Finding the Interest Rate (Part I)

Make sure the service charge is $0.00 (zero).

Change the number in the interest rate cell so that the amount in the bank in the current year is just <u>slightly</u> <u>more</u> than $100 billion (that is, $100,000,000,000.00, or a 1 followed by eleven more digits before the decimal point).

Now, go find the correct rate to a precision of 0.001%. Because we had you format the interest rate cell as a percentage, type in the numbers directly as percentages. For example, the number 9.876% is internally stored as 0.09876 (with 5 decimal places), but you should type 9.876 into the cell (with 3 decimal places). You do not need to put in the percent sign; that is done automatically for you as part of the percentage format.

We are using only 3 decimal places in the interest rate, so the correct answer is a value where subtracting 0.001% would cause the amount in the bank to go below $100 billion. Suppose, for example, that 1.234% generates more than $100 billion, but 1.233% generates a value less than $100 billion; the correct answer would be the 1.234% figure. The correct answer might be quite a bit more than $100 billion; just make certain that your final result contains at least <u>twelve</u> digits to the left of the decimal point (some students confuse millions, billions, and trillions).

Think about how you might search for the correct rate: if 9% is way too high, and 1% is way too low, try 5%, which is half way in the middle. Continue to split the range in half, discarding the half <u>not</u> containing the answer, until you find a result with sufficient precision. This is a very fast process called a *binary search*!

Printing (Part 1 of 4)

Select (click drag with the mouse, white cross) the top part of the spreadsheet from cell B1 (containing your name) down through the computed amount in the bank for 1650.

Excel 2003: In the menu click on File-Print Area-Set Print Area to select that block. Click File-Print Preview to see how the page will look when printed. Click on the Setup... button. In the Page Setup dialog box make sure that the Portrait radio button is set (but <u>not</u> the Landscape button), then click the OK button.
Excel 2007: In the Page Layout tab of the ribbon, click Print Area-Set Print Area. Click Office Button-Print-Print Preview to see how the page will look when printed. Click on Page Setup in the Print tab of Print Preview. In the Page Setup dialog box make sure that the Portrait radio button is set (but <u>not</u> the Landscape button), then click the OK button.
Excel 2010-2016: In the Page Layout tab of the ribbon, click Print Area-Set Print Area. Click the File tab, then Print to see how the page will look on the printer. Make certain that the Orientation drop-down list is set to Portrait Orientation.
Excel 2008-2011 (Mac): In the menu click on File-Print Area-Set Print Area to select that block. Click File-Print, then in the print dialog click on the Page Setup button. In the Page Setup dialog box make sure that the Portrait radio button is set (but <u>not</u> the Landscape button), then click the OK button.

Print the selected section of the spreadsheet.

 Excel 2003 & Excel 2008-2011 (Mac): Click on File-Print Area-Clear Print Area.
Excel 2007-2016: In the Page Layout tab of the ribbon, click Print Area-Clear Print Area.

 Do NOT print out all years between 1650 and 1990 – you'll get lots and Lots and LOTS of output! Let's not cut down any more trees than we have to!

 Go to the bottom of the spreadsheet, click drag over the region of years and amounts from 1990 up through and including the current year, set the print area, then preview the block and **print it** as before, and finally clear out the print area.

Printing (Part 2 of 4)

On the keyboard, enter `Ctrl` ` or `Ctrl` ~ (the ` and ~ symbols are on the same key-top). The view of the spreadsheet will change to show the formulae, and <u>not</u> their computed values. We want to make sure that your methods are correct.

 As you did before, set the print area to the top of the spreadsheet (your name and the block between 1626 and 1650), preview it, **print it**, and clear out the print area.

 Set the print area to the bottom of the spreadsheet (the block from 1990 through the current year, inclusive), preview it, **print it**, and clear out the print area.

When you are finished with all the printing tasks, enter `Ctrl` ` or `Ctrl` ~ to restore the spreadsheet view to the results instead of the formulae.

Finding the Interest Rate (Part 2)

Change the service charge to **$2.00**, and then <u>repeat the task</u> of finding the correct smallest interest rate to a precision of 0.001% that generates <u>just above</u> $100 billion in the current year.

Watch out for numbers enclosed in parentheses: if you see a red number in parentheses such as (**$100,103,234,535.56**) in your spreadsheet, it is *negative, which is wrong*! If you look closely, you will see that the amount in the bank starts at $24 in 1626, but immediately starts <u>decreasing</u>: the amount being added to the account in interest is *less* than the amount subtracted in the service charge! This is a dead giveaway that something is wrong. Negative currency amounts are shown with surrounding parentheses. You don't have $100 billion in the bank; <u>you owe the bank</u> *billions and billions* (as Carl Sagan is reputed to have said)! You must *increase* the interest rate to find a new value. This calculation is very sensitive to the initial interest rate value; your final correct answer may surprise you!

Save your spreadsheet.

Printing (Part 3 of 4)

As you did before, set the print area to the top of the spreadsheet (your name and the block between 1626 and 1650), preview it, **print it**, and clear out the print area.

Set the print area to the bottom of the spreadsheet (the block from 1990 through the current year, inclusive), preview it, **print it**, and clear out the print area.

Printing (Part 4 of 4)

On the keyboard, enter Ctrl ` or Ctrl ~ (the ` and ~ symbols are on the same key-top). The view of the spreadsheet will change to show the formulae, and <u>not</u> their computed values. Again, we want to make sure that your methods are correct.

As you did before, set the print area to the top of the spreadsheet (your name and the block between 1626 and 1650), preview it, **print it**, and clear out the print area.

Set the print area to the bottom of the spreadsheet (the block from 1990 through the current year, inclusive), preview it, **print it**, and clear out the print area.

When you are finished with all the printing tasks, enter Ctrl ` or Ctrl ~ to restore the spreadsheet view to the results instead of the formulae.

Save your spreadsheet.

<u>**Your spreadsheet work is now complete.**</u>

What Can Go Wrong

Plenty. Make certain that both final answers are greater than or equal to $100 billion, but less than a trillion dollars. Count the number of digits in your answers: $100 billion is $100,000,000,000 (twelve digits long). These calculations are extremely sensitive to the interest rate, particularly in the case where there is a service charge. The closest you can get and still keep the interest rate limited to the correct number of decimal places may give you a positive answer well above +$500 billion, or even more!

Creating the Banner Page

As you have done in previous assignments, start Microsoft Word running and create a banner page containing your name, the phrase LAB ASSIGNMENT #6, WORK AT LAB or WORK AT HOME, and the current date, all at the top of the page, hitting [Enter ←] after each line. Select these lines with the mouse. **Center** the lines, make sure that they are in the Times New Roman typeface, and change the size to **20 points**. Format the document to be single-spaced, with *no extra spacing* between the lines.

Word 2003: Save the document as **LAB6.DOC** in your Word Processing folder.

Word 2007-2016, or Word 2008-2011 (Mac): Save the document as **LAB6.DOCX** in your Word Processing folder.

In Word, **print** out your completed banner page. This page will become the cover page (page #1) of your report. This is what that page, and all banner pages for subsequent labs, should look like (with your name and the current date, where appropriate):

William T. Verts
LAB ASSIGNMENT #6
WORK AT HOME
November 1, 2013

Shutting Down

Close all programs. If Microsoft Word or Microsoft Excel asks you if you want to save any changes, you generally should answer "yes". Close down your computer normally.

What to Turn In

You will need to turn in the printout of your spreadsheet, containing the following items (check off the items in the list below):

☐ Have you designed your spreadsheet so that by changing the values in the interest rate and service charge cells, you get the correct amount in the bank for all years between 1626 and the current year? How can you determine if your calculations are correct?

☐ Did you format the cells so that they appear correctly?

☐ Are your name, WORK AT LAB or WORK AT HOME, and the current date/time at the top of the spreadsheet?

Page #1 (the banner page) must contain:
    ☐ Your name (centered),
    ☐ LAB ASSIGNMENT #6 (centered),
    ☐ WORK AT LAB or WORK AT HOME (centered),
    ☐ Current date (centered),
    ☐ No extra spaces between lines.
    ☐ Font must be Times New Roman, 20 Points.

Pages #2 through #3 ($0.00 service charge)
    ☐ Did you find the best interest rate for a $0.00 service charge?
    ☐ Are your name, date, etc., printed at the top of the spreadsheet? (page 2)
    ☐ Did you print results from the top through year 1650? (page 2)
    ☐ Did you print results from 1990 through the current year? (page 3)

Pages #4 through #5 ($0.00 service charge)
    ☐ Are your name, date, etc., printed at the top of the spreadsheet? (page 4)
    ☐ Did you print formulae from the top through year 1650? (page 4)
    ☐ Did you print formulae from 1990 through the current year? (page 5)

Pages #6 through #7 ($2.00 service charge)
    ☐ Did you find the best interest rate for a $2.00 service charge?
    ☐ Are your name, date, etc., printed at the top of the spreadsheet? (page 6)
    ☐ Did you print results from the top through year 1650? (page 6)
    ☐ Did you print results from 1990 through the current year? (page 7)

Pages #8 through #9 ($2.00 service charge)
    ☐ Are your name, date, etc., printed at the top of the spreadsheet? (page 8)
    ☐ Did you print formulae from the top through year 1650? (page 8)
    ☐ Did you print formulae from 1990 through the current year? (page 9)

Grading Policy

Lab assignments are worth 10 points each. Teaching assistants will observe the following criteria for evaluating and scoring the Lab #6 assignments that they receive.

- Any report that does not have the student's name *typed* on *all appropriate* pages (centered at the top of the banner page, and as part of the header on pages 2, 4, 6, and 8 of the report) will be *rejected*, and if submitted will receive a *zero*. If any student writes their name in by hand, instead of typing it, then the report must be rejected. **Reject any report missing a banner page.**

- 1 Point - Report must be stapled together. Remove the full point if the report is paper-clipped together or is submitted loose (even with folded corners). Remove the full point if the pages are not in this order:
    1. Banner,
    2. spreadsheet top results for $0 service charge,
    3. spreadsheet bottom results for $0 service charge,
    4. spreadsheet top formulae for $0 service charge,
    5. spreadsheet bottom formulae for $0 service charge,
    6. spreadsheet top results for $2 service charge,
    7. spreadsheet bottom results for $2 service charge,
    8. spreadsheet top formulae for $2 service charge,
    9. spreadsheet bottom formulae for $2 service charge.

- 1 Point - Printout of the banner page must be present and must contain the appropriate lines of information. Remove ½ point for every missing banner line or incorrect format (for example: a line not centered, the font not set to 20 point Times New Roman, or the lines are not single spaced with no extra spacing between lines) up to the full point possible.

- 1 Point - Remove the point for any errors in formatting the spreadsheet (missing date/time lines, incorrect formatting of borders and patterns, incorrect cell justification, incorrect numeric formats, etc.).

- 3 Points - Remove 2 points if either the first interest rate (for $0 service charge) or the second interest rate (for $2 service charge) is wrong by more than 0.001%, remove all 3 points if both are wrong by more than 0.001%. Remove 1 point if the interest rate for the $0 service charge is wrong by exactly 0.001%. Remove 1 point if the interest rate for the $2 service charge is wrong by exactly 0.001%.

- 2 Points - Values in the CURRENTLY cell at the top of the spreadsheet must match the value in the row value at the bottom of the block of calculations. Remove 1 point if these values do not match for the $0 service charge pages. Remove 1 point if these values do not match for the $2 service charge pages.

- 1 Point - Some students may ignore the restriction to stay within ±0.001% in the interest rate and carry the calculations out more decimal places in an attempt to hit $100,000,000,000 exactly. Remove the point if they do so.

- 1 Point - Remove the point if they printed out more than or fewer than the right number of rows on any sections (1626-1650, or 1990-current year).

- **5 Additional Penalty Points** - After all other scoring is completed, TAs must check the four formulae pages to ensure that students completely followed all of the directions. Remove additional points for any of the following infractions, but do not go below zero points total (in other words, even if the rest of the report *appears to be perfect*, you can still lose up to five points for solving the problem the wrong way):

Remove 2 additional points if formulae page 4 ($0, top) is missing.

Remove 1 additional point if formulae page 5 ($0, bottom) is missing.

Remove 2 additional points if formulae page 8 ($2, top) is missing.

Remove 1 additional point if formulae page 9 ($2, bottom) is missing.

Remove 1 additional point if the date formula in cell B3 is wrong.

Remove 1 additional point if the "currently" formula in cell C8 is wrong.

Remove 1 additional point if the interest rate is carried out to too many decimal places.

Remove 1 additional point if the computation formulae in cell B14 and onwards are wrong (particularly if they contain constant numbers and not formulae).

Remove 3 additional points if the computation formulae in cells C14 and onwards are obviously wrong or use the wrong method.

Lab #7 – Spreadsheets: Design & Query

Introduction & Goals

In this lab you will design a spreadsheet to obtain meaningful information from a large collection of data. This is the most complicated assignment in the book, so proceed carefully and check your work at each of the testing stations along the way. **You cannot use either Excel 2008 for the Macintosh or Excel 2010 <u>Starter</u> for Windows for this assignment.** (Later versions of Excel for the Macintosh are fine.) This assignment requires the use of Visual Basic macros, which are not enabled in either of those versions.

Some time ago we obtained some statistics from 80 countries in such areas as murder rate (murders per 1000 persons), physical quality of life (an index, where 100 is perfect), female literacy rate (percent of female population), and military expenditures (percent of the country's gross national product). Unknown data in any category have the value -1. Those data have been typed into the Excel spreadsheet `world.xlsx` (a copy of the data appears at the end of this assignment). We want to create a worksheet from those data to help us answer some questions about the countries, such as the following examples:

- What countries have a murder rate above 9.3?

- What countries spend 13% or more of their GNP on the military, have 8% or less female literacy, and have a quality of life index less than 70?

- What countries have a quality of life index greater than 50% and a military expenditure less than 5%?

The set up for this problem is long, tedious, and intricate. It is possible to make lots of mistakes if you are not careful. You will learn how to test your spreadsheet as it is being constructed to avoid having to "rip out" and rebuild large sections. Once everything has been set up correctly, you will have a system at the end of this assignment where you can easily ask the kinds of questions listed above, and see what countries match the desired criteria. For some questions *no* countries will match. As you learn more about spreadsheets and databases, you will discover that the problem described here is really more suited to a database package than to a spreadsheet package, but part of our lesson is that you can indeed perform these kinds of tasks in a spreadsheet. Knowing when to use one type of tool and when to use another is an important skill to develop.

No matter when you read this assignment, the country data that we provide to you are laughably out of date. Some of the named countries no longer exist, countries that do exist are missing from the list, and the statistical numbers for the listed countries have surely changed since we compiled the data. Be aware that it is the *process* that we are interested in exploring here, and that in "real life" your answers will be different from what we obtain in this assignment as you update the country data to reflect the actual state of the world. Just because you got the answers from a computer doesn't mean that they have any bearing on reality!

Specifics You Will Learn in This Assignment

You will learn the following things in this assignment.

- **How to use Multiple Windows and Multiple Spreadsheet Pages** – You will be copying data from one spreadsheet to another, and creating a spreadsheet requiring several separate pages. You will print each of the pages separately, and in one case you will print a page multiple times.

- **How to use Functions** – Functions are pre-built routines that come as part of any spreadsheet package. The two you will use here are SUM to add up a range of cells, and IF to have the spreadsheet choose between two alternatives based on a logical expression. Using the IF function correctly will require that you remember and review the early material about truth tables.

- **How to use Range Names** – Rather than remember cell addresses, we can give cells names and use the names as part of our formulae. Copying a formula that includes a range name treats that name as if it were absolute, instead of relative.

- **How to Format Cells and Hide Columns** – You will format parts of your spreadsheet to include shading and lines, and you will hide columns of intermediate calculations.

- **How to use Data Validation** – Excel has the ability to restrict what is entered into a cell to only one item picked from a predefined list of items. This prevents a user from entering any unacceptable values into a cell.

- **How to use the Filter or AutoFilter Database Facility** – Since we are looking up answers in a table, we will need to use the Filter facility to help establish our queries.

- **How to Write Macros** – Finally, when we get the results of our database query, we need to copy those answers to our output sheet. This task will be automated with a simple macro. (Macros are *disabled* in Excel 2008 for the Macintosh and Excel 2010 <u>Starter</u> Edition for Windows, but Excel 2011 for the Mac and the regular Excel 2010 and Excel 2013 for Windows all work just fine.)

Preparation before Starting Assignment

Read this assignment through in its entirety before doing anything. This lab does not depend on the data files you created in any earlier assignment, but you will store new files in the directories created in lab #1.

In the Laboratory

Bring your flash drive containing the folders created in lab #1 and this lab assignment. Do not come to lab without these items.

At Home

Your home machine must have a working version of Microsoft Excel and a working printer, as usual. Almost any version of Excel will work here from Excel 97 onwards, but the instructions are written for later versions of Excel for both Microsoft Windows and Apple Macintosh. However, this assignment cannot be performed on either Excel 2008 for the Mac or on Excel 2010 Starter Edition. You must be able to locate the folders created in lab #1.

Note for Mac Users

Microsoft Excel 2011 for the Mac has what seems like a combination of features from other versions of the program. All commands can be executed through the traditional menus (as does Excel 2003 for Windows and Excel 2008 for the Mac), many functions can be performed by clicking on a button in a toolbar at the top of the window (like Excel 2008 for the Mac), and it also has the ribbon (like Excel 2010-2016 for Windows). The instructions for this assignment will be targeted towards the menus for Excel 2003 for Windows and Excel 2011 for the Mac, but towards the ribbon for later versions of Excel for Windows. If you are using a Mac and want to use the toolbar or the ribbon instead of the menus, go ahead. Use whatever gets the job done.

Data Files

There is one spreadsheet data file, called `world`, provided to you in compressed form on the class Web site in a `.zip` archive. You must download it from the class web site and unpack the contents (you will need some utility on your computer that can unpack the `.zip` archive format). The unpacked file is to be placed into your Spreadsheets folder.

Step-By-Step Procedure

Start your computer up normally. Download and unpack the `world` data file to the Spreadsheets folder. See the instructions on unpacking `.zip` files in lab 4 if you've forgotten how to do this. Note that you <u>must</u> extract the `world` data file from the `.zip` archive before you can use it; you *cannot* launch Excel by double-clicking the file while it is still inside the archive. Doing so will prevent you from saving any changes to that file. Instead, open the archive, and then click-drag the `world` file from the archive into your Spreadsheets folder. After the file has been extracted successfully, you may close, or even delete, the `.zip` archive.

A text copy of the data you will use appears as reference at the end of this assignment.

Starting Up

Find and run the Microsoft Excel program (it may take several seconds to start up, so be patient). If asked for what kind of Excel file to use, answer with an Excel Workbook or Blank workbook. Maximize the window if necessary. As you did in the previous assignment, configure Excel to a "standard" look.

We will need three sheets (Sheet1, Sheet2, and Sheet3) in the notebook. If for any reason you see more than three or fewer than three sheets present, you must perform the following instructions:

Excel 7 (Office 95): Click on the Sheet4 tab, then hold down the Ctrl key while you click on the tabs for Sheet5 through Sheet16. All sheets from 4 through 16 should now be selected; click Edit-Delete Sheet, then click the OK button to delete the unneeded sheets.

Adding sheets: Next to the rightmost tab at the bottom of the window there is a small tab or plus-sign. Click that tab or plus-sign to create a new notebook page containing a new worksheet. If necessary, activate each of these new pages and configure the sheets to a "standard" look.

Deleting sheets: Right-click or two-finger click a notebook page tab and select Delete from the pop-up menu.

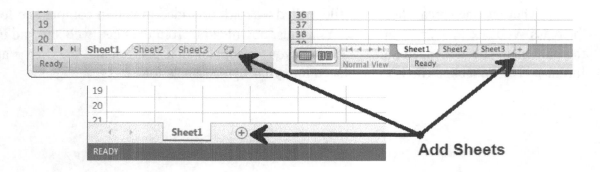

Add Sheets

<u>*Do not proceed*</u> until there are exactly <u>three notebook tabs</u> in the spreadsheet, labeled Sheet1, Sheet2, and Sheet3.

Sheet1: When you see the blank spreadsheet on screen, *right click* on the Sheet1 tab at the bottom of the page; click the Rename menu entry in the popup menu (or click Format-Sheet-Rename in the menus on a Mac), and then change the name of Sheet1 to Header.

Type your name into cell A1, either WORK AT LAB or WORK AT HOME into cell A2, and the formula =NOW() into cell A3.

Select all three cells (with the white cross), then format all three cells as **Boldface**.

Left justify all three cells.

Widen column A so that no text spills over into column B.

Use the Format-Cells... dialog box to draw a medium thick solid border outlining the three cells, and shade those cells with a medium color pattern (dark enough to show up on the printer, but not so dark that the text is obscured).

Once the three cells have been formatted correctly, and while the three cells are still selected, copy them to the clipboard as follows (we will paste this information into the second and third sheets).

Excel 2003 / Excel 2011 (Mac): Click on Edit-Copy in the menu.

Excel 2007-2016: Click on the Home tab of the ribbon and then on Copy in the Clipboard panel.

Either: Type Ctrl C at the keyboard (Windows) or ⌘C (Mac).

Sheet2: Click on the Sheet2 tab and rename it to Input Output (including the space between Input and Output). Click in cell A1 and then paste the clipboard contents:

Excel 2003 / Excel 2011 (Mac): Click on Edit-Paste in the menu.

Excel 2007-2016: Click on the Home tab of the ribbon and then on Paste in the Clipboard panel.

Either: Type Ctrl V at the keyboard (Windows) or ⌘V (Mac).

The information in the colored box that you created on the first sheet will appear here without retyping. Widen column A as necessary.

Sheet3: Click on the Sheet3 tab and rename it to Data. Click in cell A1 and paste the contents of the clipboard again. Widen column A as necessary.

Saving the File

Excel 2003: Click on File-Save or File-Save As... to save the entire spreadsheet notebook into your Spreadsheets folder as **lab7.xls** (if you type the name without typing the .xls extension, Excel will add the correct extension automatically).

Excel 2007: Click on Office Button-Save As, pick Excel Macro-Enabled Workbook, and save the file into your Spreadsheets folder as **lab7.xlsm** (set the Save as type option in the save dialog to Excel Macro-Enabled Workbook; do <u>not</u> save this as an .xlsx file).

Excel 2010-2016: Click on the File tab, then click Save As. In Excel 2013/2016 click the Browse button. Set the Save as type option in the save dialog to Excel Macro-Enabled Workbook, and save the file into your Spreadsheets folder as **lab7.xlsm** (do <u>not</u> save this as an .xlsx file).

Excel 2011 (Mac): Click on File-Save or File-Save As..., whichever is available, set the Format: option in the save dialog to Excel Macro-Enabled Workbook, and save the entire spreadsheet notebook into your Spreadsheets folder as **lab7.xlsm** (do <u>not</u> save this as an .xlsx file).

Case does not matter: the file can be called lab7, Lab7, or LAB7.

In the future, when loading an .xlsm file you may get a security warning saying that macros have been disabled, next to an Options button. Click on Options *immediately* and select the Enable this content radio button from the dialog. If you do not do this, the option will become unavailable after you make changes to the spreadsheet, thus forcing you to close and reopen the file to make the Options button visible once more.

Click on the Header tab to select that page of the lab7 spreadsheet notebook.

Your spreadsheet should now have your personal information and the current date/time present in cells A1, A2, and A3 on all three pages, and the three pages should be named Header, Input Output, and Data in that order. Your spreadsheet should be saved onto your disk (as lab7.xls in Excel 2003 and as lab7.xlsm in Excel 2007-2016 for Windows, and Excel 2011 for the Mac).

Do not proceed unless this is so.

The Second Window

In this section we will load in the spreadsheet file containing the world data and copy those data into our master spreadsheet. If something goes wrong with our spreadsheet and we lose the data, we can always recopy them in the same manner as shown here.

Excel 2003: Using File-Open, load the `world.xls` spreadsheet file into Excel. Your `lab7.xls` file is still active in Excel, but is hidden behind the `world.xls` window.

Excel 2007: Using Office Button-Open, load the `world.xlsx` spreadsheet file into Excel. Both `lab7.xlsm` and `world.xlsx` will have buttons on the task bar you will use to select between the two windows, and the `world` data will now be visible.

Excel 2010-2016: Click on the File tab, then on Open, and then load the `world.xlsx` spreadsheet file into Excel. If you get a warning message saying that the file originated from an Internet location, click the Enable Editing button. Both `lab7.xlsm` and `world.xlsx` will have buttons on the task bar you will use to select between the two windows, and the `world` data will now be visible.

Excel 2011 (Mac): Using File-Open, load the `world.xlsx` spreadsheet file into Excel. Your `lab7.xlsm` file is still active in Excel, but may be hidden behind the `world.xlsx` window. Maximize the window.

Look carefully at the `world` data, but <u>do not</u> make any changes to this file.

Click drag (using the white cross mouse cursor) over all data in the `world` file to select all of the cells containing information (five columns and 81 rows of information). Copy those cells to the clipboard.

Excel 2003: In the Window menu, select the `lab7.xls` file at the bottom of the list (the `world.xls` file will vanish, but is still safely loaded into Excel).

Excel 2007-2016: Click the button on the task bar for `lab7.xlsm` (the `world.xlsx` file will vanish, but is still safely loaded into Excel).

Excel 2011 (Mac): In the Window menu, select the `lab7.xlsm` file at the bottom of the list (the `world.xlsx` file will vanish, but is still safely loaded into Excel).

Click on the tab for the Data page of the `lab7` spreadsheet notebook.

Click on cell A5 to set the cursor position. Finally, paste the `world` data into the `lab7` spreadsheet starting at cell A5.

Set the width of all columns so that all data are visible. To do this, click-drag <u>on the right side boundary of a cell in the column header</u> to set the size of the column manually, or double-click on that boundary to have Excel set the column width to the optimum size.

Save your spreadsheet now.

Building the Input/Output Table

In this section we will be constructing an input table for us to use to enter data values into the spreadsheet and see the results. In order to make some later formulae easy to write, we will be naming twelve input cells with special names. We will also be formatting the table so that it looks nice on the screen and printer.

Go to the Input Output section (click on its tab).

In cell G1 type the word **YES** (all capitals) and in cell G2 type the word **NO** (also all capitals). These cells will be referenced in a later step.

Construct the table shown in the next image, putting **Ask?** in cell B7 and **Military** in cell C6. Manually type in the labels shown in the shaded areas of the table. Center each label, and make all labels boldface. Do not type anything in the white areas at this time. Widen the first column as shown.

Click drag over the region containing the labels Military, Literacy, Murder, and Quality to select those four cells, then *right click* on the selected region and pick Format Cells... from the popup menu. Click the Border tab in the Format Cells dialog box, click on the medium thick solid line width in the Style box and Outline in the Presets list. Click on the Patterns tab (Excel 2003) or Fill tab (Excel 2007-2016, Excel 2011 for the Mac), select a medium or light color value, and then click the OK button.

Repeat this process for the region of cells containing Ask?, Low-Value, and High-Value. Use the same color shade in Patterns that you did in the previous step.

Repeat this process for the cell containing Names, and for the cell containing Total.

Draw the outline box with medium-thick lines (no colored shading) for the twelve cells containing the names *ASK_1*, *ASK_2*, etc. Draw the outline box with medium-thick lines (no colored shading) for the cell to the right of Total.

Don't type in anything right now in the cells that are white.

	A	B	C	D	E	F	G	H
1	William T. Verts						YES	
2	WORK AT HOME						NO	
3	7/1/2013 22:50							
4								
5								
6			Military	Literacy	Murder	Quality		
7		Ask?	ASK_1	ASK_2	ASK_3	ASK_4		
8		Low-Value	LOW_1	LOW_2	LOW_3	LOW_4		
9		High-Value	HIGH_1	HIGH_2	HIGH_3	HIGH_4		
10								
11		Names			Total			
12								

Excel 2003 / Excel 2011 (Mac): Click on the cell labeled *ASK_1* in the image, then on Insert-Name-Define. In the Names in workbook: box, type ASK_1 (do not forget the underscore), and then click the OK button. Nothing will appear in the cell on screen.

Excel 2007-2016: Click on the cell labeled *ASK_1* in the image. Click on the Formulas tab in the ribbon, and then click the Define Name entry in the Defined Names panel. In the Name: box type ASK_1 (do not forget the underscore), and then click the OK button. Nothing will appear in the cell on screen. If you forget the underscore, the name ASK1 will <u>not</u> work because there is a spreadsheet cell with that name as its address.

Click on each successive cell, and give the cell the <u>name</u> listed in italics from the sample table. You will be performing this action a total of twelve times, once for each name (do not forget the underscores in the names):

> *ASK_1*
> *ASK_2*
> *ASK_3*
> *ASK_4*
> *LOW_1*
> *LOW_2*
> *LOW_3*
> *LOW_4*
> *HIGH_1*
> *HIGH_2*
> *HIGH_3*
> *HIGH_4*

Nothing will appear on screen in these twelve cells as you name them.

To test that you have done everything correctly, click once in turn on each of the twelve cells that you just named. As you select each cell, the <u>name</u> that you defined for that cell will appear in the drop down list above the upper left corner of the spreadsheet work area. Use this technique to verify that all twelve cells have been named correctly.

Common errors at this point include forgetting to name one of the twelve cells, giving a cell a name that is not spelled correctly, or giving one cell two different names at the same time (that is, applying a range name to the wrong cell). All of these problems can be repaired. In Excel 2010-2016 for Windows, click on the Formulas tab of the ribbon, then on Name Manager. In Excel 2011 for the Mac, click on Insert-Name-Define. In either case a dialog box pops up that will allow range names to be created or deleted, and possibly even renamed or reassigned to new cells, depending on the version of Excel in use.

Excel 2003 / Excel 2011 (Mac): Click on cell C7. In the menu, click Data-Validation, and in the Settings tab of the dialog box that pops up, set Allow: to **List**, <u>un</u>check the Ignore Blank check box, and type the formula **=G1 : G2** into the Source box. Click OK to close the dialog.

Excel 2007-2016: Click on cell C7. Click on the Data tab of the ribbon, then in the Data Tools panel on Data Validation-Data Validation. In the Settings tab of the dialog box that pops up, set Allow: to **List**, <u>un</u>check the Ignore Blank checkbox, and type the formula **=G1 : G2** into the Source box. Click OK to close the dialog.

Cell C7 will now have a drop-down button on its right side. Click this button and select NO, then click it again and select YES. Cell C7 may now contain only those two values (the values YES and NO from cells G1 and G2).

<u>**Repeat this process**</u> to set identical drop-down buttons on cells D7, E7, and F7. In all cases use the same formula =G1 : G2 in the Source box.

Now, for cells C8 : F9 type in the initial numerical values as shown in the following table, and then <u>center</u> the text and numbers as shown (set the column widths appropriately). Notice that the cursor is in cell C7, which is showing the drop-down button at its right side.

	A	B	C	D	E	F	G	H
1	William T. Verts						YES	
2	WORK AT HOME						NO	
3	7/1/2013 22:50							
4								
5								
6			Military	Literacy	Murder	Quality		
7		Ask?	YES	YES	YES	YES		
8		Low-Value	0	95	0	95		
9		High-Value	10	100	10	100		
10								
11		Names			Total			
12								

<u>*Do not proceed*</u> to the next step until your table and the Input Output page looks like the image above and has had the twelve range names created correctly.

Save your spreadsheet now.

Building New Column Labels

Now we need to construct five new columns of formulae, next to the world data in the Data sheet, which will help determine which countries match the search criteria entered into the table on the Input Output sheet.

Click on the tab for the Data page of the spreadsheet notebook.

Cell E5 should contain the label that says QUALITY; in the cell to its right (F5) type the label PICK1. Make sure the cursor is on the PICK1 cell. Click on the lower right corner of the cell (it is a little black button in some versions of Excel), and then drag the selection (with the black cross) to the right for three more cells. This will copy the PICK1 label to the three cells to the right, but due to the nature of the extend-copy function, the PICK1 label will be copied as PICK2, PICK3, and PICK4, respectively.

To the right of the PICK4 label, enter the label MATCH. You should now have five new column labels: PICK1, PICK2, PICK3, PICK4, and MATCH.

What These New Columns Mean

The PICK1 column is to contain yes-or-no information about the Military category based on the ASK_1, LOW_1, and HIGH_1 cells from the input output table. The formula in each row of the PICK1 column will ask whether or not the corresponding country matches the criteria expressed by the user in the ASK_1, LOW_1, and HIGH_1 cells. If so it will return the numeric value 1, and if not it will return the numeric value 0. When complete, the PICK1 column will appear to contain a list of random 1s and 0s. This should remind you of a truth table.

Correspondingly, PICK2 will contain yes-or-no information about the Literacy category, based on information from the ASK_2, LOW_2, and HIGH_2 cells, PICK3 will contain information about the Murder category based on the ASK_3, LOW_3, and HIGH_3 cells, and PICK4 will contain information about the Quality category based on the ASK_4, LOW_4, and HIGH_4 cells. Our next task is to create formulae that generate those 1s and 0s.

The basic format of the formula is =IF(___,1,0), where the blank will be filled in with a complex true-or-false expression, described below. The result of this formula is guaranteed to be either 1 or 0, but which value is actually returned will depend on what the user enters in the input output table.

Once the four columns of IF functions have been created, any country with a 1 in all four PICK columns will match all of our search criteria and is a country we want to know about. Any country that contains a 0 in any or all of the four corresponding columns does not match our search criteria and can be excluded from consideration. It is possible that all countries may match our search criteria, and it is also possible that none of them will.

Entering the First IF Formula

Move the cursor to the cell one row below the PICK1 column header (next to the first row of data, for Afghanistan in this case).

 Write a formula in this cell to return 1 if Afghanistan matches our search criteria for the Military category, and returns 0 otherwise. (See below for a discussion of this formula.)

The circumstances where we want 1 returned by the IF are:

- The Military category <u>was</u> selected (the cell named ASK_1 contains the string YES) <u>and</u> the corresponding country (Afghanistan) spent on the military an amount between the values in the cells named LOW_1 <u>and</u> HIGH_1, inclusive.

- The Military category <u>was not</u> selected (the ASK_1 cell doesn't contain YES).

In any other circumstance the formula should return 0.

Suppose the cell which contains Afghanistan's military expenditure has address <u>X33</u> (it does not have this address; you will have to figure this cell address out for yourself); then the formula that you would type in is as follows:

=IF(OR(AND(ASK_1="YES",<u>X33</u>>=LOW_1,<u>X33</u><=HIGH_1),ASK_1<>"YES"),1,0)

Replace the <u>X33</u> with the ***actual cell address*** of Afghanistan's military expenditure. This may seem like an overly complicated formula, but it is pretty easy to figure out. The following diagram shows how to interpret the text of the expression.

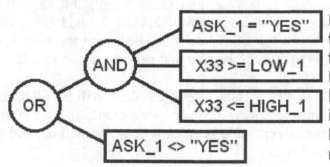

Expression is TRUE if either the bottom box is true, or all three of the top boxes are true, but at no other time. When this happens, either we are interested in the category and the cell X33 is between the limits, or else we are not interested.

The OR result will be true if either of two things happens: either all three of the AND conditions are true (meaning that the country matches our search criteria and should be considered), or ASK_1 is <u>not</u> "YES" (meaning that we weren't interested in that category). If the OR result is true, then the IF formula will return 1. The only way for the IF formula to return 0, then, is for ASK_1 to be "YES", but the corresponding data value (<u>X33</u> in our example) is out of range (either less than LOW_1 or greater than HIGH_1).

Copying & Testing the First IF Formula

Click on the cell in the PICK1 column where you just entered the IF formula. Click on the lower right (black) corner button (the cursor will change to the black cross), drag and extend the box down to the bottom row of the table of data, and then release the button. You should see a column of 1s and 0s appear, one for each country. If you change the corresponding ASK_1 cell value on the Input Output page to NO, all values should appear as 1 (a good way to test, but remember to change the cell value back to YES after your tests).

 Do not proceed until you get this column right. Check the column to make sure that the 1s appear where they should and that the 0s appear where they should.

Entering & Testing the Other Three IF formulae

 Move the cursor to the cell below the PICK2 column header. Type in another IF formula, just like you did earlier, except that we want to compute the literacy rate this time. Use ASK_2 instead of ASK_1, LOW_2 instead of LOW_1, and HIGH_2 instead of HIGH_1, and use the appropriate data cell (for example, if we used X33 for the military, we would use Y33 for the literacy rate). Copy the formula down to the bottom row of data, and test the column by changing the literacy input cells.

 Generate <u>two</u> more IF formulae, just like you did before, to compute the results for the murder rate (PICK3, using ASK_3, LOW_3, and HIGH_3) and the quality of life (PICK4, using ASK_4, LOW_4, and HIGH_4), then copy them down to the bottom row of data.

You will now have four columns of 1s and 0s to the right of the original data. <u>None</u> of the columns should contain all 1s or all 0s at this time. All four columns will contain a <u>mixture</u> of 1s and 0s, if you entered the initial data correctly into the input output table and created the formulae correctly.

 Do not proceed until all four columns contain a mixture of 1s and 0s, which change correctly when you change the appropriate input cells.

The Last Nasty Formula

Under the MATCH column header, enter a formula that outputs the value 1 if <u>all</u> four cells to its left (in the PICK1, PICK2, PICK3, and PICK4 columns) contain 1, and outputs the value 0 if <u>any</u> of them contain 0.

There are *many* correct ways to accomplish this task, some more efficient than others. You can do it with an IF function, as you did before, you may use a purely computational approach, or you may use a combination of approaches. If you use an IF function in your solution, it will be *much simpler* than what we used for the four "pick" formulae.

Think about this and try to come up with a solution on your own without help. This concept should sound really familiar by now. The following diagram shows what we want. Study the relationship between the four "pick" columns and the MATCH column.

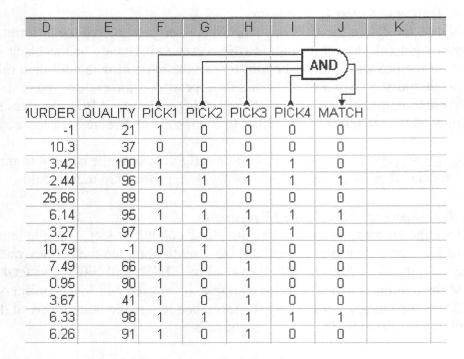

MURDER	QUALITY	PICK1	PICK2	PICK3	PICK4	MATCH
-1	21	1	0	0	0	0
10.3	37	0	0	0	0	0
3.42	100	1	0	1	1	0
2.44	96	1	1	1	1	1
25.66	89	0	0	0	0	0
6.14	95	1	1	1	1	1
3.27	97	1	0	1	1	0
10.79	-1	0	1	0	0	0
7.49	66	1	0	1	0	0
0.95	90	1	0	1	0	0
3.67	41	1	0	1	0	0
6.33	98	1	1	1	1	1
6.26	91	1	0	1	0	0

Once complete, copy the formula down throughout all of the rows.

 There should be 17 entries in this column equal to 1, and all the rest will be equal to zero. *Do not proceed* until the MATCH column contains 17 entries equal to 1.

Formatting the Block

Select (with the white cross) across all five new columns and across all rows in the table, then center the cells. Narrow all five of the new columns as much as possible (i.e., shrink them without losing information).

The First Useful Result

Click on the Input Output tab. Make sure that the input values in the 12 cells are the initial values entered in an earlier step (Military=YES, 0, 10; Literacy=YES, 95, 100; Murder=YES, 0, 10; and Quality=YES, 95, 100).

Click in the empty box (surrounded by a dark line) to the right of the word Total.

 Write a formula here to add up all of the cells containing 1s and 0s in the MATCH column of the Data sheet. You don't need to know specific cell addresses here. As soon as you enter the formula =SUM(click on the Data tab, then click drag over all of the 1s and 0s in the MATCH column. Close off the formula by typing the) and then hit the [Enter ↵] key. Do not return manually to the Input Output tab; hitting [Enter ↵] will take you back there automatically. If all goes well you should see 17 appear in the total box.

Save your spreadsheet.

Testing

Test your formulae to see if you got everything entered correctly up to this point. Select topics (Military, Literacy, etc.) by picking YES or NO from the drop-down lists associated with ASK_1 through ASK_4, and entering ranges of numbers to look for in the Low-Value and High-Value cells of that topic. The spreadsheet recalculates everything and marks the qualifying countries in the MATCH column, then displays the number of matches in the total box.

- All four ASK entries are NO: because of the way the formulae were constructed, the total should be the number of countries in the entire list (80 by my count).

- All four ASK entries are YES, all Low-Value entries are -1, and all High-Value entries are 100: all countries match, so the total should be 80 here as well.

- All four ASK entries are YES, all four Low-Value entries are 100, and all four High-Value entries are 0: because the low values are greater than the high values (a situation that does not make sense), the total must be zero.

- All four ASK entries are YES, Military is between 0 and 10, Literacy between 95 and 100, Murder between 0 and 10, and Quality between 95 and 100: the total should be 17, and there will be a 1 in the MATCH column next to the rows for Austria, Barbados, Canada, Denmark, Finland, France, Germany-West, Ireland, Italy, Japan, Luxembourg, New Zealand, Norway, Sweden, Switzerland, the United Kingdom, and the United States.

What we have built so far is a *database*, spreadsheet style. We've gone through all this work just to get one column of ones and zeroes that correspond to our input request. Now, we use that information to extract the names of the selected countries. This kind of problem is more appropriate to a database package than to a spreadsheet, which allows us to ask these kinds of questions without all the messing around setting up formulae. When you read about databases, think back on this assignment, and try to imagine how much simpler it would be in a database package than in a spreadsheet!

If the computed total in the Input Output page is always zero (instead of initially 17), then it is likely that in one or more formulae, either the PICK or the MATCH formulae, you may have used "1" and "0" (wrong) instead of 1 and 0 (right). Quoted strings have the numerical value zero, even if they look like numbers. Remove the quotes.

Similarly, errors in the PICK formulae can also lead to wrong totals as well. For example, check to make sure that the PICK2 formula refers only to ASK_2, LOW_2, and HIGH_2, and not to ASK_1 or LOW_3 or something else.

Explaining Queries

In the next section you will tell the spreadsheet how to list the country names under the Names label in the Input Output section. Notice that there are no entries for India or Russia, and the German bloc (yes, that's spelled b-l-o-c) is still listed as two separate countries! How do you update the database? To pick out the answers, a **_query_** needs to know three things:

- **_Where the data are located._** (The big table in the Data sheet)
- **_How to select the data._** (Picking countries where MATCH = 1)
- **_Where to put the results._** (Underneath Names in the Input Output sheet)

Setting up those three items is a bit tricky, so pay close attention to the following instructions! You may have to fiddle around with them to get them to work correctly!

Query Preliminaries

 In the input box on the Input Output page, set all four ASK entries to YES, all Low-Value entries to -1, and all High-Value entries to 100. The value of the Total cell should be 80.

 Do not proceed until all 80 entries in the MATCH column are 1.

Setting the Filter (or AutoFilter)

Click on the tab for the Data page of the spreadsheet notebook.

Click to select any cell <u>inside</u> the block of data (it doesn't matter which cell; in the next step Excel will automatically determine the extent of the data).

 Excel 2003 / Excel 2011 (Mac): Click on Data-Filter or Data-Filter-AutoFilter.
Excel 2007-2016: Click the Data tab in the ribbon, and then select Filter from the Sort & Filter panel.

Little buttons will appear in the row of names at the top of each column of data. These buttons activate drop-down lists, showing all of the different values in that column.

Excel 2003 / Excel 2011 (Mac): Clicking on one of those buttons then picking a value causes all rows to disappear *except* for those containing that value in the column. The rows that disappear are still present; they have been hidden from view temporarily. Click the same drop down button, then select All from the list, and any row hidden by that column will again become visible.

Excel 2007-2016: All criteria are automatically selected; once you click a button, you should click on Select All until all check boxes are cleared, then check the desired search criteria. The rows that disappear are still present; they have been hidden from view temporarily. Click the same drop down button, then pick Select All from the list, and any row hidden by that column will again become visible.

To practice with the Filter, click on the button in the Literacy column, and select 100 from the bottom of the list. All countries will disappear except those with 100% literacy. Next, click the button in the Quality column and select 99. Now you will see only those countries with 100% literacy AND 99% quality of life. This is how we will extract the countries that match our search criteria (by selecting 1 as the search value in the drop-down list associated with the MATCH column).

Restore the settings on the Filter so that all countries are visible again.

Save your spreadsheet now.

If you have done everything correctly up to this point, the contents of the Data sheet should have Filter buttons in cells A5 through J5.

Do not proceed unless this is so.

Creating the Update Macro

This is one of the trickiest parts of the entire assignment. We will now create a **_macro_**, which is a small spreadsheet program to automate a complicated task. That task is to update the rows shown by the Filter, and then copy the resulting visible country names to the output region on the Input Output sheet. (Macros are not enabled in either Excel 2008 for the Mac or in the Starter Edition of Excel 2010 for Windows, which is why you cannot use either package for this assignment.)

To create a macro, we will have the spreadsheet start recording our actions as we perform them manually. This means that we have to get every step absolutely correct, or the resulting macro will blindly do the same dumb things we did. We may have to stop recording the macro, throw it out, and start over a couple of times before we get it right.

Verify again that all 80 country names are visible in the Data page (none are hidden by the Filter). If any country names are hidden, make them visible again. Verify that all four ASK entries are YES, all Low-Value entries are -1, and all High-Value entries are 100.

Click on the Input Output tab, and then set the cursor to the empty cell below the cell containing Names.

Excel 95 / Excel 2011 (Mac): Click on Tools-Record Macro-Record New Macro or Tools-Macro-Record New Macro. In the dialog box that pops up, click on the Options >> button if present, then click on the Shortcut Key check box to fill it in ⊠).

Excel 97, 2000, XP, and 2003: Click on Tools-Macro-Record New Macro...

Excel 2007-2016: Click on the View tab in the ribbon, then on Macros, then on Record Macro...

Change the macro name to Update, put your own name in the Description: box (replacing any previous contents), and in the Ctrl+ or Option+Cmd+ box replace any character there with the **u** character (this is how we will run the macro). Finally, click on the OK button.

Excel 2003: A "stop recording" button will appear on screen.

Excel 2007-2016, Excel 2011 (Mac): No button appears.

EVERYTHING YOU DO is now being recorded as part of the macro, so be careful! The following steps describe the tasks to be performed by the macro.

The Macro Steps

1. Click on the Input Output tab. I know that we are in the Input Output page already, but we want the macro to select that page automatically when it runs.

2. Click drag to select (with the white cross) all cells from the cell below Names down at least 85 <u>more</u> rows (enough for all names in the table plus a few extra; this takes us well beyond the actual row 85 in the sheet to about row 100). Do this even if the range is already selected.

3. Hit the [Del] key (Windows) or Edit-Clear Contents (Mac). This erases the contents of those selected cells (currently empty).

4. Click the Data tab.

5. In the MATCH column open the drop-down list and pick 1 from the list of values. If Afghanistan is not the first country or if Zimbabwe is not the last, then you have made an error in either the PICK columns or the MATCH column, and must stop this macro and fix the problem, then try again.

    In Excel 2007-2016, you can <u>only</u> pick 1 from the list of values. Unfortunately, this records the wrong item in the body of the macro itself. We will fix this in a later section. Click OK to close the filter dialog.

6. Click drag to select (with the white cross) over all country names from the first country (Afghanistan) down to and including <u>one blank cell below</u> the last country (Zimbabwe) in the list. The blank cell is used to ensure that there will always be at least one cell to copy, even if no countries match the search criteria. Do this even if the range is already selected.

7. Click Ctrl C (Windows) or ⌘C (Mac) to copy the selected area.

8. Click on the Input Output tab.

9. Click to set the cursor on the cell just below Names.

10. Click Ctrl V (Windows) or ⌘V (Mac) to paste the selection.

11. **Excel 2003 / Excel 2011 (Mac):** Click the stop macro button if one is visible, or click on Tools-Macro-Stop Recording.

Excel 2007-2016: Click on the View tab in the ribbon, then Macros, then Stop Recording.

Viewing the Macro Source Code

Excel 95: There will now be a fourth tab on the bottom of the spreadsheet, labeled Module1. Click on the tab and rename it to Macros.

Excel 97, 2000, XP, 2003 (Windows), and 2011 (Mac): View the macro by clicking Tools-Macro-Macros..., clicking on Update (the name of the macro) in the dialog box, and then clicking the Edit button. The Visual Basic language editor will automatically launch, containing the contents of your macro.

Excel 2007-2016: Click in the View tab of the ribbon, then on Macros, then on View Macros. In the dialog pick the macro that you created and click the Edit button.

This sheet contains the instructions, written in the Visual Basic language, that correspond to your macro. You could have written this code by hand, but it is not recommended that you do so until you get more experience with macros.

The Macro Body Reality Check

If you have done everything correctly, the body of the macro will look very similar to the following text. Visual Basic will appear in its own separate window.

```
Sheets("Input Output").Select
Range("B12:B100").Select
Selection.ClearContents
Sheets("Data").Select
ActiveSheet.Range("$A$5:$J$85").AutoFilter Field:=10
Range("A6:A86").Select
Selection.Copy
Sheets("Input Output").Select
Range("B12").Select
ActiveSheet.Paste
```

Excel 2003: Leave Visual Basic running, but switch back to Excel by clicking on its taskbar button.

Excel 2007-2016, Excel 2011 (Mac): Unfortunately, the macro body is slightly incorrect in later versions of Excel. We need to add text to the end of the line that references the Filter, because it does not use the correct search criteria. On that line, add a comma, the word Criteria followed by a 1 (not a lowercase L), a colon, an equal sign, and the number 1 in quotes. You <u>must</u> type this in correctly or the macro won't work. The end of the line should look as follows:

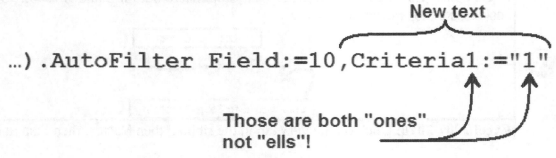

Make this correction in Visual Basic and click File-Close and Return to Microsoft Excel.

The Final Modification

Click on the Header tab.

In cells A5 through A7 of the Header page, type a three line English description of the **_purpose_** of this spreadsheet, with no more than 60-70 characters per line. This description must be something that you would find useful if you were to come back to it in a year's time; simply saying that it tests macros, etc., is *not* acceptable. (You may want to come back to this step and fill it in later, after you have a chance to run a few of the queries.) In Excel 2000 and later the formatting lines and shading from cells A1:A3 may appear in A5:A7 as you enter the new data; if so then reset the formatting in A5:A7 to black text on a white background with no border lines.

Excel 2003 / Excel 2011 (Mac): Click in cell A10, then on Insert-Name-Paste, and click on Paste List in the dialog box that pops up. You will see a table appear in the spreadsheet, called a data dictionary, of all cell names that you have defined. It is often a useful piece of documentation. If you have done everything correctly the spreadsheet is now completely operational.

Excel 2007-2016: Click in cell A10, then on the Formulas tab in the ribbon, then on the Use In Formula entry of the Defined Names panel. You will see a drop-down list containing all of the defined range names (ASK_1, ASK_2, etc.). At the end of that list is an entry called Paste Names. Click on Paste Names, and in the pop-up dialog click on Paste List.

Save your spreadsheet.

Running Queries

Click on the Input Output tab. To run any query, you must type into the input table the categories of interest (YES or NO in ASK_1 through ASK_4), and for each YES category the range of acceptable low and high values. In the total box you will see the number of matching countries, but the list of names won't be automatically updated until you run the macro. The macro erases the current list of matching countries, updates the Filter rows, and then copies the resulting country names back to the output section of the Input Output page.

Running the First Query

Enter the original query data (all four ASK entries are YES, Military between 0 and 10, Literacy between 95 and 100, Murder between 0 and 10, and Quality between 95 and 100). You should see the total equal to 17, as before. Hit [Ctrl]u, (Windows) or Option-⌘u and the names of those 17 countries will appear before you under the cell containing Names.

Do not proceed until your query system works correctly.

Printing the First Query Pages

Make sure you are in the Input Output page. Print-preview this page. You should see the entire page as it will be printed appear in miniature on screen. If the preview appears in Landscape mode, set the orientation to Portrait. When all is correct, print the page.

Click on the Data page.

Preview it, set its orientation to Portrait if necessary and print it as well.

On the keyboard, click [Ctrl] ` or [Ctrl] ~ (the ` and ~ symbols are on the same key-top, and this works with both Windows and Mac versions of Excel). The view of the spreadsheet will change to show the formulae, and <u>not</u> their computed values. We want to make sure that your methods are correct.

<u>Widen</u> the four PICK columns and the MATCH column so that the formulae are completely visible.

Preview it, set its orientation to Landscape, and print it as well. This printout will come out on multiple pages.

When you are finished with all the printing tasks, click on click [Ctrl] ` or [Ctrl] ~ to restore the spreadsheet view to the results instead of the formulae. <u>Narrow</u> the PICK and MATCH columns to their previous widths.

Running and Printing the Second Query

 Go back to the Input Output page. Set up the second query: Military=NO (do not change the LOW or HIGH numbers), Literacy=YES(95-100), Murder=YES(5-15), and Quality=YES(95-100). The low and high input values for the military column can be left unchanged. Run the query again. The list should contain 9 countries.

 Print the Input Output page in Portrait mode again (do not print the Data page).

Running and Printing the Third Query

 Set up the third query: Military=YES(25-50), Literacy=NO (do not change the numbers), Murder=NO (do not change the numbers), and Quality=YES(50-100). Run the query again. The list will contain 2 countries (Iraq and Israel).

 Print the Input Output page in Portrait mode again (do not print the Data page).

Final Spreadsheet Printing

 Click on the Header tab, and print that page in portrait mode.

 Excel 2003-2016: Load the macro into Visual Basic and click File-Print... in its menu, then click on the OK button.

Excel 2011 (Mac): Load the macro into Visual Basic. Visual Basic in Excel for the Mac does not have an option to print, so select all the text with ⌘A and copy it to the clipboard with ⌘C. Bring up the familiar TextEdit application (in Finder-Applications), paste the text in with ⌘V and print from there.

Shut down Visual Basic by clicking on File-Close and Return to Microsoft Excel in its menu.

Creating the Banner Page

As you have done in previous assignments, start Microsoft Word and create a banner page containing your name, the phrase LAB ASSIGNMENT #7, either WORK AT LAB or WORK AT HOME, and the current date, hitting Enter⏎ after each line. Select these lines with the mouse.

Center the lines, make sure that they are in the Times New Roman typeface, and change the size to **20 points**.

Format the document to be single-spaced, with *no extra spacing* between the lines.

Word 2003: Save the document as **LAB7.DOC** in your Word Processing folder.

Word 2007-2016 (Windows), 2011 (Mac): Save the document as **LAB7.DOCX** in your Word Processing folder.

Print out your completed banner page. This page will become the cover page of your report.

William T. Verts
LAB ASSIGNMENT #7
WORK AT HOME
November 15, 2013

Shutting Down

Close all programs (including Visual Basic if necessary). You generally should answer "yes" if Microsoft Excel (or Visual Basic) asks you if you want to save any changes.

Close down your computer normally.

What to Turn In

You will need to turn in the printout of your spreadsheet (7+ pages total), containing the following items (check off the items in the list below):

Page #1 (the banner page) must contain:
- ☐ Your name (centered),
- ☐ LAB ASSIGNMENT #7 (centered),
- ☐ WORK AT LAB or WORK AT HOME (centered),
- ☐ Current date (centered),
- ☐ No extra spaces between lines.
- ☐ Font must be set to 20 Point, Times New Roman.

Page #2 (the Header page):
- ☐ Page must be printed in Portrait mode,
- ☐ Cells A1 to A3 contain your name, workplace, & current date/time,
- ☐ Cells A1 to A3 are in a shaded box,
- ☐ Cells A5 to A7 contain a three line description of the spreadsheet purpose,
- ☐ Cells A10 and below contain a table of the defined range names.

Pages #3 through #5 (Input Output pages for each of three queries):
- ☐ Pages must be printed in Portrait mode,
- ☐ Cells A1 to A3 contain your name, workplace, & current date/time,
- ☐ Cells A1 to A3 are in a shaded box,
- ☐ Input Output box has correct borders and shading, label text is in boldface,
- ☐ Query #1: Total=17 and there are 17 country names listed under Names,
- ☐ Query #2: Total=9 and there are 9 country names listed under Names,
- ☐ Query #3: Total=2 and there are 2 country names listed under Names.

Page #6 (Macro page):
- ☐ Text of macro must contain your name (as a comment),
- ☐ Keyboard shortcut must be **u**,
- ☐ Macro must be named **Update**,
- ☐ Body of macro must contain the required commands (about 10 lines).

Page #7 (Data page <u>results</u> for Query #1):
- ☐ Page must be printed in Portrait mode,
- ☐ Cells A1 to A3 contain your name, workplace, & current date/time,
- ☐ Cells A1 to A3 are in a shaded box,
- ☐ Data table contains 10 columns and 17 rows of data below the column headers.

Page #8+ (Data page <u>formulae</u> for Query #1):
- ☐ Page must be printed in Landscape mode,
- ☐ Cells A1 to A3 contain your name, workplace, & the formula for the date/time,
- ☐ Cells A1 to A3 are in a shaded box,
- ☐ Printout must show formulae (will appear on more than one page.),
- ☐ Columns must be widened to show formulae in their entirety.

Grading Policy

Lab assignments are worth 10 points each. Teaching assistants will observe the following criteria for evaluating and scoring the Lab #7 assignments that they receive.

- Any report that does not have the student's name *typed* on *all* appropriate pages (centered at the top of the banner page, as part of the header on every spreadsheet page, and in the body of the macro) will be *rejected*, and if submitted will receive a *zero*. If any student writes their name in by hand, instead of typing it, then the report must be rejected. **Reject any report missing a banner page.**

- 1 Point - Report must be stapled together. Remove the full point if the report is paper-clipped together or is submitted loose (even with folded corners). Remove the full point if the pages are not in the order listed here:
  1. Banner,
  2. header,
  3. input/output (query 1),
  4. input/output (query 2),
  5. input/output (query 3),
  6. macro
  7. data (query 1 results),
  8.+ data (formulae).

- 1 Point - Printout of the banner page must be present and must contain the appropriate lines of banner information. Remove ½ point for every line of the banner page that is missing or incorrect (for example: a line not centered, the font not set to 20 point Times New Roman, or the lines are not single spaced with no extra spacing between lines), up to the full point possible.

- 1 Point - Remove the point for any errors in formatting the spreadsheet (missing date/time on any sheet, incorrect formats for numbers, borders or patterns, pages printed in landscape mode, etc.).

- 1 Point - Remove the point if the description of the purpose of the spreadsheet is missing from the Header page. Remove ½ point if it contains fewer than 3 total lines or does not contain a "reasonable" analysis of the purpose.

- 1 Point - Remove the point if the data dictionary (list of range names and corresponding ranges) is missing from the Header page. Cell addresses may be different between different students' reports; they will depend on where the students placed the input output block. Remove ½ point if there are fewer than 12 names in the block, or if it is obvious that there are mistakes (such as two range names with the same addresses, for example).

- 1 Point - The first query result should have Total = 17 and have 17 country names listed. Check to make sure that the 17 names are correct (Austria, Barbados, Canada, Denmark, Finland, France, Germany-West, Ireland, Italy, Japan, Luxembourg, New Zealand, Norway, Sweden, Switzerland, the United Kingdom, and the United States) and that the query input values are correctly entered (all four ASK entries are YES, Military is 0 to 10, Literacy is 95 to 100, Murder is 0 to 10, and Quality is 95 to 100).

  Remove the whole point if this page is missing, or if any mistakes are found. A common mistake is to set up a query but then forget to run the macro – this leads to a mismatch between the number of countries in the total and the names of the matching countries.

- 1 Point - The second query result should have Total = 9 and have 9 names listed. Same grading rules as for the first query.

- 1 Point - The third result printout should have Total = 2 and have 2 names listed (IRAQ and ISRAEL). Same grading rules as for the first query.

- 1 Point - The macro page should be essentially what was listed in the Visual Basic image given on a previous page. Page may be printed in either portrait or landscape. Remove ½ point for each of the following infractions, but do not exceed 1 point total. Remove ½ point if the Keyboard Shortcut: line is missing. Remove ½ point if the name of the macro is not Update. Remove ½ point if many extraneous lines are present. Remove ½ point if any vital macro command is missing. Remove ½ point if the range of cells to clear contains fewer than 80 cells. Cell addresses should appear "reasonable".

- 1 Point - The printout of the Data page should match the first query. There should be 17 rows of data, corresponding to the 17 matching countries. All MATCH entries should be equal to 1. Remove the point if this page is missing, or if the data do not match the first query.

- **5 Additional Penalty Points** - After all other scoring is completed, TAs must check the formulae pages to ensure that students completely followed all of the directions. Remove additional points for any of the following infractions, but do not go below zero total points (in other words, even if the rest of the report *appears to be perfect*, you can still lose up to five points for solving the problem the wrong way):

Remove all 5 additional points if the formulae pages are missing or the columns are sized so that the formulae are not completely visible.

Remove 1 additional point if the PICK1 formula is wrong.

Remove 1 additional point if the PICK2 formula is wrong.

Remove 1 additional point if the PICK3 formula is wrong.

Remove 1 additional point if the PICK4 formula is wrong.

Remove 1 additional point if the MATCH formula is wrong.

The Contents of the "world" File (for reference only)

NAMES	MILITARY	LITERACY	MURDER	QUALITY
AFGHANISTAN	7	5.8	-1	21
ANGOLA	14.2	19.3	10.3	37
AUSTRALIA	3.2	-1	3.42	100
AUSTRIA	1.2	100	2.44	96
BAHAMAS	-1	-1	25.66	89
BARBADOS	1	97.7	6.14	95
BELGIUM	3.1	-1	3.27	97
BERMUDA	-1	97	10.79	-1
BOTSWANA	3.3	-1	7.49	66
BRUNEI	7.9	72.8	0.95	90
BURUNDI	3.5	25.7	3.67	41
CANADA	2.3	95.7	6.33	98
CHILE	4.2	93.8	6.26	91
COLOMBIA	1.4	-1	2.54	82
CONGO	2.6	55.4	1.06	64
CYPRUS	-1	88.4	2.06	93
DENMARK	2.4	100	5.77	98
DOMINICA	-1	-1	2.67	88
DOMINICAN REPUBLIC	1.2	76.8	9.32	75
ECUADOR	-1	56.9	4.53	79
EGYPT	8.5	26.8	1.53	60
FIJI	1.2	80.9	2.89	83
FINLAND	1.5	100	5.62	99
FRANCE	4.1	98.7	4.63	100
GABON	2.1	-1	1.12	54
GERMANY,WEST	3.3	100	4.51	97
GREECE	7.2	90.6	1.83	97
HONG KONG	-1	80.9	1.64	95
HUNGARY	2.2	98.6	3.72	93
INDONESIA	3.9	65.4	0.9	63
IRAQ	50	26	-1	62
IRELAND	1.8	100	1.08	96
ISRAEL	27.1	88.7	1.83	96
ITALY	2.7	96.3	5.25	98
IVORY COAST	1.2	-1	1.78	49
JAPAN	1	100	1.47	99
JORDAN	14.1	64.4	2.72	77
KENYA	4.1	49.2	4.53	58
KOREA,SOUTH	5.4	87.9	1.36	88
KUWAIT	5.3	-1	1.06	84
LEBANON	7.3	64.2	19.2	79
LESOTHO	2.9	84.5	53.19	61
LIBYA	12.9	62	1.6	66
LUXEMBOURG	0.8	100	5.25	97
MALAWI	5.6	63.2	2.93	37
MALAYSIA	1.7	63.2	1.97	81
MALDIVES	-1	82	1.76	67
MALTA	0.9	95.9	4.24	94
MAURITIUS	0.3	76.4	2.33	83
MOROCCO	5.6	58.7	0.78	54
NETHERLANDS	3.2	100	12.26	99
NEW ZEALAND	1.9	100	2.54	96
NIGER	0.8	5.8	0.21	28

NIGERIA	1.8	31.5	1.69	47
NORWAY	2.9	100	0.92	99
PAPUA NEW GUINEA	1.7	31.3	9.23	54
PHILIPPINES	1.8	87.5	42.51	79
PORTUGAL	3.5	74.6	4.6	91
QATAR	5.8	50.1	1.71	73
RWANDA	1.5	37.2	6.71	45
SAUDI ARABIA	21.7	34.6	1.15	56
SENEGAL	2.8	14.2	1.67	36
SEYCHELLES	-1	59.6	7.69	88
SINGAPORE	5.7	74	2.73	91
SPAIN	2.4	89.9	2.16	98
SUDAN	3.3	6.5	4.46	41
SWEDEN	3.1	100	5.74	99
SWITZERLAND	2.2	100	2.24	99
SYRIA	16.6	24.3	2.25	71
TANZANIA	3.3	-1	8.67	63
THAILAND	4	84.5	16.56	82
TOGO	2.5	27.5	0.16	48
TRINIDAD & TOBAGO	1	93.6	6.76	90
TURKEY	4.5	50	1.41	73
UNITED ARAB EMIRATES	7.4	66.3	1.79	74
UNITED KINGDOM	5.4	100	1.37	97
UNITED STATES	6.4	95.3	7.91	98
VENEZUELA	1.6	87.2	9.93	87
ZAMBIA	4.1	58.3	9.73	62
ZIMBABWE	6.2	66.8	21.11	67

Lab #8 – Spreadsheets: Road Trip

Introduction & Goals

In this assignment you will use a spreadsheet to collate some numbers about an imaginary road trip from Boston, Massachusetts to Vancouver, British Columbia. As you drive along, you cross the border between the United States and Canada several times, and buy gasoline as you find it in both countries. In the United States gasoline is sold by the gallon and in Canada by the liter. In the United States distances are measured in miles and in Canada in kilometers. Since we have a car made for the U.S. market, its odometer records distance in miles only. We will assume that we always pay in U.S. currency, and that the Canadian gas stations will give us a price based on the current exchange rate between U.S. and Canadian dollars. (In this day of wildly variable gas prices, where gas may be $2.00 to $4.00+ per gallon, the numbers used in this assignment will seem a bit quaint and out-of-date. They are, but the techniques still apply regardless of the actual current prices.)

For each stop along the way, we record the name of the town where we bought gasoline, the amount of gasoline purchased (in gallons or liters), how much we paid for it (in U.S. dollars), and how far we traveled on that leg of the trip (in miles). Once we have gathered our data about our trip, we would like to see how many kilometers we traveled on each leg, the number of gallons purchased, the number of liters purchased, our miles per gallon and dollars per gallon measure, and our kilometers per liter and dollars per liter measure.

Once the basic conversions have been made, we will compute our engine efficiency as the average miles per gallon and average kilometers per liter experienced over the trip. Finally, we will graph the fuel efficiency in miles per gallon and price in dollars per gallon.

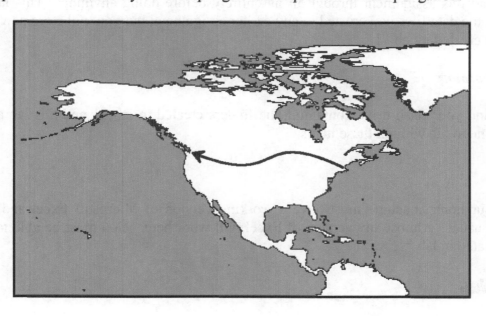

Specifics You Will Learn in This Assignment

You will learn the following things in the completion of this assignment:

- **Data Entry** – In this assignment, you will be typing in a large table of data. You will learn to identify those places where you can simplify your task by copying single values to large blocks of cells, instead of typing the same things over and over. In "real world" projects you may find that your job depends on how accurately you create and verify the correctness of your data tables.

- **Units Conversion with Spreadsheets** – Knowing how to convert from one unit of measurement to another is a vital skill in today's world, and not just in sciences such as chemistry and physics. Here is a practical problem in units conversion that you may well encounter in real life. It is important that you understand how to encode such problems into the formulae that you type into a spreadsheet.

- **Graphing Results** – While raw tables of numbers contain a lot of information, they don't convey much in the way of visual trends. A properly designed graph can do a far better job at showing what is happening overall in the data. You will learn how to create graphs and place them directly into the spreadsheet.

Preparation before Starting Assignment

Read this assignment through in its entirety before doing anything. This lab does not depend on the data files you created in any earlier assignment, but you will store new files in the directories created in lab #1.

In the Laboratory

Bring your flash drive containing the folders created in lab #1 and this lab assignment. Do not come to lab without these items.

At Home

Your home machine must have a working version of Microsoft Excel and a working printer, as usual. Almost any version of Excel will work here. You must be able to locate the folders created in lab #1.

Data Files

There are no data files provided for this assignment.

Step-By-Step Procedure

Start your machine up normally. You should have the Spreadsheets folder on your disk.

Starting Up

Find and run the Microsoft Excel program (it may take several seconds to start up, so be patient). If asked for what kind of Excel file to use, answer with an Excel Workbook or Blank workbook. Maximize the window if necessary.

As you did in the previous assignment, configure Excel so that it has exactly three notebook pages named Sheet1, Sheet2, and Sheet3.

Sheet1: Change the name of Sheet1 to Header. Type your name into cell A1, WORK AT LAB or WORK AT HOME into A2, and the formula =NOW() into A3. Select all three cells (with the white cross), and then format all three cells as **Boldface**. Left justify these three cells. Widen column A so that no text spills over into column B. Format these cells as you did in the previous assignment: draw a medium thick solid border outlining the three cells, and shade those cells with a medium color pattern (dark enough that it shows up on the printer, but not so dark that the text is obscured).

Once the three cells have been formatted correctly, and while they are still selected, copy them to the clipboard. We will paste this information into the second and third sheets.

Sheet2: Click on the Sheet2 tab and rename it to Input Output (including the space between Input and Output). Click in cell A1 and then paste the contents of the clipboard. The information in the colored box that you created on the first sheet will appear here without retyping. Widen the column as necessary.

Sheet3: Click on the Sheet3 tab and rename it to Data. Click in cell A1 and then paste the contents of the clipboard. The information in the colored box that you created on the first sheet will appear here without retyping. Widen the column as necessary.

Excel 2003: Click on File-Save to save the entire spreadsheet notebook as `lab8.xls` into your Spreadsheets folder.

Excel 2007: Click on Office Button-Save to save the entire spreadsheet notebook as `lab8.xlsx` into your Spreadsheets folder.

Excel 2010-2016: Click on the File tab, then on Save. In Excel 2013/2016 click Browse. Save the entire spreadsheet notebook as `lab8.xlsx` into your Spreadsheets folder.

Excel 2008 / 2011 for the Mac: Click on File-Save or File-Save As... to save the entire spreadsheet notebook as `lab8.xlsx` into your Spreadsheets folder.

Do not proceed unless the spreadsheet has three pages labeled Header, Input Output, and Data, has your name, WORK AT LAB or WORK AT HOME, and current date/time on all three pages in a shaded box, and has been saved as `lab8`.

Building the Input/Output Table

Click on the Input Output tab. Underneath and to the right of the title cells, starting in cell B5, create two tables that look like the following image. Do <u>not</u> type anything into the cells labeled *result* at this time (we will create formulae for those cells later).

- Type the numbers and text labels you see in the image below into your spreadsheet and justify them as shown (hint: the word Input is right justified in cell B5 and the word Units is left justified in cell C5).

- Make all of your text labels **boldface** (but leave the numeric cells alone).

- Where you see lines and shading, select the appropriate range of cells, right click on the range, and then use the Format Cells entry in the pop-up menu to set those attributes correctly.

- Widen the columns appropriately.

Input	Units		Output	Units
2.54	cm/in		result	Miles
12	in/ft		result	Km
5280	ft/mi		result	Gallons
100	cm/m		result	Liters
1000	m/km		result	Dollars
3.785	L/gal		result	MPG Average
result	km/mi		result	KPL Average

Define a range name for the cell containing the number 3.785 as L_PER_GAL (use underscores in the name, not blanks).

This number represents the number of liters in a gallon of liquid measure. You will use the range name L_PER_GAL later in your formulae to convert gasoline between gallons and liters, instead of embedding the constant 3.785 directly into those formulae.

In the *result* cell next to the km/mi label, create a formula that calculates the number of kilometers in a mile, based on the distance measurements in the cells above it.

Define a range name for this cell as KM_PER_MI (again, notice the underscores).

For purpose of cross-checking, the expected answer is around 1.6, but you will lose points if we catch you typing in a constant here instead of calculating it with a formula! A result around 0.6 indicates that you have solved for miles-per-kilometer instead of kilometers-per-mile. Format the cell as a number with 6 decimal places, and widen the column if necessary to show the number. Leave all other *result* cells blank for now.

Save your spreadsheet now.

Building the Data Table

Click on the Data tab, and type in the following data (seven columns overall, including the row numbers), starting with the word **City** in cell C5. Set the $ column format to Currency with 2 decimal places (except for Boston), and set the Volume column format to Number with 2 decimal places (except for Boston). Set the justification of the cells to what you see in the following diagram, set the text labels to **boldface**, and set the lines and shading to what you see.

Notice that several entries in the State/Province column are the same (several stops in Ontario, a couple each in Minnesota and Michigan, and so on). In order to save time and reduce the number of typing errors, I suggest that you type each duplicated name only once, and then copy the contents of the cell to the other places that require the same value.

Similarly, instead of typing a whole bunch of individual L and G characters in the Codes column, I suggest that you type a single L code for Montreal, copy the L throughout the remainder of that column, then go back and fill in the G codes where necessary. Make sure that when you type in the Code column you type only the *single* character L or the *single* character G. Do not put any spaces around the characters (click on the correct button in the toolbar to center them instead). If you accidentally put spaces around these characters, later formulae that depend on them will fail to give the correct results.

	City	State/Province	Miles	$	Volume	Code
0	Boston	Massachusetts	none	none	none	none
1	Montreal	Quebec	310	$40.05	35.56	L
2	Toronto	Ontario	335	$41.55	36.23	L
3	Detroit	Michigan	237	$17.05	6.41	G
4	Mackinaw City	Michigan	292	$23.62	8.53	G
5	Sault Ste. Marie	Ontario	53	$7.79	6.47	L
6	Wawa	Ontario	132	$16.70	14.27	L
7	Marathon	Ontario	116	$15.37	12.91	L
8	Thunder Bay	Ontario	169	$20.38	17.77	L
9	Duluth	Minnesota	191	$14.16	5.46	G
10	Minneapolis	Minnesota	156	$13.17	4.99	G
11	Fargo	North Dakota	237	$20.02	7.65	G
12	Winnipeg	Manitoba	218	$26.94	25.78	L
13	Regina	Saskatchewan	357	$41.80	37.54	L
14	Swift Current	Saskatchewan	156	$23.67	20.36	L
15	Medicine Hat	Alberta	144	$18.63	17.58	L
16	Calgary	Alberta	191	$25.46	22.59	L
17	Great Falls	Montana	278	$21.95	8.12	G
18	Butte	Montana	155	$13.53	5.17	G
19	Spokane	Washington	318	$24.68	9.28	G
20	Seattle	Washington	282	$22.94	8.55	G
21	Vancouver	British Columbia	168	$24.70	21.19	L

Save your spreadsheet now.

Creating Labels for the Formulae Columns

In the Data page, click on the cell to the right of the label containing the word Code. Enter the label KM in that cell, then GAL in the next cell to the right, MPG in the cell after that, then $/G, then L, then KPL, and finally $/L. These seven new column labels represent (respectively) <u>k</u>ilometers, <u>g</u>allons, <u>m</u>iles <u>p</u>er <u>g</u>allon, dollars per gallon, <u>l</u>iters, <u>k</u>ilometers <u>p</u>er <u>l</u>iter, and dollars per <u>l</u>iter. Make the labels **boldfaced** and <u>centered</u>, if they are not set that way already. Enter the word none for the Boston row underneath all seven new labels, and then <u>right justify</u> these seven cells.

 An efficient way to enter none in all seven cells is to enter it once (under KM), then drag copy it to the other six cells using the (black) square in the lower right corner of the cursor cell (where the mouse pointer turns into a black cross).

The Formulae Columns

Now we start the most difficult portion of this assignment. Under each of the new column labels we are going to create a formula, using unit conversions, which will be copied down through the remaining rows of the table. I expect you to think about and create each formula yourself, without help, verify that it returns the expected result, and then copy the formula to the bottom of the table. Only if you get really, really stuck are you to ask one of the lab assistants for help (and they will only give you guidance — they are *not* to give you the correct formula outright).

In general, you will be using only multiplication and division to perform unit conversions. For example, since we have the number of kilometers per mile safely computed and tucked away in the KM_PER_MI cell, we can use that number to convert between kilometers and miles, as in the following two equations:

$$Miles \times \frac{1.6\,Km}{1\,Mi} \rightarrow Kilometers$$

$$Kilometers \div \frac{1.6\,Km}{1\,Mi} \rightarrow Miles$$

Instead of using the ~1.6 constant, you would of course use the KM_PER_MI range name.

 KM (Kilometers Traveled During This Leg of the Trip): In the KM column, underneath the word none, create a formula to compute the number of kilometers traveled on the leg from Boston to Montreal. The formula you create depends on the number of miles traveled on that leg (in a cell in the current row of the table) and the KM_PER_MI range name (created in an earlier step on the Input Output page).

Does the answer make sense? Because there are about 1.6 kilometers in a mile, should the resulting number be larger or smaller than the number of miles traveled?

When you get the formula correct, copy it down throughout the rest of the column.

<u>GAL</u> **(Gallons of Gasoline Purchased):** In the GAL column we want to compute the number of gallons of gasoline consumed during each leg of the trip. Unfortunately, sometimes we bought gasoline in gallons, and sometimes in liters. The letter in the Code column tells us which interpretation to use for the Volume column.

If the Code value is "G" the value in the Volume column represents gallons. If the Code is "L" the corresponding volume is in liters, and it will have to be converted to gallons using the L_PER_GAL range name defined earlier.

To do this properly, write a formula that uses an IF statement to ask about the code character and returns the corresponding correct value. A "pseudocode" version of this instruction is outlined below (you must convert it into the correct Excel syntax):

>IF the Code is "G" THEN return the current Volume (it is already in gallons),
>   ELSE convert the Volume from liters to gallons (using L_PER_GAL).

Copy the formula throughout the remainder of the column.

Does the resulting column contain reasonable looking amounts, or are you getting numbers that indicate you have a 100-gallon tank on your car? (Most private vehicles have gas tanks that hold between 10 and 25 gallons.)

Are the amounts in the Volume column for "G" codes the same as what you get as the result of this formula? They should be! (Why is that?)

Since there are slightly less than 4 liters per gallon (as you notice from the L_PER_GAL cell on the Input Output page), are the amounts in the Volume column for "L" codes roughly 4 times the amount you get as the result of this formula?

<u>MPG</u> **(Miles Driven Per Gallon of Gasoline Burned):** In the MPG column, write a formula based on the Miles and the GAL columns, that computes the number of miles per gallon achieved during that leg of the trip.

Copy the formula throughout the remainder of the column.

Are these numbers reasonable, or does your car actually get 90+ miles to the gallon? The values you see will be somewhere between 29 and 37 mpg.

For example, if cell X10 represented miles, and Y10 represented gallons, how do you compute the mpg? Is it =X10/Y10, =Y10/X10, or =X10*Y10?

$/G (Dollars Paid Per Gallon of Gasoline Purchased): In the $/G column, write a formula to compute the number of dollars paid per gallon of gasoline purchased, and copy it throughout the column as before.

Are the price per gallon numbers commensurate with reality, or are you paying too much or too little? If you pay $10 for 7 gallons of gas, for example, are you paying $1.43 per gallon or $0.70 per gallon?

Note that you will pay considerably more for a gallon of gas in Canada than you will in the United States. (The prices we are using might not be realistic today!)

L (Liters of Gasoline Purchased): In the L column, write a formula to compute from the GAL column and the L_PER_GAL cell the number of liters of gasoline purchased, then copy the formula throughout the column.

This formula does <u>not</u> need to use an IF function. The number of liters can be computed directly from the volume of gallons purchased and the L_PER_GAL conversion constant.

Are these numbers reasonable? Based on the conversion factor from liters to gallons, should the liters number be larger than or smaller than the corresponding gallons number?

Are the volumes you get here exactly the same as the Volume column when the Code is "L"? They should be! (Why is that?)

KPL (Kilometers Driven Per Liter of Gasoline Burned): In the KPL column, write a formula to compute the number of kilometers driven per liter of gasoline burned, then copy it throughout the column. Are these numbers reasonable (between 12 and 16 kilometers per liter)?

$/L (Dollars Paid Per Liter of Gasoline Purchased): In the final $/L column, write a formula to compute the price as the number of dollars paid per liter of gasoline purchased, then copy it throughout the column. Are these numbers reasonable, assuming that the dollars column is correct and the liters column is correct?

Do not proceed until all seven new columns contain formulae which generate the correct values. Check that all values "make sense" in the context in which they are generated.

Formatting the Seven new Columns

Format all of the cells in this new block of seven columns with 2 decimal places: format columns $/G and $/L as currency and all other columns as simple numbers (depending on your version of Excel, these cells may be already formatted correctly).

Narrow the width of all seven columns so that the minimum space is occupied by each (i.e., double click in the column header on the right boundary between columns to have Excel automatically set the size).

Draw a box outlining all of the data cells.

Draw a shaded box outlining the column title cells (if Excel hasn't already done so).

Save your spreadsheet now.

Computing the Final Results

Click on the Input Output tab. In the output block, write five new formulae to compute the total miles and kilometers traveled, the total gallons and liters of gasoline purchased, and the total cost of the trip. Format these five cells with 2 decimal places (all should be simple numeric except for the total cost which should be formatted as currency).

In the lower two cells of the output block, write two new formulae using only the results from the upper section of the output block to compute the average number of miles per gallon and average kilometers per liter experienced over the trip. Both these formulae use simple division, but do not use the AVERAGE function. Format these two cells as numeric with 2 decimal places.

Save your spreadsheet now.

At this point your spreadsheet formulae have all been entered. No other changes should be necessary to any of the notebook pages, formulae, formats, numbers, or column widths. From what we have generated, we can examine the numbers to tell us about our fuel efficiency (mpg or kpl), our costs ($/gal or $/l), and our total trip distances and costs. Unfortunately, while all of the information is present in the spreadsheet, it is not very easy to extract it from the piles of numbers that we have generated. What remains for us now is to create graphs for the data to make them understandable.

Before proceeding, you might want to take a few minutes and review the numbers in the Data tab again. Did you type in the table of distances correctly? Did you type in the conversion formulae correctly? Do the resulting numbers make sense? Did the final formulae on the Input Output page return reasonable looking amounts? (For example, how far is it from Boston to Vancouver? 100 miles? 10,000 miles? What is a reasonable value?) Are all the cells formatted correctly? Did you save your spreadsheet on your disk?

Building the First Graph

The first graph will be used to display all of the MPG (miles per gallon) numbers from the data table. We will want this to be a line chart in order to show trends over time. As the trip progressed, did the gas mileage improve or not, or did it stay about the same? While we could show the data with a bar chart, a line chart is a better choice because it "connects the dots" of the data points. The line segments thus formed then provide a visual record of the change, or slope, between adjacent data points that is much more difficult to infer from a bar chart, and nearly impossible to do so from the raw numerical data.

Before we build the first graph, click on the Data page, and then select all the numeric data in the MPG column (click-drag over all of the <u>numbers</u> in that column, not including the "none" at the top).

Excel 2003: Click on Insert-Chart... in the menu.

Chart Wizard - Step 1 of 4 - Chart Type: In this step we are to choose the type and subtype of chart to display. Make sure that Chart type: is on Line, and Chart sub-type: is on Line with markers displayed at each data value.

Click on the Next > button when this is correct.

Excel 2007-2016: Click on the Insert tab in the ribbon, then on Line in the Charts panel, and select 2D Line-Line with Markers. A chart will appear in the Data page; we will move it onto its own page later.

Excel 2008 / 2011 for the Mac: Click on Insert-Chart... in the menu. A toolbar will appear showing chart types. Pick the Line category, and then choose Marked Line from the displayed samples. A chart will appear in the Data page; we will move it onto its own page later.

Next, we need to set up the chart with the location of the data labels we wish to plot.

Excel 2003: Chart Wizard - Step 2 of 4 - Chart Source Data: In this dialog box, there are two notebook tabs: the Data Range tab is the default because it can capture most simple graph data definitions, but the Series tab allows us to customize and "fine tune" the graph data definitions minutely. Click on the Series tab. The Values: edit box should already be filled in with the correct cell addresses for the MPG column.

Click once in the Name: edit box, then type Miles Per Gallon and *your name*.

Click once in the Category (X) axis labels: edit box. The blinking cursor will appear there. Scroll the Data page until you can see the cells under the City column, then click-drag over all city names from Montreal through Vancouver (omit Boston). The Category (X) axis labels: edit box will be filled in with the correct cell addresses.

As you tab and click around the dialog box, you will notice that the preview window will show a small version of the graph as it is being constructed. The title of the graph will also appear to the right of the graph in a "legend" box, but don't worry about this – we will get rid of the legend box in the next step.

Click on the Next > button when all items are correct.

Excel 2007-2016: Click in the Design tab of the ribbon, then on the Select Data button in the Data panel. Click the Edit button in the Horizontal (Category) Axis Labels box of the Select Data Source dialog; the dialog will be temporarily replaced by a small Axis Labels dialog box. Click drag over all city names from Montreal through Vancouver (omit Boston), then click the OK button to clear the Axis Labels box, and click OK again to clear the Select Data Source box.

Excel 2008-2011 (Mac): Click on Chart-Source Data..., and in the Select Data Source dialog box click the edit button to the right of the Category (X) axis labels box. The dialog will be temporarily replaced by a much smaller box containing an edit line. Click drag over all city names from Montreal through Vancouver (omit Boston), and then click the button to re-expand the dialog (you should see the correct cell range in the X axis labels). Finally, click the OK button to clear the Select Data Source dialog.

The chart, before final formatting, should look similar to the following image:

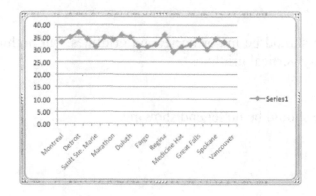

Next, we need to tweak a few of the options to turn a pretty picture into information.

Excel 2003: Chart Wizard - Step 3 of 4 - Chart Options: This dialog box has six notebook tabs. We will need to set or check options in all of them.
Excel 2007-2010: Click on the Layout tab in the Chart Tools panel of the ribbon. We will need to set or check options for many of these settings.
Excel 2013/2016: In the Design tab of Chart Tools click on Add Chart Element. You will see entries such as Axes, Axis Titles, Chart Title, etc.
Excel 2008 (Mac): In the toolbar there is a button labeled Toolbox. Click that button to make the Formatting Palette dialog appear (you may also do this by clicking on View-Toolbox-Formatting Palette in the menu).
Excel 2011 (Mac): Clicking on the chart should add a purple Chart Layout tab to the ribbon, showing Chart Title, Axis Titles, Legend, etc.

Using those tools, we need to set the following items:

Axes:

Axes should show both horizontally and vertically.

Axis Titles:

The X axis title should be **Gasoline Stops**, and it should be horizontal, left-to-right, and below the axis. The Y axis title should be **MPG**, and it should be rotated vertically.

Chart Title:

The chart title should be **Miles Per Gallon** and *your name* above the chart.

Data Labels:

Each data point in the chart should be set to have its actual numeric value showing next to the symbol on the right.

Data Table:

The data table should <u>not</u> be showing.

Gridlines:

There should be major horizontal gridlines, but nothing else (no minor gridlines, nor any vertical gridlines).

Legend:

There should be no legend showing.

The final step is to make the chart appear on a page of its own in the spreadsheet.

Excel 2003: Chart Wizard - Step 4 of 4 - Chart Location: This dialog box is used to determine where in the Excel spreadsheet to place the new graph. Click on the As new <u>s</u>heet: radio button, then in the corresponding edit box name the new sheet as **MPG**.

Finally, after all of these steps are complete, click on the <u>F</u>inish button.

Excel 2007-2016: Click on the Design tab in the Chart Tools panel of the ribbon, and then on Move Chart. A Move Chart dialog will appear. Select the New Sheet radio button, and in the corresponding edit box name the new sheet as **MPG**. Click OK.

Excel 2008-2011 (Mac): *Right-click* the chart and select Move Chart... from the pop-up. In the Move Chart dialog, select the New sheet radio button, and name the chart **MPG**.

A new notebook page, labeled MPG, will appear as part of your current notebook.

Save your spreadsheet now.

Reality Check for the First Graph

Click on the MPG tab to view your graph. If you have performed all of the steps correctly, this first graph should appear to be very similar to the following image. Examine the following image very carefully, and compare it against the version that you just created.

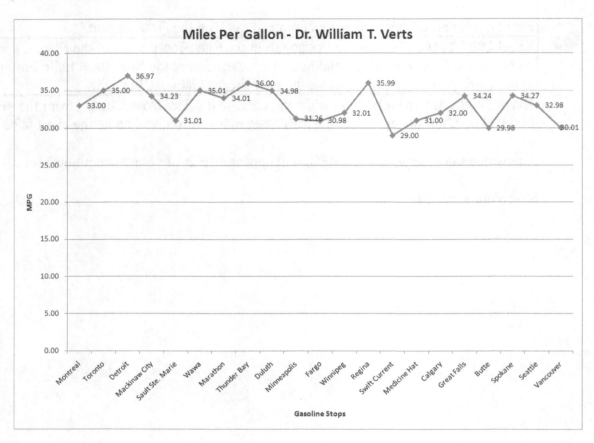

 Don't do this step if your graph is correct: If the graph does *not* look correct, you can always delete the graph and start over by *right-clicking* on the MPG notebook tab and selecting <u>D</u>elete from the pop up menu. Otherwise, it is possible to correct minor mistakes by editing the graph. You might find it conceptually easier to start over from scratch, then once you become comfortable with the graph generation process you might try being adventurous by editing an existing graph.

 Do not proceed until this graph is correct.

Building the Second Graph

Now we need to build a second graph in the same manner as before. In this graph we want to construct a column (standard bar) chart of the $/G (dollars per gallon) column. Select the Data page and click drag over all numeric values in the $/G column, not including the "none" at the top.

Excel 2003 or Excel 2008-2011 (Mac): Insert a new chart as before, but make sure that the chart type is Column and the chart subtype is Clustered Column.

Excel 2007-2016: Insert a new chart as before, but make sure that the chart type is a Column, 2-D Column, Clustered Column chart.

As before, we have a number of settings to verify and adjust:

- The x-axis data series labels should still be the list of city names from Montreal through Vancouver (not including Boston).

- The single series of data should be all numbers from the $/G column (not including the "none" value for Boston).

- The title for the x-axis should be **Gasoline Stops**, as before.

- The title for the y-axis should be **$/G**.

- The title for the entire chart should be **Dollars Per Gallon** and *your name*.

- There should be both horizontal axes and vertical axes displayed.

- There should be major gridlines for the y-axis, but nowhere else (i.e., there should be horizontal grid lines, but not vertical grid lines).

- The legend should be deleted.

- Each bar in the column chart should have a data value associated with it, above the top of the bar.

- The chart should be moved to its own page in the spreadsheet, with **PRICES** as its tab name.

Save your spreadsheet now.

Reality Check for the Second Graph

Click on the PRICES tab to view your graph. If you have performed all of the steps correctly, this graph should appear to be very similar to the following image. Examine the image very carefully, and compare it against the version that you just created.

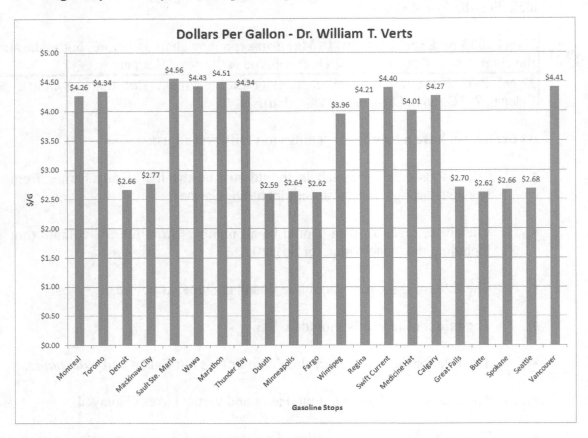

Don't do this step if your graph is correct: As before, if the graph does *not* look correct, you can always delete the graph and start over by *right-clicking* on the PRICES notebook tab and selecting Delete from the pop up menu, or you can edit the graph.

Do not proceed until this graph is correct.

Final Documentation

Click on the Header tab, and starting in cell A5 type *at least three but no more than five lines* of English text describing the purpose of the spreadsheet (more than five lines would interfere with the next step). This documentation must include the problem setup, as well as a description of the results and graphs. Format the cells without shading or lines. If Excel applies shading or lines to these cells automatically (which might happen in the older Excel 2000), remove those formats.

Below the documentation, click in cell A10.

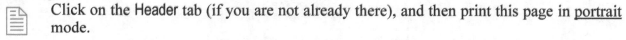

Excel 2003 or Excel 2008-2011 for the Mac: Generate a table of the range names (both of them) by clicking on Insert-Name-Paste, then clicking on Paste List in the dialog box that pops up.

Excel 2007-2016: Click on the Formulas tab in the ribbon, then on Use in Formula in the Defined Names panel, and select Paste Names. Click on Paste List in the dialog box that pops up.

Save your spreadsheet now. Your spreadsheet is complete.

Printing

Click on the Header tab (if you are not already there), and then print this page in portrait mode.

Click on the Input Output tab, and then print this page in portrait mode as well.

Click on the Data tab, and then print this page in landscape mode. The columns should have been resized so that everything fits on one page.

Click on the MPG tab, and then print this page (the miles-per-gallon chart) in landscape mode.

Click on the PRICES tab, and then print this page (the dollars-per-gallon chart) in landscape mode.

Click on the Input Output tab, then key in ⌈Ctrl⌉ ` to show formulae instead of results. Widen the columns to show all the formulae, and then print this page in landscape mode. Key in ⌈Ctrl⌉ ` to show results once more. Narrow the columns appropriately.

Click on the Data tab, then key in ⌈Ctrl⌉ ` to show formulae instead of results. Widen the columns to show all the formulae, and then print this page in landscape mode. Key in ⌈Ctrl⌉ ` to show results once more. Narrow the columns appropriately.

Save your spreadsheet now.

Creating the Banner Page

As you have done in previous assignments, start up Microsoft Word and create a banner page containing just your name, the phrase LAB ASSIGNMENT #8, either WORK AT LAB or WORK AT HOME, and the current date, hitting [Enter←] after each line.

Center the lines, make sure that they are in the Times New Roman typeface, and change the size to **20 points**.

Format the document to be single-spaced, with *no extra spacing* between the lines.

Word 2003: Save the document as **LAB8.DOC** in your Word Processing folder.

Word 2007-2016, or Word 2008-2011 for the Mac: Save the document as **LAB8.DOCX** in your Word Processing folder.

Print out your completed banner page from Word. This page will become the cover page of your report.

William T. Verts
LAB ASSIGNMENT #8
WORK AT HOME
November 27, 2013

Shutting Down

Close all programs. If Microsoft Excel asks you if you want to save any changes, you generally should answer "yes". Close down your computer normally.

What to Turn In

You will need to turn in the banner (1 page) and all of the printouts from your spreadsheet (7 pages), containing the following items (check off the items in the list below):

Page #1 (the banner page) must contain:
- ☐ Your name (centered),
- ☐ LAB ASSIGNMENT #8 (centered),
- ☐ WORK AT LAB or WORK AT HOME (centered),
- ☐ Current date (centered),
- ☐ No extra spaces between lines.
- ☐ Font must be set to 20 Point Times New Roman.

Page #2 (the Header page):
- ☐ Cells A1 to A3 contain your name, workplace, and date/time in a shaded box,
- ☐ cells A5 to A7 contain a 3 to 5 line description of the spreadsheet purpose,
- ☐ cells A10 and below contain a table of the defined range names,
- ☐ printed in <u>portrait</u> mode.

Page #3 (the Input Output page):
- ☐ Cells A1 to A3 contain your name, workplace, and date/time in a shaded box,
- ☐ input table contains the six given constants and the computed value,
- ☐ output table contains five sums and two averages,
- ☐ tables are properly outlined, with shaded titles, text label cells in boldface,
- ☐ printed in <u>portrait</u> mode.

Page #4 (the Data page):
- ☐ Cells A1 to A3 contain your name, workplace, and date/time in a shaded box,
- ☐ table contains <u>*seven*</u> columns of original data (includes column to left of cities),
- ☐ table contains seven columns of computed values (formatted with 2 decimals),
- ☐ table is properly outlined, with shaded titles,
- ☐ printed in <u>landscape</u> mode.

Page #5 (the MPG graph page):
- ☐ Graph is a line graph,
- ☐ data values are next to each data point,
- ☐ City names (except Boston) are X axis labels,
- ☐ X axis title is Gasoline Stops,
- ☐ Y axis title is MPG,
- ☐ title is Miles Per Gallon and student's name,
- ☐ printed in <u>landscape</u> mode.

Page #6 (the PRICES graph page):
    ☐ Graph is a column (standard bar) chart,
    ☐ data values are above each data point,
    ☐ City names (except Boston) are X axis labels,
    ☐ X axis title is Gasoline Stops,
    ☐ Y axis title is $/G,
    ☐ title is Dollars Per Gallon and student's name,
    ☐ printed in <u>landscape</u> mode.

Page #7 (the Input Output page, may print on more than one page):
    ☐ Formulae printed **and are completely visible**.

Page #8 (the Data page, may print on more than one page):
    ☐ Formulae printed **and are completely visible**.

Grading Policy

Lab assignments are worth 10 points each. Teaching assistants will observe the following criteria for evaluating and scoring the Lab #8 assignments that they receive.

- Any report that does not have the student's name *__typed__* on *__all__* pages (centered at the top of the banner page, as part of the header on every spreadsheet page, and in the title line of both graphs) will be *__rejected__*, and if submitted will receive a *__zero__*. If any student writes their name in by hand, instead of typing it, then the report must be rejected. **Reject any report missing a banner page.**

- 1 Point - Report must be stapled together. Remove the full point if the report is paper-clipped together or is submitted loose (even with folded corners). Remove the full point if the pages are not in the order listed here (banner, header, input output, data, MPG graph, $/G graph, input output formulae, data formulae).

- 1 Point - Printout of the banner page must be present and must contain the appropriate lines of banner information. Remove ½ point for every line of the banner page that is missing or incorrect (for example: a line not centered, the font not set to 20 point Times New Roman, or the lines are not single spaced with no extra spacing between lines), up to the full point possible.

- 1 Point - Remove the point for any errors in formatting the spreadsheet (missing date/time on any sheet, incorrect number, border, or pattern formats, incorrect portrait/landscape paper orientation, etc.).

- 1 Point - Remove the point if the description of the purpose of the spreadsheet is missing from the Header page. Remove ½ point if it contains fewer than 3 total lines or does not contain a "reasonable" analysis of the purpose.

▪ 1 Point - Remove the point if the data dictionary is missing from the Header page. Cell addresses may be different between different students' reports; they will depend on where the students placed the input output block. Remove ½ point if there are fewer than 2 names in the block, or if it is obvious that there are mistakes.

▪ 3 Points - Input Output and Data page values must be correct. TAs must check the formulae pages. Remove points as follows, up to the maximum of 3 points. **Remove 2 points if the Input Output formulae are not completely visible. Remove 2 points if the Data formulae are not completely visible.** Remove ½ point if any of the six input constants were entered incorrectly. Remove ½ point if the KM_PER_MI value is computed incorrectly. Remove ½ point if any of the five output sums were computed incorrectly. Remove ½ point if either of the output averages were computed incorrectly. Remove ½ point for each column of the Data table that contains any computational mistake, but do not exceed the 3 points total for this section.

▪ 1 Point - MPG graph. Remove points as follows, up to the full point possible. Remove ½ point if the graph is not a line graph. Remove ½ point if the data values are obviously incorrect (i.e., wrong series). Remove ½ point if the data values are missing next to each data point. Remove ½ point if the city names are not the X axis labels. Remove ½ point if the X title is not Gasoline Stops. Remove ½ point if the Y title is not MPG. Remove ½ point if the main title is not Miles Per Gallon and the student's name.

▪ 1 Point - $/G graph. Remove points as follows, up to the full point possible. Remove ½ point if the graph is not a column (standard bar) chart. Remove ½ point if the data values are obviously incorrect (i.e., wrong series). Remove ½ point if the city names are not the X axis labels. Remove ½ point if the X title is not Gasoline Stops. Remove ½ point if the Y title is not $/G. Remove ½ point if the main title is not Dollars Per Gallon and the student's name.

Lab #9 – Databases: Handedness Statistics

Introduction & Goals

In this assignment you will start using the Microsoft Access database package. Sorry, Macintosh users: Microsoft Access is only for Windows PCs. You will learn the basics of getting around: creating tables by importing data from a text file, printing reports, and performing simple queries. The file that will be provided contains 246 records of information, gathered from a Computer Literacy class long ago. Each data record describes a single person and contains their birth date, their sex ("M" for male, or "F" for female), their handedness ("L" for left-handed, "R" for right-handed, or "A" for ambidextrous), and their lecture section ("1" or "2"). We will import that text file into Access, save it as a database table, and then get the database package to help us ask questions about that table. We will then create some reports on the results of those questions, and send them to the printer.

Note that the next assignment, lab #10, will depend on the results from this assignment. You will not be able to perform lab #10 unless you have completed lab #9 first. Don't lose your files! You may wish to do lab #10 at the same time as lab #9; they are both fairly short.

Specifics You Will Learn in This Assignment

You will learn the following things in the completion of this assignment:

- **Importing Comma Delimited Data into a Table** – Rather than provide you with a pre-built database table, and rather than forcing you to type in 246 records by hand, we will provide you with a text file that you can view and edit in Notepad. This text file can be imported into Access, and automatically converted into the internal form that Access needs to use.

- **Creating Simple Queries about the Data** – Given that the data have been stored in the correct form, we need to be able to ask questions about it. Such a question is called a query. You will learn how to create a query, how to modify it, and how to save it as part of the database.

- **Creating Reports** – Once you know your answers, you have to be able to print them out. This involves creating a report, also saved as part of the database, which shows the information extracted from the queries.

Preparation before Starting Assignment

Read this assignment through in its entirety before doing anything. This lab does not depend on the data files you created in any earlier assignment, but you will store new files in the directories created in lab #1. The results from this assignment will be used in lab #10.

In the Laboratory

Bring your flash drive containing the folders created in lab #1 and this lab assignment. Do not come to lab without these items.

At Home

Your home machine must have a working version of Microsoft Access on a Windows PC (no Macintosh) and a working printer, as usual. Almost any version of Access will work here from Access 97 onwards, but the instructions here are written for much later versions. You must be able to locate the folders created in lab #1.

Data Files

There is one data file, a text file called `handed.txt`, provided to you in compressed form on the class Web site in a `.ZIP` archive. You must download it from the class Web site and unpack the contents just as you did in earlier assignments. The file is to be placed in the Databases folder on your disk. The last page of this assignment shows a complete listing of this text file.

Step-By-Step Procedure

Start your machine up normally. You should have the Databases folder on your disk or flash drive.

Starting Up

Download and unpack the `handed.txt` file to your Databases folder. Review the procedure for unpacking `.ZIP` files if you do not remember how to do so.

This step is to familiarize you with the data that you will be importing into Access. Open up a copy of Windows Notepad. Using File-Open, navigate to the Databases folder on your disk and load in the `handed.txt` file.

 Scroll up and down through the file to see what it looks like, but **DO NOT MAKE ANY CHANGES TO THE FILE!**

Each line of the data corresponds to all of the information about a single student. Since the data file contains 246 lines, we have information about 246 distinct students. The first line of the data file will appear as follows:

$$1/23/69,"L","F","1"$$

This line means that the corresponding student was a left-handed female, born on January 23, 1969, and was enrolled in the morning lecture ("1" is the morning lecture, "2" is the afternoon lecture). The sex field will only be "M" for male or "F" for female, but the handedness field may be "L" for left-handed, "R" for right-handed, or "A" for ambidextrous (which means that the person can use either hand equally well). The largest proportion of any population of people will be right-handed.

The data are in "comma and quote delimited format" which means that commas are used to separate the individual items on each line. Text items are surrounded by quotes because (in the general case) they are allowed to contain blanks, and it is important to know where the text strings start and stop. Comma delimited data are easy to edit in a text editor, and almost all large spreadsheet and database programs such as Excel and Access (among many others) can import data in that form.

When you finish examining the data, click on File-Exit to close Notepad (do ***not*** click on File-Save. If Notepad asks you if you want to save any changes, click on the NO button).

Starting Access

Find and start the Microsoft Access database program. It may already be established as an icon on the desktop, or you may have to go through the menus.

Access 2003: In the initial dialog box that pops up as soon as you start Access create a new blank database and save it as **lab9.mdb** in the Databases folder of your disk. You will see a new, blank database child-window appear on screen. This window has several page tabs along the side (they are along the top in Access 97 and earlier).

Access 2007-2016: From the initial page of Access create a new blank database, click the browse button (the tiny button to the right of the File Name edit box in the right-most panel of the screen or dialog box) to locate the Databases folder of your disk, and type in **lab9.accdb** as the name of the file. Click the Create button. The new database completely fills the Access window.

All types of objects, including tables, queries, screen forms, and reports, will be stored in the database itself. Even though the database is completely empty the file takes up a considerable amount of space on your disk (around 100K in Access 2000/2003, 284K in Access 2007, 324K in Access 2010, and 328K in Access 2016).

Do not proceed until you have a blank database saved as lab9 in the Databases folder of your disk or flash drive.

Importing the Data

In this step we need to have you convert the text file into a database table. You may start this process, called ***importing the data***, in several ways.

Access 2003: You may click in the menu on File-Get External Data-Import..., or you may click on New in the Tables tab of the lab9 database window, and then select Import Table from the New Table dialog box that pops up. It does not matter which method you use.

You will see an Import dialog box appear. Make sure that the Look in: list box points to your Databases folder, where you unpacked the handed.txt file from the lab9.zip archive file. You will not see the file name appear until you go down to the Files of type: list box, click on its drop down arrow, and select Text Files from the list (this option can find *.txt files). The handed.txt file should now appear in the main window of the dialog box; click once on its name, and then on the Import button. The Text Import Wizard or Import Text Wizard dialog box will appear.

Access 2007-2013: Click in the ribbon on External Data, then click Text File in the Import panel. Make sure the setting is Import the source data into a new table in the current database, then click the Browse button and look for the handed.txt file. Click OK until you see the Import Text Wizard appear.

Access 2016: Click in the ribbon on External Data, then click the New Data Source button. In the menu that pops up, click From File, then Text File. In the Get External Data dialog box that appears, click the Browse button and look for the handed.txt file. Click OK until you see the Import Text Wizard appear.

We will now step through the (many) screens of the wizard, but only a few options need to be changed.

The Import Wizard

1. You should see the first few records of the data, and the Delimited radio button should be filled in (⊙). If it is not filled in, then make it so. Click Next > once.

2. You should see a group of radio buttons, with Comma filled in (⊙) as the delimiter, a double quote (") as the Text Qualifier, and *no* check mark (☐) in the First Row Contains Field Names check box. Make no changes here. Click Next > once.

3. **Access 2003:** You should see the radio button In a New Table filled in (⊙) as the place to store the data. Make no changes here unless necessary. Click Next > once.
   Access 2007-2016: Nothing to do here.

4. You should see the top few lines of the table on screen with field names Field1, Field2, Field3, and Field4. (The Field2 and Field3 names may be partially obscured.)

Access 2003: In older versions of Access you can change the names of the field by clicking on each field name column header in turn and replacing it in the Field Name: edit box with a new name. There seems to be a bug in Access 2003 which permits only the first field to be changed. The work-around for Access 2003 is to click on the Advanced button, which brings up a new Import Specification dialog box, as shown below.

Change Field1 to Birthdate, Field2 to Hand, Field3 to Sex, and Field4 to Class. Make no other changes here (no fields will be indexed, and we wish to import all of the fields). Click the OK button to close the Import Specification dialog.

Access 2007-2016: Click on each field name in turn and rename it. Change Field1 to Birthdate, Field2 to Hand, Field3 to Sex, and Field4 to Class. Make no other changes here (no fields will be indexed, and we wish to import all of the fields).

Click Next > once.

5.   You should see the Let Access add Primary Key radio button filled in; change this by clicking on the No primary key radio button to fill it in (⊙). Click Next > once.

6.   In this final box the Import to Table: edit box should already contain the name HANDED. Leave this unchanged. Make no other changes here. Click on the Finish button.

You may get a message box saying that the `handed.txt` file has been successfully imported into table HANDED. Clear this message box.

Access 2010-2016: You will get a dialog box asking if you wish to save these import steps. Close the dialog without checking the Save import steps check box.

Scrolling Through the Data

The HANDED table name should now be visible in the Tables section of the database. If there is any other table present (such as Table1), close it.

Access 2003: Click on the name HANDED (if it is not already highlighted), then click on the Open button.

Access 2007-2016: Double-click the name HANDED to open it in the right hand panel.

Scroll up and down, and use the controls like those on a VCR or DVD player, to get comfortable with moving through the table, but make no changes to the data at this time.

The First Action

Access 2003: *Right-click* on the Birthdate column header, then select Sort Ascending from the pop up menu. Scroll through the table to verify that it is sorted.

Access 2007-2016: *Right-click* on the Birthdate column header, then select Sort Oldest to Newest from the pop up menu. Scroll through the table to verify that it is sorted.

Close the table by clicking on the window's ✖ button. When the dialog box pops up asking if you want to save your changes, click on the Yes button. The database table will vanish, but all the records will be sorted by birth date on the disk.

Creating the First Query

We are now going to ask the database to show us all records where the corresponding person was born on or after January 1, 1972.

Access 2003: Click on the Queries tab, then on the New button to build a new query. In the New Query dialog box that pops up there will be several ways listed of creating queries. Make sure that Design View is highlighted so we can build a query from scratch, and then click OK.

Access 2007-2016: Click on the Create tab in the ribbon, then on Query Design in the Queries panel.

A query form will appear where you fill in the specific information about the question you are asking. Before you are allowed to make changes to the query form, however, you must select the source for the data used in the question. A Show Table dialog box will pop up on top of the query form, and from this dialog you choose the tables (or results from previous queries) to use as the data sources for this query.

In the Show Table dialog box that pops up in this case, the HANDED table should be the only thing present (or if not, any other tables are empty), and it should be highlighted. Select HANDED, click the Add button *once* to add HANDED to the query form, then click the Close button.

1. Click in the leftmost Field: box of the query. A button will appear; click it, then select the Birthdate field from the list. The Field: box will be automatically filled in with Birthdate, and the Table: box will be automatically filled in with HANDED. Click in Sort:, click on the button, and select Ascending from the list. Make sure that the Show: check box is checked (☑). Click on the Criteria: box, then type in (manually) the phrase **>=#1/1/1972#** into the box.

2. Click in the second Field: box. Make this query field be the Hand field (the Table: will automatically be HANDED), and make sure the Show: check box is checked (☑).

3. Click in the third Field: box, and make that one Sex, and make sure the Show: check box is checked (☑).

4. Click in the fourth Field: box, and make that one Class, and make sure the Show: check box is checked (☑).

Access 2003: In the menu, click on Query-Run.

Access 2007-2016: In the upper left corner of the ribbon click the Run button.

The query form will vanish, to be replaced by a view of the table containing only those records where the person was born after January 1, 1972. By my count, there should be 71 matching records (the number of records is shown at the bottom of the window).

Access 2003: If you make a mistake, click on View-Design View to go back to the query form. Make your corrections, and then run the query again with Query-Run.

Access 2007-2016: If you make a mistake, click on View in the ribbon (next to the Run button) to go back to the query form. Make your corrections, and then run the query again with Query-Run.

Close the query by clicking on its ✕ button, and in the dialog box that pops up asking if you want to save your query, click on the Yes button. In the Save As dialog box, replace the Query Name: with the name **Youngsters**, then click the OK button. The Youngsters query will now appear as part of the database.

Creating and Printing the First Report

Access 2003: Click on the Reports tab of the database, then on the New button. In the New Report dialog box that pops up, click on AutoReport: Tabular to select the type of report we will build. In the Choose the table or query... drop down list, select the Youngsters query, and then click the OK button.

Access 2007-2016: Select Youngsters, next click on the Create tab in the ribbon, then on Report Wizard in the Reports panel. Click the >> symbol to select all fields, and then click Next once.

When you see the question about adding grouping levels, simply click Next again.

When you see the question about sort order, click Next once more.

When you see the question about how to lay out your report, select Tabular and Landscape. Verify that the checkbox Adjust the field width... has a check mark ☑ in it so everything fits across the page. Click Next.

Access 2007: If you see a question about style, leave the setting on Office and click Next.

In the last question, leave the title Youngsters, leave the radio button set on Preview the report, and click Finish.

Access will automatically create a landscape formatted report containing all of the fields from our table. You can see an entire page at a time by clicking on the image of the report. You may not be able to read all of the text, but you will be able to see how the report is formatted for the printer. Use the VCR controls to view all of the report pages.

Access 2003: In the menu click on View-Design View.

Access 2007-2016: Click the Close Print Preview button.

The page view of the report will go away, to be replaced by the design view for your report. You will see several "bands" across the page, with names such as Report Header, Page Header, Detail, Page Footer, and Report Footer. The name of the report (Youngsters) will be in the report header section.

We need to have you make some small changes to the report design to include your name and "Work at Lab" or "Work at Home" as part of the report.

Access 2003: There will also be a small tool window that pops up next to the report design. In the tool window, the upper left button is labeled with a large italic *Aa*, and if you float the mouse over this control you will see the word Label appear in a little yellow box. Click on this button to select text entry mode.

Access 2007-2016: In the Design tab of the ribbon, click on the *Aa* button in the Controls panel.

Click in the Report Header band, to the right of the word *Youngsters*, and type in your name. Repeat the process to enter either *Work at Lab* or *Work at Home* as a label underneath your name. View the report in Report View. The report may look just fine, but it is also possible that the columns may be too narrow to show either the headers or the data. In the following view, the Birthdate column is too narrow to show all the dates.

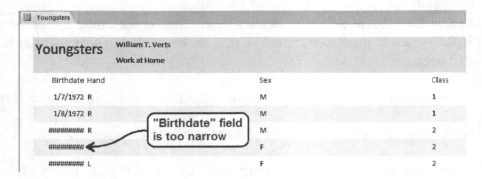

If this happens, you will need to fix it. Show the report in Design View, click on the appropriate items in the Page Header or the Detail bands, and then resize the items by dragging one or more of the little square handles on the control. This is shown below.

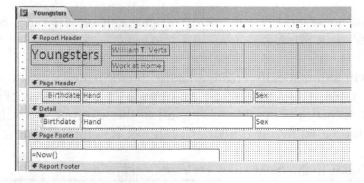

 Make certain that the items in the Detail band are wide enough to display all the data, and that the labels in the Page Header view are the same width. You may have to fiddle with several fields to get everything sized correctly. Switch back and forth between Design View and Report View until everything is correct. Also, if the text you inserted (name, etc.) does not look right, you can *click-drag* a label to a new position, or *double-click* on a label to change its caption.

STOP *Do not proceed* until the report looks correct, and contains all of the items that we require of you.

Access 2003: Click on File-Print... in the menu.

Access 2007: Click on Office Button-Print-Print.

Access 2010-2016: Click on the File tab, then Print-Print.

In the Print dialog box that pops up, make sure that the All radio button is filled in (⊙) in the Print Range radio group. Click on OK to **print the report** (it likely will be three or four pages, with your name on the first page).

Click on the ✕ button in the report window. You will get a message box asking if you wish to save the changes to the design of the report. Click on the <u>Y</u>es button.

Access 2003: The next dialog box will ask you what to call this report, and its name will already be filled in with the name of the query from which the report was generated (Youngsters). Make no changes, and click the OK button. The report window will vanish, but the Reports tab of the database will now contain the Youngsters report that you just generated.

 If you find that you need to reference the report again, you can simply click on the name of the report (Youngsters), then on either the Preview or Design buttons, and from there you can make changes to the design (or print it).

 Access 2007-2016: If you find that you need to reference the report again, you can simply right-click on the name of the report (Youngsters), then on Design View, and from there you can make changes to the design.

Creating the Second Query

This time, we are interested in knowing all available information about left-handed females from our table. As you did in the first query, create a new query using HANDED as the data source.

We wish to add all four fields to this query just as we did in the first query. To make this task easier than what we did before simply *double-click* on the Birthdate field name in the field name box and it will be automatically copied to the query design grid. *Double-click* on the Hand, Sex, and Class fields in turn to add those fields to the query.

Since we are interested in the left-handed females in the table enter the string **="F"** in the Criteria: box of the Sex field and enter **="L"** in the Criteria: box of the Hand field. Set the Sort: entry in the Birthdate field to sort in <u>descending</u> order.

Run the query (you should get 24 records).

Close the query window, and save the query with the name **Lefty Ladies**.

Creating and Printing the Second Report

As you did for the first report, create a new landscape, tabular report for the Lefty Ladies query results.

As you did before, change the design of the report to include your name, and either *Work at Lab* or *Work at Home*, in the Report Header.

Also, change the widths of the labels and fields for Hand and Birthdate to make all of the labels and data visible, as needed.

Preview the results again. Edit the report design as necessary to make the report look correct.

 Print this second report (likely two or more pages, with your name and work area printed on the first page).

Close the report and save it as **Lefty Ladies**.

Creating the Third Query

In this query we want to know how many people fall into each of the six categories of sex and handedness (how many lefty females, how many lefty males, righty females, righty males, ambidextrous females, and ambidextrous males).

As you did before, create a new query using the HANDED table as the data source.

Add the Hand, Sex, and Class fields to the design grid of the query, but *do not* add the Birthdate field.

Up in the tool bar or ribbon there is a button labeled with the Greek sigma character (Σ); click it (alternatively, you could click on View-Totals in the menu).

This action adds a Total: line to the query design, so we can calculate totals for the fields. The Total: line for all three fields will be automatically set to Group By, which means to group common field values together. Click on the Total: line for the Class field, then on the drop down list button, and finally select Count from the drop down list.

The query is now complete (the Show: entries for fields Hand, Sex, and Class all contain check marks ☑, the Total: lines for Hand and Sex are listed as Group By, and Class is listed as Count).

Run the query.

You will see six records in the result, one for each of the six combinations of handedness and sex, along with the count for each of those categories in a new field called CountOfClass. The six numbers will sum to the number of records in the table (246).

Close this query, and save it with the name **Categories**. The query result after it has been renamed should appear as follows (Access 2003 on the left, Access 2013 on the right):

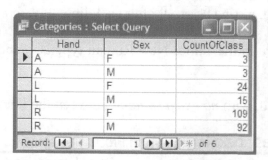

Creating and Printing the Third Report

As you did for the other two reports, go to the Reports tab, create a new landscape, tabular report for the Categories query results. Since there are only six records, this report will fit on a single page.

Change the design of the report to include your name, and either *Work at Lab* or *Work at Home*, in the Report Header band, and then view the results again. Make corrections to the design as necessary.

 Print this third report (one page).

Close the report and save it as **Categories**.

Taking Stock of the Situation

Let's take a breather, and verify that everything is where it should be. At this time, there should be only the Lab9 database window on screen, with the HANDED table, the queries named Categories, Lefty Ladies, and Youngsters, and the reports also named Categories, Lefty Ladies, and Youngsters.

 Do not proceed unless the database contains all seven of these objects.

Creating the Banner Page

As you have done in previous assignments, start up Microsoft Word and create a banner page containing your name, the phrase LAB ASSIGNMENT #9, WORK AT LAB or WORK AT HOME, and the current date, hitting ⌷Enter←⌸ after each line.

Center the lines, make sure that they are in the Times New Roman typeface, and change the size to **20 points**.

Format the document to be single-spaced, with *no extra spacing* between the lines.

Word 2003: Save the document as **LAB9.DOC** in your Word Processing folder.

Word 2007-2016: Save the document as **LAB9.DOCX** in your Word Processing folder.

Print out your completed banner page in **portrait mode**. This page will become the cover page of your report.

William T. Verts
LAB ASSIGNMENT #9
WORK AT HOME
December 6, 2013

Shutting Down

Close Microsoft Word. In Access, close the database table by clicking on the ✕ button in its window. The window should vanish without complaint. Click on File-Exit to close down Microsoft Access. Close down your computer normally.

What to Turn In

You will need to turn in the printout of your database project, containing the following items (check off the items in the list below):

Page #1 (the banner page) must contain:
- ☐ Your name (centered),
- ☐ LAB ASSIGNMENT #9 (centered),
- ☐ WORK AT LAB or WORK AT HOME (centered),
- ☐ Current date (centered),
- ☐ No extra spaces between lines.
- ☐ Font must be set to 20 Point Times New Roman.

Next Pages (the Youngsters report):
- ☐ Your name & *Work at Lab* or *Work at Home* must be on the 1ST page,
- ☐ report must contain 71 records,
- ☐ report must be landscape,
- ☐ report must contain all four fields, in the order Birthdate, Hand, Sex, Class,
- ☐ Birthdate and Hand fields must be resized so *Birthdate* is entirely visible,
- ☐ all birthdates must be on or after January 1, 1972
- ☐ birthdates must be sorted in <u>ascending</u> order.

Next Page (the Lefty Ladies report):
- ☐ Your name & *Work at Lab* or *Work at Home* must be on the 1ST page,
- ☐ report must contain 24 records,
- ☐ report must be landscape,
- ☐ report must contain all four fields, in the order Birthdate, Hand, Sex, Class,
- ☐ Birthdate and Hand fields must be resized so *Birthdate* is entirely visible,
- ☐ all Hand fields must contain "L" and all Sex fields must contain "F",
- ☐ birthdates must be sorted in <u>descending</u> order.

Last Page (the Categories report):
- ☐ Your name & *Work at Lab* or *Work at Home* must be on the 1ST page,
- ☐ report must contain 6 records (one each for Hand and Sex combinations: "A"&"F", "A"&"M", "L"&"F", "L"&"M", "R"&"F", "R"&"M"),
- ☐ report must be landscape,
- ☐ report must contain <u>three</u> fields, in the order Hand, Sex, and CountOfClass,
- ☐ the sum of the CountOfClass fields over the six records must be 246.

Grading Policy

Lab assignments are worth 10 points each. Teaching assistants will observe the following criteria for evaluating and scoring the Lab #9 assignments that they receive.

- Any report that does not have the student's name _typed_ on the header page and the first page of _all three_ reports and will be _rejected_, and if submitted will receive a _zero_. If any student writes their name in by hand, instead of typing it, then the report must be rejected. **Reject any report missing a banner page.**

- 1 Point - Report must be stapled together. Remove the full point if the report is paper-clipped together or is submitted loose (even with folded corners). Remove the full point if the pages are not in the order listed here (banner, Youngsters, Lefty Ladies, and Categories).

- 1 Point - Printout of the banner page must be present and must contain the appropriate lines of banner information. Remove ½ point for every line of the banner page that is missing or incorrect (for example: a line not centered, the font not set to 20 point Times New Roman, or the lines are not single spaced with no extra spacing between lines), up to the full point possible.

- 1 Point - Remove the point for any errors in formatting the reports (missing name on any report title page, etc.).

- 3 Points - Youngsters report: Remove all 3 points if the Youngsters report is missing. Otherwise, score as follows. Remove 1 point if the records are not in <u>ascending</u> order on Birthdate. Remove 1 point if any dates in the Birthdate field are prior to January 1, 1972. Remove 1 point if there are more than or fewer than 4 fields in the report, or if the fields are not in the proper order (Birthdate, Hand, Sex, and Class), or if the _Birthdate_ label is clipped, or if resized fields and labels don't line up.

- 3 Points - Lefty Ladies report: Remove all 3 points if the Lefty Ladies report is missing. Otherwise, score as follows. Remove 1 point if the records are not in <u>descending</u> order on Birthdate. Remove 1 point if there are more than or fewer than 4 fields in the report, or if the fields are not in the proper order (Birthdate, Hand, Sex, and Class). Remove 1 point for any records where Hand does not contain an "L", or Sex does not contain an "F", or if there are not exactly 24 records in the report, or if the _Birthdate_ label is clipped, or if resized fields and labels don't line up.

- 1 Point - Categories report: Remove the point if the report is missing, or has any values different from the screen image presented earlier in this assignment.

The Contents of HANDED.TXT

The `handed.txt` file contains 246 lines of comma-delimited text, that all appear as follows. Fields represent in order: Birthdate, Hand, Sex, and Class ("1" or "2").

```
1/23/69,"L","F","1"      5/12/69,"L","F","1"      10/4/71,"R","F","1"      10/9/72,"R","M","2"
10/3/68,"R","F","1"      10/29/70,"R","M","1"     1/2/69,"R","M","1"       12/18/69,"R","M","2"
5/16/68,"R","F","1"      6/10/68,"R","M","1"      9/21/72,"R","F","1"      3/27/72,"R","M","2"
1/8/72,"R","M","1"       4/14/72,"R","M","1"      8/12/72,"L","M","1"      1/10/72,"R","M","2"
5/1/49,"R","F","1"       3/5/69,"R","F","1"       7/3/72,"R","F","1"       9/10/68,"R","M","2"
1/26/54,"R","F","1"      3/7/71,"R","F","1"       9/23/39,"R","M","1"      5/25/71,"R","M","2"
2/15/69,"R","F","1"      4/15/71,"R","M","1"      10/13/70,"R","F","1"     1/4/71,"R","M","2"
6/4/71,"L","M","1"       12/10/71,"R","F","1"     8/27/71,"R","F","1"      3/31/71,"R","F","2"
4/25/69,"L","F","1"      2/14/72,"R","F","1"      8/22/72,"R","F","1"      9/6/72,"R","F","2"
1/17/69,"L","M","1"      1/3/71,"R","M","1"       12/24/71,"R","F","1"     9/25/72,"R","M","2"
9/12/69,"R","F","1"      5/9/72,"R","M","1"       3/20/69,"L","M","1"      3/1/72,"R","M","2"
7/30/69,"R","M","1"      5/15/72,"R","M","1"      10/2/72,"R","F","1"      8/17/72,"R","M","2"
10/14/70,"R","M","1"     7/15/71,"R","M","1"      10/30/71,"R","M","1"     4/13/72,"L","M","2"
4/27/69,"R","F","1"      12/29/70,"R","M","1"     3/9/72,"R","M","1"       4/24/72,"R","F","2"
1/6/69,"R","F","1"       8/8/66,"R","F","1"       7/10/72,"R","F","1"      11/4/72,"L","F","2"
5/23/71,"L","F","1"      3/4/71,"R","M","1"       5/1/72,"L","F","1"       11/21/71,"R","F","2"
7/14/71,"R","M","1"      10/13/71,"R","M","1"     5/1/72,"R","F","1"       9/30/68,"R","M","2"
3/19/69,"L","F","1"      9/7/71,"L","F","1"       8/6/69,"L","F","1"       6/13/69,"R","M","2"
3/13/68,"R","M","1"      3/10/69,"R","M","1"      5/19/72,"R","F","1"      4/2/71,"R","M","2"
3/29/68,"R","F","1"      4/26/69,"R","M","1"      8/13/71,"R","F","1"      3/20/72,"R","F","2"
12/5/72,"L","F","1"      9/29/68,"R","M","1"      3/27/72,"R","M","1"      11/14/69,"L","F","2"
10/24/71,"R","F","1"     8/12/72,"R","F","1"      7/27/71,"R","M","1"      1/11/69,"L","F","2"
2/8/71,"R","M","1"       9/18/71,"L","M","1"      4/7/70,"R","M","1"       10/9/72,"R","F","2"
9/20/70,"R","M","1"      5/23/71,"R","F","1"      5/29/68,"R","M","1"      2/9/72,"R","F","2"
6/29/69,"R","M","1"      4/2/68,"R","M","1"       10/24/70,"R","F","1"     10/9/68,"R","F","2"
11/27/70,"R","F","1"     5/1/71,"L","M","1"       12/8/70,"R","M","1"      9/10/71,"R","F","2"
1/25/69,"R","F","1"      12/19/70,"R","F","1"     5/21/69,"R","M","1"      9/9/72,"R","F","2"
2/27/70,"R","M","1"      6/21/72,"R","M","1"      7/1/69,"R","F","1"       12/9/68,"R","M","2"
5/11/71,"R","F","1"      8/22/69,"R","F","1"      2/19/72,"R","F","1"      12/5/69,"R","M","2"
3/7/70,"R","F","1"       3/31/72,"A","M","1"      9/27/72,"R","F","1"      1/23/70,"R","F","2"
4/4/69,"R","F","1"       8/19/67,"L","M","1"      1/27/72,"R","F","1"      6/16/70,"R","M","2"
6/15/71,"R","F","1"      1/11/69,"R","F","1"      8/28/72,"R","F","1"      3/16/72,"L","F","2"
1/24/70,"R","M","1"      9/26/68,"R","F","1"      3/17/72,"L","F","1"      5/22/72,"R","M","2"
11/22/71,"L","M","1"     4/28/69,"A","F","1"      5/4/72,"R","F","1"       12/23/71,"R","M","2"
6/21/69,"R","M","1"      11/6/72,"R","F","1"      8/22/72,"R","M","1"      4/3/69,"R","M","2"
7/12/67,"R","M","1"      9/8/71,"R","M","1"       4/6/72,"R","M","1"       5/29/72,"L","F","2"
7/25/69,"R","F","1"      5/25/71,"R","F","1"      11/23/70,"L","F","1"     8/12/64,"R","F","2"
8/10/69,"R","M","1"      9/29/71,"R","F","1"      12/11/70,"R","F","1"     11/30/71,"R","F","2"
3/17/72,"R","F","1"      6/13/72,"R","F","1"      8/1/68,"R","F","1"       2/26/72,"L","M","2"
6/11/69,"R","F","1"      7/23/69,"R","F","1"      8/5/70,"R","M","1"       7/26/69,"R","F","2"
7/11/69,"L","F","1"      4/5/72,"R","F","1"       4/12/65,"R","M","1"      7/25/69,"R","F","2"
3/20/69,"L","F","1"      11/24/56,"R","M","1"     12/26/62,"R","F","2"     9/24/70,"R","M","2"
12/13/69,"R","M","1"     8/18/71,"R","M","1"      12/24/64,"R","F","2"     7/22/69,"R","M","2"
5/1/69,"R","M","1"       8/25/72,"R","F","1"      9/13/71,"A","F","2"      1/19/73,"R","F","2"
6/19/69,"R","M","1"      7/28/71,"R","M","1"      1/13/72,"R","F","2"      4/19/72,"R","F","2"
4/14/65,"R","M","1"      10/26/56,"R","M","1"     7/25/72,"R","F","2"      6/18/72,"R","F","2"
1/19/70,"R","M","1"      6/28/72,"R","F","1"      12/27/64,"R","F","2"     1/18/72,"L","F","2"
8/19/72,"R","M","1"      2/16/49,"A","M","1"      7/20/60,"R","F","2"      3/15/71,"R","F","2"
1/27/69,"R","F","1"      8/11/72,"R","M","1"      6/10/50,"R","M","2"      6/8/72,"A","M","2"
4/11/64,"L","M","1"      5/20/71,"L","M","1"      3/17/71,"R","M","2"      9/2/69,"R","F","2"
4/7/72,"R","F","1"       8/13/72,"L","F","1"      4/15/69,"R","M","2"      1/29/69,"R","F","2"
2/25/69,"R","F","1"      4/30/63,"R","F","1"      4/10/69,"R","F","2"      10/24/68,"R","M","2"
10/6/69,"R","M","1"      2/4/71,"R","M","1"       1/11/71,"R","F","2"      6/6/72,"R","F","2"
1/7/72,"R","M","1"       7/28/71,"R","F","1"      6/27/69,"R","F","2"      11/3/69,"R","F","2"
3/31/71,"R","M","1"      7/7/71,"R","F","1"       10/29/66,"R","M","2"     8/15/72,"R","M","2"
12/12/72,"R","F","1"     9/17/68,"R","M","1"      10/3/69,"R","F","2"      4/30/49,"L","M","2"
1/28/72,"R","F","1"      3/8/69,"R","F","1"       12/21/68,"L","M","2"     10/12/71,"A","F","2"
11/30/70,"R","F","1"     7/30/69,"R","F","1"      6/8/72,"R","M","2"       9/16/70,"R","F","2"
3/15/71,"R","M","1"      4/18/69,"R","F","1"      5/12/50,"R","F","2"      3/16/69,"L","F","2"
12/27/69,"R","M","1"     1/25/71,"R","F","1"      7/23/69,"R","F","2"      12/16/68,"R","M","2"
9/25/71,"L","F","1"      12/12/72,"L","F","1"     11/20/68,"R","M","2"
8/19/70,"L","M","1"      10/12/49,"L","F","1"     3/2/72,"R","M","2"
```

Lab #10 – Databases: Joining Tables

Introduction & Goals

In this assignment you will continue using the Microsoft Access database package with the database that you constructed in the previous assignment. Sorry, Macintosh users: Microsoft Access is only for Windows PCs. You will create two new database tables, then combine (join) those two tables with the HANDED table to create a composite result. You will also combine those tables with the result of the queries you created in lab #9 to create new results.

Specifics You Will Learn in this Assignment

You will learn the following things in the completion of this assignment:

- **Creating New Database Tables** – You will create two short tables manually, containing very few records each. You will learn about database structure and the different data types available in Access.

- **Creating Join Queries about the Data** – Once the new tables have been constructed, we need to combine them with the HANDED table and the result of the Categories query in the HANDED database from the previous assignment. You will also print a report of the results.

- **Direct Printing of Tables** – You can send tables and query results directly to the printer without first creating reports for them. Unfortunately, we can't edit what is sent to include our names and identifying information, so we will send only a single small object to the printer in this fashion.

Preparation before Starting Assignment

Read this assignment through in its entirety before doing anything. This lab depends on the data files you created in lab #9. Make sure to have the `lab9` database file you created in the previous assignment (if you weren't careful when saving the file, Microsoft Access may have renamed it to `handed`). Do not perform this assignment unless that previous one has been completed correctly, and that the HANDED database contains the HANDED table, three queries (Categories, Lefty Ladies, and Youngsters) and three reports (with the same names as the queries).

In the Laboratory

Bring your flash drive containing the folders created in lab #1, the database created in lab #9, and this lab assignment. Do not come to lab without these items.

At Home

Your home machine must have a working version of Microsoft Access on the PC (no Macintosh) and a working printer, as usual. Almost any version of Access will work here from Access 97 onwards, but the instructions here are written for much later versions.

Data Files

There are no new data files for this assignment. You must be able to locate the `lab9.mdb` or `lab9.accdb` file that you created in lab #9 and the folders created in lab #1.

Step-By-Step Procedure

Start your machine up normally. You should have available your Databases folder containing `lab9`.

Starting Up

In Windows (not in Access) find and open your Databases folder. ***Right-click-drag*** the `lab9` file to another part of the same window, and in the pop-up boxes select <u>C</u>opy here. Right-click on the new file called either `Copy of lab9` or `lab9 - Copy`, select <u>R</u>ename from the pop-up menu, and then rename the file to **lab10.mdb** (Access 2003) or **lab10.accdb** (Access 2007-2016) Double-click on the `lab10` file to cause Access to start up and load it into a window. If this does not work, you may also start Access normally and select the `lab10` file once Access is running. If you get any warning about active content being disabled, enable the content. Your database will appear on screen.

Creating the First New Table

We are going to build a new table that maps the code letters "L", "R" and "A" onto the spelled-out words "Left-Handed", "Right-Handed" and "Ambidextrous".

Access 2003: Click on the Tables tab, then on the New button, to create a new table. Click on Design View, then on the OK button.

Access 2007-2016: In the Create tab of the ribbon, click on Table, then on View-Design View. Save the table as **Hand Map**. In the Design panel of the ribbon, turn <u>off</u> the Primary Key setting.

In the first Field Name box, type in the name **Hand Name** (replacing any pre-existing field name). In the Data Type column, set the type to Short Text (or Text) if not already that type. In the Description line to the right, type in the phrase **Code for handedness: L, R, or A**. In the Field Properties notebook at the bottom of the screen set the following options:

- set the Field Size entry to **1**
- set the Validation Rule entry to **="L" Or ="R" Or ="A"**
- set the Allow Zero Length entry to **No**
- set the Required entry to **Yes**
- set the Indexed entry to **Yes (No Duplicates)**

Leave all other options unchanged, keeping their default values.

In the second Field Name box, type in the name **Hand Text**. The data type is also Short Text (or Text). In the Description line, type in **Expanded version of handedness**. In the Field Properties notebook set the Field Size to **12** and the Required entry to **Yes**.

Click on the ✕ button in the table design window, and in the message box asking if you want to save your changes click the Yes button.

 Access 2003: In the Save As box, name the new table **Hand Map**, and click the OK button.

You will get a message box asking if you wish to create a primary key for the table. Answer by clicking No that you <u>do not</u> want to create a primary key.

Access 2007-2016: Nothing to do here; the table was named earlier.

Open the new Hand Map table. You will see your new table appear on screen, with the two fields Hand Name and Hand Text that you defined. The next step is to add the new data to those fields.

 A note about the "validation rule" that you entered into the description of the table a little while ago. The rule ="L" Or ="R" Or ="A" means that the corresponding field (Hand Name) can only be one of the three listed values. If you attempt to enter, or accidentally enter, another value, you will get an error message from Microsoft Access forbidding you from entering the bogus value.

 You will now add three records to the table. In the first entry for Hand Name, type **L**, and in the first entry for Hand Text type **Left-Handed**. In the second entry type **R** and **Right-Handed**, respectively. In the third entry type **A** and **Ambidextrous**, respectively. Mind your spelling and capitalization! This table is now complete and should look like the image below. Close its window by clicking on the ✕ button. The Access 2003 view is shown on the left, and the Access 2013/2016 view is shown on the right:

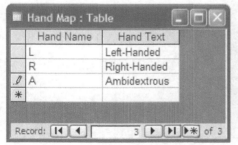 

Creating the Second New Table

It is exactly the same process to build the second table (**Sex Map**) as it was for the first. Create a new table, remove the primary key, and create the fields as follows

The first field will be called **Sex Name** with the following options:
- set the Data Type entry to **Short Text** (or **Text**)
- set the Description entry to **Code for Sex: M or F**
- set the Field Size entry to **1**
- set the Validation Rule entry to **="M" Or ="F"**
- set the Allow Zero Length entry to **No**
- set the Required entry to **Yes**
- set the Indexed entry to **Yes (No Duplicates)**

Leave all other options unchanged, keeping their default values.

The second field will be called **Sex Text** with the following options:
- set the Data Type entry to **Short Text** (or **Text**)
- set the Description entry to **Expanded version of Sex**
- set the Field Size entry to **6**
- set the Required entry to **Yes**

<u>Do not</u> define a primary key.

Click the View button (or ✕ out of the design view). If asked to save, click Yes.

Open the Sex Map table, and enter two records: one has field Sex Name=**M** and field Sex Text=**Male** and the other has Sex Name=**F** and Sex Text=**Female**. It does not matter in what order you enter these records, as you can see from the following image. The validation rule will prevent you from entering any illegal values into the Sex Name field. Mind your capitalization! When complete, close the Sex Map table by clicking on its ✕ button. The Access 2003 view is shown on the left, and the Access 2013/2016 view is shown on the right:

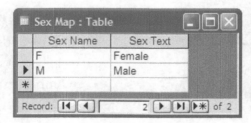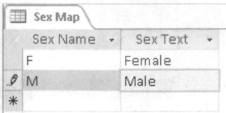

Creating the First Join Query

Create a new query using Query Design (Design View). In the Show Table box, Add all three tables (Hand Map, HANDED, and Sex Map, in that order). You will see the three forms appear in the query. Close the Show Table box.

We will now add four fields from the three tables to the query design: Birthdate and Class from HANDED, Sex Text from Sex Map, and Hand Text from Hand Map. Double-click on each of these four field names, in order, and you will see them appear in the query design. Notice how the fields in the query design show which table they come from.

 If you make mistakes in selecting the fields, you can easily correct your mistakes in a number of ways:

- If you picked the fields in the wrong order, you can move fields around in a two-step process. First, click on the thin gray line at the top of the field that you wish to move (just above the Field: row). This selects the entire column, which will turn black. Next, click drag on that thin line to move the column to the desired position, and then click away from the column to deselect it.

- If you wish to delete a column entirely, click on the thin gray line at the top of the field that you wish to delete (just above the Field: row as before), then hit the [Del] key. The column will vanish.

- If you selected the wrong table or wrong field in a column, click on the Table: drop down list or on the Field: drop down list in that column and select the correct value(s).

In the Birthdate field, also select Sort: Descending.

Our final step in setting up the query is to establish the relationships between the three tables. Using the mouse, click-drag from the Hand Name field in the Hand Map table onto the Hand field of the HANDED table. When you release the mouse, a line will be drawn between those two fields, indicating that we wish those fields to match (contain the same values) when selecting records from the tables for the join. Similarly, click drag from the Sex Name field of Sex Map onto the Sex field of HANDED, and a line will be drawn between those two fields.

 Do not proceed until the final query configuration is correct.

Run the query. You will see all 246 records appear, but with fully expanded, spelled out words instead of the one letter codes for both sex and handedness.

Close the query window by clicking on the ✕ button, then save the query with the name **Expanded View**.

Creating the Second Join Query

The second join query will be essentially *identical* to the first, except that we will choose to use the Lefty Ladies query result as a data source instead of the HANDED table (in the Show Table dialog, click the Both tab to see all tables and queries). Let's see if you can set this up without extensive help! (You can refer back to the instructions for the first join query.) Set up the new query yourself this time.

Run the query. Since the Lefty Ladies query result only contained 24 records, there will only be 24 records here as well. All 24 of them will have Female in the Sex Text field and Left-Handed in the Hand Text field.

Close the query window by clicking on the ✕ button, then save the query with the name **Expanded Lefty Ladies**.

Creating a Summary Query

Create a new query using Query Design (Design View) as you have done before.

Select as the data source the Categories query, and then close the Show Table box.

Select the CountOfClass field only (double click on CountOfClass in the Categories box).

Click on the sigma (Σ) in the tool or ribbon bar to add the Total: line to the query, and then change its entry from Group By to Sum.

Run the query.

The result will be a table with one field and one record, and the field will be named SumOfCountOfClass. (I have seen a few cases where this field name was created backwards as ClassOfCountOfSum in Access 2003; ignore this error if you see it.) Widen the column so that you can see the entire field name by click-dragging the right-hand border of the field name.

If you did everything correctly, the sum will be 246 (we just added up the six numbers in the CountOfClass field of the Categories query result: 3+3+24+15+109+92=246). The result should look like the following image. The Access 2003 view is shown on the left, and the Access 2013/2016 view is shown on the right:

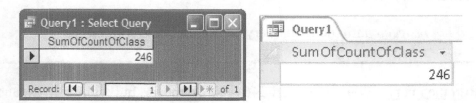

Close the query window by clicking on the ✕ button, then save the query as **Sum**.

Printing the Summary Query

Open up the Sum query result that we just saved.

Preview the query result on screen. Expand the window and zoom in on the data to make sure that the report is formatted correctly (so that you can see the entire field name, for example).

 When the preview looks OK, print out the page, then close the Sum query window.

 Since we printed this page without first generating a report, this page will print out without your name at the top. This is the **_only_** printout that you are allowed to turn in with this assignment that will not include identifying information!

Creating and Printing the First Report

Create a new landscape, tabular report for the Expanded View query result. In Design add your name and either *Work at Lab* or *Work at Home* to the Report Header band as you did in the previous assignment. If necessary, appropriately widen the labels and fields so that nothing gets clipped off, as you did in lab #9. Preview your new design.

 Print the report. In the dialog box that pops up, click on the Pages radio button in the Print Range box, then enter **1** into the From: box and **3** into the To: box, then click the OK button. Since this report would be normally at least 12 pages in length, we can save some trees by printing only the first three pages, which will still be enough for us to tell if you did everything correctly.

Close the report window, and save it as a report named **Expanded View** (which should be the default).

Creating and Printing the Second, Third, and Fourth Reports

Create a new landscape, tabular report for the Expanded Lefty Ladies query result. Add your name and either *Work at Lab* or *Work at Home* to the Report Header band as you did earlier. Change the size of the labels and fields so that nothing gets clipped off, as necessary, as you did in lab #9. Preview your new design.

 Print that report. Close the report and save it as **Expanded Lefty Ladies**.

 Create and **print** a landscape report for the Sex Map table (add your name and either *Work at Lab* or *Work at Home* to the Report Header band, as you normally do). This report will be a single page in length. Close and save the report as **Sex Map**.

 Create and **print** a landscape report for the Hand Map table (add your name and either *Work at Lab* or *Work at Home*, to the Report Header band, as you normally do). This report will be a single page in length. Close and save the report as **Hand Map**.

Taking Stock of the Situation

The database now contains:

- Three <u>tables</u>
    - Hand Map
    - HANDED
    - Sex Map

- Six <u>queries</u>
    - Categories
    - Expanded Lefty Ladies
    - Expanded View
    - Lefty Ladies
    - Sum
    - Youngsters

- Seven <u>reports</u>
    - Categories
    - Expanded Lefty Ladies
    - Expanded View
    - Hand Map
    - Lefty Ladies
    - Sex Map
    - Youngsters

There will not be a report for the Sum query, since we printed that table directly.

 Do not proceed until this is so.

Creating the Banner Page

As you have done in previous assignments, start up Microsoft Word and create a banner page containing your name, the phrase LAB ASSIGNMENT #10, WORK AT LAB or WORK AT HOME, and the current date, hitting Enter↵ after each line.

Center the lines, make sure that they are in the Times New Roman typeface, and change the size to **20 points**.

Format the document to be single-spaced, with *no extra spacing* between the lines.

Word 2003: Save the document as **LAB10.DOC** in your Word Processing folder.
Word 2007-2016: Save the document as **LAB10.DOCX** in your Word Processing folder.

Print out your completed banner page in portrait mode. This page will become the cover page of your report.

William T. Verts
LAB ASSIGNMENT #10
WORK AT HOME
December 13, 2013

Shutting Down

Close Microsoft Word. Close the database table by clicking on the ✕ button in its window. The window should vanish without complaint. Close down Microsoft Access. Close down your computer normally.

What to Turn In

You will need to turn in the printout of your database project, containing the following items (check off the items in the list below):

Page #1 (the banner page) must contain:
- ☐ Your name (centered),
- ☐ LAB ASSIGNMENT #10 (centered),
- ☐ WORK AT LAB or WORK AT HOME (centered),
- ☐ Current date (centered), no extra spaces between lines,
- ☐ Font must be set to 20 Point Times New Roman.

Page #2 – Sum (data only, will not contain your name)
- ☐ Printout must contain 1 record and 1 field,
- ☐ field name is SumOfCountOfClass (or ClassOfCountOfSum)
- ☐ value of the field is 246.

Page #3 – Sex Map (report)
- ☐ Your name & *Work at Lab* or *Work at Home* must be on the 1ST page,
- ☐ report must contain 2 records,
- ☐ report must contain 2 fields (Sex Name and Sex Text),
- ☐ the four data values must be entered correctly,
- ☐ capitalization and spelling of data items must be correct.

Page #4 – Hand Map (report)
- ☐ Your name & *Work at Lab* or *Work at Home* must be on the 1ST page,
- ☐ report must contain 3 records,
- ☐ report must contain 2 fields (Hand Name and Hand Text),
- ☐ the six data values must be entered correctly,
- ☐ capitalization and spelling of data items must be correct.

Pages #5 through #7 – Expanded View (report)
- ☐ Your name & *Work at Lab* or *Work at Home* must be on the 1ST page,
- ☐ report must be three pages long (the 1ST three pages of the report only),
- ☐ report must be landscape,
- ☐ report must contain four fields, in the order Birthdate, Class, Sex Text, Hand Text,
- ☐ report must be sorted in <u>descending</u> order on Birthdate,
- ☐ report field and label widths must be modified so no fields are clipped off.

Pages #8+ – Expanded Lefty Ladies (report) (May be only one page, may be more.)
- ☐ Your name & *Work at Lab* or *Work at Home* must be on the 1ST page,
- ☐ report must contain 24 records,
- ☐ report must be landscape,
- ☐ report must contain four fields, in the order Birthdate, Class, Sex Text, Hand Text,
- ☐ report must be sorted in <u>descending</u> order on Birthdate,
- ☐ report field and label widths must be modified so no fields are clipped off.

Grading Policy

Lab assignments are worth 10 points each. Teaching assistants will observe the following criteria for evaluating and scoring the Lab #10 assignments that they receive.

- Any report that does not have the student's name *typed* on the header page and the first page of *__all four__* main reports (not including the results of the SumOfCountOfClass query) will be *__rejected__*, and if submitted will receive a *__zero__*. If any student writes their name in by hand, instead of typing it, then the report must be rejected. **Reject any report missing a banner page.**

- 1 Point - Report must be stapled together. Remove the full point if the report is paper-clipped together or is submitted loose (even with folded corners). Remove the point if the pages are not in order
  1. Banner,
  2. Sum,
  3. Sex Map,
  4. Hand Map
  5.-7. Expanded View,
  8+. Expanded Lefty Ladies.

- 1 Point - Printout of the banner page must be present and must contain the appropriate lines of banner information. Remove ½ point for every line of the banner page that is missing or incorrect (for example: a line not centered, the font not set to 20 point Times New Roman, or the lines are not single spaced with no extra spacing between lines), up to the full point possible.

- 1 Point - Remove the point for any errors in formatting the reports (missing text on any report title page, capitalization or spelling errors in any data tables, not landscape, fields out of order in any query result, etc.).

- 1 Point - Sum printout. Remove the full point if the report is missing. Remove ½ point if the width of the SumOfCountOfClass name is so short that the name is partially hidden. Remove ½ point if the value is not 246.

- 1 Point - Sex Map report. Remove 1 point if report is missing or contains any incorrect data.

- 1 Point - Hand Map report. Remove 1 point if report is missing or contains any incorrect data.

- 2 Points - Expanded View report. Remove the full 2 points if the report is missing. Otherwise, score as follows, up to 2 points total. Remove 1 point if there are more than or fewer than 4 fields. Remove 1 point if there are no expanded fields ("L" instead of "Left-Handed"). Remove ½ point if there are not exactly three pages. Remove ½ point if the table is not sorted in descending order on Birthdate. Remove ½ point if the Birthdate label is clipped, or labels sized incorrectly.

- 2 Points - Expanded Lefty Ladies report. Remove the full 2 points if the report is missing. Otherwise, score as follows, up to 2 points total. Remove 1 point if there are more than or fewer than 4 fields. Remove 1 point if there are no expanded fields ("L" instead of "Left-Handed"). Remove ½ point if the table contains more than or fewer than 24 records. Remove ½ point if the table is not sorted in descending order on Birthdate. Remove ½ point if any label is clipped, or labels sized incorrectly.

ALL YOUR LAB ASSIGNMENTS ARE NOW COMPLETE!

Chapter 3: Extra Credit Project

Introduction

This chapter contains the description of an extra credit assignment that should satisfy all folks who want to make up for a poor midterm grade. With luck it should be interesting as well. This project will consume a fair amount of time outside class, and is not part of the assigned lab work. I do not want you to attempt to work on this project casually: this is not something that you can do over the course of the last weekend before the final exam. If you are going to attempt this project at all then get started early.

Ground Rules

This project is to be worked on individually; you are not to solicit help from other students in the class. If you need help, then you must visit your instructor during regular office hours (or set up an appointment). The TAs have no part of this assignment – you may ask them for help if you get stuck using one of the software packages, but you may NOT ask them for help on the assignment itself.

The final report is due at the time you take the final exam. No projects will be accepted after that time. Submit a self-addressed 9×13 envelope with your report if you wish it to be returned to you after the end of the semester (please include sufficient postage; extra loose stamps can be returned to you).

General Form of the Project

There are several options for research projects that will be described below; pick only one. If you have a particular interest that you wish to research, please talk to your instructor first to work something out. You may pursue any of these topics, or design your own, as long as you can make a convincing argument that your topic satisfies the requirements for the project.

Regardless of the project option you choose, you are to perform some research, work up a set of spreadsheets based on your research, plot spreadsheet graphs that show the trends of the data you have gathered, draw some conclusions based on those data and those graphs, and then write a report explaining your findings and your conclusions. In your report justify your conclusions by citing both the appropriate references from the bibliography and the spreadsheets and graphs that you create. You may use a database if you have access to data appropriate for analysis by a database package. No more than 50% of your research sources may be from the Internet, and no more than half of those (less than or equal to 25% overall) may be from on-line encyclopædia (such as Wikipedia).

There are two major reasons for structuring this project as I have. First, by doing the research, you learn far more about your chosen subject than I could possibly teach you in class. Second, by following the instructions laid out here, you prove that you know how to use the software packages that you have learned throughout the semester.

Specific Requirements

1. NO HANDWRITTEN REPORTS will be accepted.

2. You must use the word-processing and spreadsheet software you were taught this semester.

3. All of your work must be submitted on laser printer or ink-jet paper: your spreadsheets, your graphs and your reports.

4. Make sure that your writing is grammatically correct; your spelling and your grammar will be checked, and points will be removed for any errors. Use the spelling checker on your report before submitting it.

5. Submit your final report with a plastic cover, title page, and bibliography.

6. The title page must contain the title of your document in boldface, your name, and your student number, and the due date, all centered, but no page number.

7. Your name must appear centered at the top of every page (except for the title page), in the header area.

8. All pages must be numbered, except for the title page, with page #1 on the first page of the report text. Page numbers must be centered at the bottom of the page, in the footer area.

9. The text of your report (not including spreadsheets and graphs) must be at least 15 pages in length, double spaced, fully justified on both left and right margins, properly indented, and with an extra line between paragraphs.

10. There must be at least two properly referenced spreadsheets and two properly referenced graphs in your report. Graphs and spreadsheets should be inserted (electronically, not pasted in with glue) on separate and properly numbered pages of their own after the 15 pages of your text and before the bibliography.

11. Use the Times New Roman typeface, 12 points in size, for all of your text. If you quote computer terms you may use the Courier or Arial typefaces for those items (such as A:\LOTUS or Program Manager for example).

12. The bibliography must start on a new page, with the word **BIBLIOGRAPHY** in boldface and centered at the top of the page, and with a page number at the bottom. Make titles boldface, and italicize the names of any journals you cite. If you include sources from the Internet you must also include the complete URL to each referenced site.

13. No more than 50% of the references included in the bibliography can come from the Internet. You must use, primarily, sources from a regular library.

The Project Descriptions

These project descriptions contain the general outline of what I expect you to find in your research. You may not find all the items listed here, and you may find something during your research that is interesting and/or critical to your report that <u>isn't</u> listed here. These are only suggestions. You are doing <u>research</u>: I can't predict what you will find!

Option #1: *History of Computing*

Research the history of modern computing, from the 1940s to the present. Show the evolution of computing systems from the large mainframe machines at central sites through the modern microprocessor machines owned and operated by single users at private locations. Show (i.e., plot graphs to show) how costs have decreased from the early machines to the present in terms of dollars per bit of memory and dollars per instruction performed. Show the average number of instructions executed per second over the same period (show this for mainframes, minicomputers, microcomputers, and supercomputers). Also, show the average number of bytes of memory available to a typical machine over this same period. If you wish, show the costs for various software packages available for microcomputers since 1980, such as Lotus 1-2-3, Microsoft Office, dBase, and WordPerfect. Compare those costs with similar packages produced by competitors of those listed.

Based on your research, make a projection for personal computers and personal computer software ten years from now. Show how much a byte of memory will cost, how many bytes of memory an average machine will be expected to have, how many instructions it can execute per second, and how much it will be expected to cost. If you wish, show the same projections for supercomputers as well.

Option #2: *History of Space Flight*

Research the history of space flight, from the 1950s to the present. Show the advance of technology from the early days to the present, in particular where such advancement impinges on computing devices. Document the transfer of technology from the aerospace industry to the private sector by showing what innovations that we use in everyday life came from the various space programs (computing, medical, materials technology, environmental, etc.)

Show (create spreadsheets and graphs to show) the costs per year of the manned and unmanned space programs from the 1950s to the present. Compare the annual monetary allocations by Congress with the requests by NASA over the same period. Compare the costs of these programs with the estimated amount returned by the associated research. Compare these costs with the other major costs of government: debt service, social programs, military expenditures, etc. If you wish, you may consider the military influence on the various space efforts and the implications that have resulted thereby. You also may research the space programs for the former Soviet Union and current Commonwealth of Independent States, the European Space Agency, the Japanese, and the Chinese.

Based on your research, make projections for ten years from now on how much money will be spent on aerospace efforts, and how much return will be seen on the investments through research and technology transfer. Compare the manned and unmanned programs, and based on your research make a judgment about the relative merits of each.

Option #3: *History of Women in Science*

Research the history of women in the sciences and mathematics from the 17TH century to the present. Across those years estimate the percentage of the total population of scientists who are women, and compare their average incomes to the incomes of men in the sciences. You may break down the population according to fields such as social sciences, medicine, physics, chemistry, mathematics, computer science, etc. Show (create spreadsheets and graphs to show) the trends over the years and make predictions of what these numbers will be ten, twenty, and thirty years from now. Justify your predictions.

As one small part of this project you may wish to create a database of women scientists. If you do, include for each person their name, their field, their birth and death dates and a short description of one of their major contributions to their field. You also may include other data if desired, such as income, number of years as a productive scientist, whether or not they were married, number of publications, etc. Include a formatted report of this database with the rest of your document.

Option #4: *Cost Benefits of Mining Asteroids*

Explore the cost benefits of bringing a near-Earth asteroid, one kilometer in diameter, into Earth's orbit and mining it for its raw materials. You must consider percentages of iron, nickel, silicon, and water, but your model may also consider the presence of rare elements. Consider the differences in composition and distribution between the various types of asteroids (carbonaceous chondrites, silicates, stony-iron, achondrite, etc.). Make assumptions about how long it would take to create the infrastructure to capture an asteroid and what that infrastructure would cost, how much of the asteroid's mass would be thrown away as fuel for the trip, how long it would take to disassemble the asteroid, and how much the introduction of that quantity of raw materials would have on the planetary economy, and the cumulative effects of capturing multiple asteroids at regular intervals. Predict the effects of the technology fallout that this project would have on the economy.

Create a spreadsheet for your basic model, and then refine the model by attempting to tie down as many of these variables as possible. There are a lot of ways to do this assignment and lots of potential for spreadsheets and graphs.

Consider the percentages of rare and/or strategic metals (such as rhenium, osmium, palladium, etc.). Consider the terrestrial sources of such metals and the effects of political boundaries on their acquisition. Consider the effects of different distributions of elements on the final value of the asteroid. Consider the masses and distances of known asteroids and estimate how much energy it would take to move them from their current orbits into Earth orbit (this might be a good candidate for a database). Check the financial section of the newspaper to get current market values for each of the elements you extract from your asteroid, research how these values change over time, and estimate the effects that the sudden influx of extraterrestrial minerals would have on the global economy and political situations (particularly if asteroids are captured at regular intervals). Examine the environmental benefits of reducing Earth based mining in favor of space based mining.

In the text portion of your report include a description of your model, your assumptions, and your results. Finally, make a GO / NO-GO decision: are the benefits worth the trip? Justify your conclusions.

This portion of the extra credit term paper assignment has been in the Workbook for many years, but very few students have pursued this option. Mining asteroids seemed too esoteric and infeasible to be a serious topic. In April of 2012, however, a company called Planetary Resources (http://www.planetaryresources.com/) announced a bold and ambitious plan to do just that. Backed by a number of famous billionaires, they intend to develop and deploy the technologies to reduce the cost of access to space, create fuel depots in space, alter the trajectories of asteroids to either "bring them home" or keep them from smacking into us, and eventually mine them for their metallic and other resources. It will be a long road, and many people are skeptical about the potential of success, but it is a project worth watching.

Project Check List

- ☐ Report must:
    - ☐ have a plastic cover,
    - ☐ have a title page,
    - ☐ have a bibliography, and
    - ☐ be on laser printer (or good quality ink-jet) paper.

- ☐ The title page contains:
    - ☐ the title of your document in boldface (centered),
    - ☐ your name and student number (centered),
    - ☐ the date that the report is due (centered).

- ☐ The text of your report:
    - ☐ is spell checked,
    - ☐ is at least 15 pages in length (not including spreadsheets and graphs),
    - ☐ is in Times New Roman 12 point font,
    - ☐ is double spaced,
    - ☐ is fully justified on both left and right margins,
    - ☐ is properly indented (½ inch on the first line), and
    - ☐ has an extra line between paragraphs.

- ☐ Your name must be:
    - ☐ centered,
    - ☐ at the top of the page (in the header), and
    - ☐ on every page except on the title page.

- ☐ Page numbers must be:
    - ☐ centered,
    - ☐ at the bottom of the page (in the footer), and
    - ☐ on every page except on the title page.

- ☐ Spreadsheets (at least two) must:
    - ☐ be on their own titled and numbered pages between the text and the bibliography,
    - ☐ be properly documented to correspond with the text.

- ☐ The graphs (at least two) must:
    - ☐ be on their own titled and numbered pages between the text and the bibliography,
    - ☐ correspond to any spreadsheets.

- ☐ The bibliography must:
    - ☐ start on a new page with its own page number,
    - ☐ have the word **BIBLIOGRAPHY** in boldface (centered) at the top of the page,
    - ☐ have titles of citations in boldface,
    - ☐ have the names of any journals you cite in italics,
    - ☐ have one blank line between each citation,
    - ☐ have each citation formatted with a hanging indent.

Chapter 4: Exam Preparation

Introduction

This chapter contains a study guide suitable for a midterm and a final examination. One thing to remember about computer science exams is that rote memorization of facts is far less important than the understanding of *process*. Raw data you can always look up later in a manual, notes, or in an on-line help system; what I expect of you is to know how to solve problems using the techniques that you have learned.

Exam Review

History

What were some of the contributions to computing of: Blaise Pascal / Gottfried Leibniz / Joseph Marie Jacquard / Charles Babbage / Lady Ada Augusta of Lovelace / Herman Hollerith / Alan M. Turing / Konrad Zuse / John von Neumann / Margaret Hamilton? What was the Difference Engine / ENIAC / Harvard Mark I? What kind of calculator is an abacus? A slide rule? What was the Antikythera machine? What is a punched card, and how does it store information? What is the difference between analog equipment and digital equipment?

Mathematics

What is a bit / byte / nybble / word / truth table / gate? How can we represent integers (both signed and unsigned) and floating point numbers using bits? How do powers of 2 relate to logarithms base 2? Can all integers be represented by a fixed number of bits? Can all fractions be represented by a fixed number of bits? What is special about the numbers $\frac{1}{10}$, $\sqrt{2}$, or π in floating-point? How & when are functions AND / NAND / OR / NOR / XOR / XNOR / NOT used? (DeMorgan's Theorems, too.) How does a half-adder or a full-adder work? How many patterns can be represented using some fixed number of digits in some base? How are numbers converted between decimal and another base (in both directions)? How do you count in a base? What does the kilo-, mega-, giga-, or tera- prefix mean? How do they differ from their "normal" meanings? Given a number in one unit, how do you convert it to another unit? Given a problem involving units, how do you reason about units to solve the problem? How would you use a spreadsheet to solve unit conversion problems?

Hardware

What are RAM / ROM / CPU / chip / keyboard / mouse / network card / Ethernet / Wi-Fi / modem / terminal / terminal emulator? What is the structure of a disk (tracks / sectors / etc.)? What is a floppy disk / hard disk / flash drive? Is a 3½" diskette or a flash drive a hard disk? What is write-protection on a disk? How do you set & remove it for 5¼" and 3½" diskettes? What are the differences between CD-R, CD-RW, DVD-R, DVD-RW, etc.?

Operating Systems and Files

What is an Operating System? A Disk Operating System? What services are provided by an OS? What is preemptive vs. cooperative multitasking? Can you run several copies of the same application simultaneously? What are the differences between a Graphical User Interface (GUI) and a Command Line Interface (CLI)? What is a file? What are the uses, advantages, and disadvantages of each kind of file: .TXT, .BMP, .JPG, .GIF, .PNG, .WAV, .MP3, .WMA, .AVI, .WMV, .MOV, .MP4, .MPEG? What is a subdirectory or folder? What is a path and how do you change it? What is the root? What are the differences between MS-DOS and UNIX? What are the differences between Microsoft Windows and Apple Macintosh? How do modern Macs use UNIX?

MS-DOS

What is meant by "Bootstrapping" the operating system? What OS software is stored in ROM / RAM / DISK? How do you change the logged (default) disk drive or the logged directory? How do you "override" the current (default) drive and path in DOS commands? How does the current (default) path relate to the DOS prompt? What is the correct form for a DOS file name? How do you use wildcards (* and ?) in DOS file names? How does a file server fit in to all this? How and when are COPY / ERASE / DEL / RENAME / TYPE / DIR / CLS / CD / MD / RD etc. (and their synonyms) used? What does the FORMAT command do? What is the difference between CD, CD., CD .. and CD \ ? What are the differences between internal and external commands?

UNIX

How do we connect to a UNIX server? What's a server / username / password / email? On a Macintosh, how can we access the internal UNIX operating system? How are the following UNIX commands used: passwd / ls / cat / cd / pwd / chmod / cp / mv / rm / mkdir / rmdir / emacs / finger / logout / elm / telnet / ftp? How are MS-DOS commands similar to or different from UNIX commands? (Which uses /, which uses \ to separate path names?) How are UNIX wildcards (* and ?) used? What are file permissions?

Windowing Operating Systems

What benefits do multiple windows give you? What is a window / icon / scroll bar / scroll button / check box / radio button / drop-down list? How do you move / maximize / minimize / resize / scroll / close a window? How do you use the keyboard or mouse to perform commands? How do you move between windows? With the mouse, how and when are pointing / clicking / double-clicking / right-clicking / click-dragging / drag & drop used? What is the clipboard? Does "drag-and-drop" require the concept of a clipboard? How do you use the clipboard to move material between documents or within a document in copy / cut / paste operations? Is it saved when you shut the computer off? How do you select a region of text with the mouse? When do you use the right mouse button? What do you do when there is no right mouse button? How do you move between windows? What are the differences and similarities between Microsoft Windows and the Apple Macintosh? How do you start an application running? What is a multiple document interface (MDI) application? How do versions of Windows differ? How do versions of Mac OS/X differ? How are they the same?

The Internet and the Web

What is the difference between the Internet and the Web? How do you connect to a remote server over the Internet? What is an IP address? What is the client-server model? What is a packet? What is a "packet sniffer"? What is the difference between HTTP and HTTPS? What is a URL and how do you specify one? How do you create UNIX subdirectories and HTML documents so that a browser can find your home page automatically, as long as your URL is known? What is the DNS? How do you use `ftp` to transfer files to and from remote sites? What's the difference between `ftp` and `telnet`? Why are there now encrypted versions of `telnet` and `ftp`? How are UNIX `telnet` and `ftp` different from versions you run on a Mac or Windows PC? Why do you usually log in to a remote `ftp` site with the username "anonymous"? Why are time zones important when you use `ftp` or a Web browser? How do you use a Web browser? What are HTTP and HTML? Can you use a `.txt` file as a simple Web page? How might you write a page of HTML code to be viewed on the Web? What is an HTML tag? How do you specify HTML colors? How do you create a hypertext link to another page? How do you include an in-line image? How is an intra-page link different from an external link? What provisions do you make when you create your home page for people using text-only browsers or computers with limited colors? What are styles / style sheets / CSS? How do you link to an external style sheet / use an internal STYLE block / use a STYLE attribute in a tag? What is JavaScript? What is an SVG file? How do you link to a JavaScript or SVG file? What are the differences between presentation attributes and style attributes?

Word Processing

What is a word processor? How are word processors different from text editors? What features would you expect from any word processor? What is WYSIWYG? Are Windows WordPad, Mac Text Edit, or Microsoft Word WYSIWYG? Why or why not? How do you highlight & format text (characters, paragraphs, whole document)? How is the mouse used to select text or perform commands? What is drag-and-drop? How is a typeface different from a font? What is a style in a word processor? How are fonts measured in points? What is a serif? What is kerning? What is an indent (first-line, hanging, etc.), and how do you set them? How does search-and-replace work? Describe techniques for moving paragraphs in a document and between documents. What is mail-merge?

Spreadsheets

What is a spreadsheet? What advantages do computerized spreadsheets have over paper spreadsheets? What is a spreadsheet formula? How do you use the menu and the mouse? What if anything is wrong if a cell containing numbers appears as `*****` or `#####`? What do you do if it happens? What happens if a text label is too long to fit in a cell? How do you left-/center-/right-justify the contents of a cell? What are the differences between relative, absolute, and mixed cell addressing? What are ranges and range-names? How do you format or erase ranges of cells? How do you name a range of cells? Where are range names used? How do you copy or move formulae? If you copy or move a formula, what portions change, if any? How do you calculate the result of an expression? What is arithmetic precedence? In an expression, how do you know what to compute first? How do you use built in functions: SUM, MAX, MIN, AVERAGE, COUNT, IF, DATE, SQRT, ABS, etc.? In an IF, how do you use AND, OR, and NOT? How are they like truth tables? How do you use truth tables and DeMorgan's theorems to simplify conditional expressions in `IF` formulae? What is a circular reference? What is a chart? How do you set: chart types, series, titles, legends, etc.? Under what circumstances do you use the different types of charts (bar, stacked-bar, line, pie, etc.)? What is a macro? How are macros defined / created / named / run? How do you do "database-type" work in a spreadsheet? What is the Filter or AutoFilter in Excel? What can you do with a spreadsheet that you can't do with a database (as easily or at all)? What are the advantages / disadvantages of the "diamond" spreadsheet layout? How would a 3-dimensional or notebook-metaphor spreadsheet handle the need addressed by the diamond form? How do you insert or delete rows and columns? How would a modern spreadsheet use the clipboard to transfer information to other documents? How would an "alternative" spreadsheet such as Improv address the problem of copying formulae? Show the results of a spreadsheet formula or know how to write a formula that performs some given task.

Databases

What is a database / database table / DBMS / record / field (two definitions for field)? How do databases differ from spreadsheets? What are relational databases, flat-file databases, hierarchical database, and network databases? What can you do with a database that you can't do with a spreadsheet (as easily or at all)? What is a table / report / form / query? What is a data type, and why is the notion of type important in databases? What are the major data types in your database package? What are the differences between the structure of a table and the contents (data records) in a table? What are default values for a table structure, and why are they used? What are validity checks or validation rules, and why are they important? What things must you establish for each field in a new database structure? What are indexed fields, and why are they important? What happens when you have more than one index? What are 1:1 relationships, 1:many relationships, and many:many relationships? What is QBE (Query-By-Example)? How is QBE used to join two or more databases into a resulting database? What are inner, full outer, left outer, and right outer joins? How is QBE used to extract records containing certain characteristics? How do you sort a table? What is the difference between ascending and descending order in a sort? What is the difference between sorting and indexing? How do you generate a report for a table? How do you modify that report? How do you calculate sums / counts / averages for all records matching certain characteristics? How do you insert / delete / edit / search for records in a database?

Programming

What is a program? What are the differences between an assembler / a compiler / an interpreter? What is a variable? What is source code? What is an `.exe` (Windows) or an `.app` (Mac) file? What permissions must be set to run a program under UNIX? How are data types used in different languages? What is a syntax error? What is a run-time error? What is the edit-compile-test cycle? What is an integrated development environment? How do flowcharts illustrate program execution? Can programs run forever without stopping? How do you debug a program? How are languages such as JavaScript and Python used in conjunction with Web pages?

Sample Midterm Exam

<1>   1 Point questions

	1. True or False: A 3½-inch diskette is a "hard disk".
	2. True or False: A USB flash drive is a "hard disk".
	3. What power of 2 gives me 64?
	4. How many bits are necessary to represent all unsigned integers from 0 up through and including 255?
	5. In the HTML color **#F37FD0**, what is the decimal (base 10) value for green?
	6. Is the HTML color named **Fuchsia** a *browser safe* color?
	7. What is the *short hex* code for the HTML color **LightSlateGray**?
	8. The logarithm base 3 of 14 is 2.40217350. When converting the number 14 to base 3, *how many digits* will be required?
	9. What is the *octal* (base 8) value of the UNIX file permissions code **rwxr-x---**?
	10. Sam Jones has a username of **szjones** and a ID of **31415926**. What is his initial password on **elsrv3**?
	11. How many bytes are in a file of 10 kilobytes?
	12. There are two ways of representing the symbol é in HTML. Write down either one of them.
	13. A Web address has **.tv** at the end. What does this mean?
	14. Convert the decimal number 87 into binary.
	15. What is the *binary sum* of binary numbers 1001 and 0011?
	16. What is the *largest signed integer* that will fit into 7 bits?
	17. What is the product of complex numbers $(4+2i)$ and $(3-3i)$?
	18. If it is 6:00pm here in Massachusetts, should I download a large file from a mirror in Paris or from one in Denver?
	19. Can I run a telnet session, an ftp session, and a Web browser over the same link to the Internet at the same time?
	20. Can I log in to the same UNIX account with both an encrypted telnet and an encrypted ftp at the same time?

<2>   8 Points – Trace the following gate circuit and show its output for all combinations of input values.

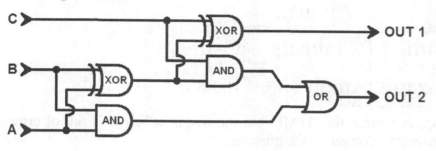

In			Out 2	Out 1
A	B	C		
0	0	0		
0	0	1		
0	1	0		
0	1	1		
1	0	0		
1	0	1		
1	1	0		
1	1	1		

<3>   5 Points – Short Answer – After using PuTTY on a PC (in ssh mode) or use ssh on a Mac (in the Terminal program) to log in to the **elsrv3** server, I immediately attempt to edit the <u>existing</u> **index.html** file with **emacs**, but the editor shows an empty file. Why?

<4>   7 Points – A UNIX file named **lizard.jpg** currently has permissions **r--r-----**, but I want them to be **rw-rw-r--** instead. Using only the *symbolic* form of **chmod**, what UNIX command would I type in to affect this change?

<5>   5 Points – Short Answer – I've told you this semester that the **elsrv3** server is a computer located in the COMPSCI building on the north end of the UMass campus. Suppose that I've been lying to you all along, and the <u>actual</u> physical location of the server was in a roadside diner named "Jake's Drive-In" on Interstate 80 in Nebraska. Would it matter to you whether or not I lied as far as the solution of our assignments is concerned? Why or why not?

<6> 10 Points – Here is a table that I want to create in HTML:

Animals		
Birds	Mammals	Fish
Lizards	Amphibians	Insects

This is my first attempt at writing the HTML, but the fragment below is full of errors, both in syntax and in content. Correct all the mistakes.

```
<TABLE BOARDER>
    <TR>
        <TD COLSPAN-"3" ALIGN="Center>Animals</TD>
    </TR>

        <TD>Bugs</TD>
        <TD>Mammals</TD>
        <TD>Fish</TD>

    <TR>
        <TD>Lizards<TD>
        <TD>Amphibians</TR>
        <TD>Insects</TD>
    <TR>
/TABLE
```

<7> 5 Points – In the address for the class site listed below, identify the protocol, the host address, the username, the folder path, and the resource:

`http://people.cs.umass.edu/~verts/coins105/coins105.html`

<8> 5 Points – Short Answer – Many students, in attempting to log in to the server, got an error message saying either "Connection reset by peer" or "ssh-exchange-identification" or "Server unexpectedly closed connection". What has happened here?

<9> 10 Points – Write an HTML fragment (not a complete Web page) that links to the Web page `http://www.starwars.com/` when clicking on the graphic image named `StarWars.jpg` (the alternate text for the image must be `Image goes here` and the fly-over title must be `Use the force, Luke`).

<10> 10 Points – In the **STYLE** block of my Web page, I want the following definitions:
1. The background color of the **BODY** of the page should be yellow,
2. All **P** paragraphs should be fully justified,
3. All **H1** headings should be in the Arial typeface,
4. All **H2** headings should be green.
Fill in the **STYLE** block below to set this up:

```
<STYLE TYPE="text/css">



</STYLE>
```

<11> 5 Points – Examine the picture to the right for the following questions.

1. The letters are each around 144 points high. How many inches is that?

2. On the picture, indicate by circling <u>all</u> places where *<u>kerning</u> can be <u>strongly</u> applied*.

3. Does the typeface have serifs, or is it sans-serif?

<12> 5 Points – In Microsoft Word, I create a style definition that is stored <u>only</u> in the current document, and is not available to any other Word documents. Is this equivalent in HTML to the **STYLE="_____"** attribute in a tag, the **<STYLE TYPE="text/css">** block, or an external **.css** file?

<13> 10 Points – Short Answer – How are text characters as defined on a modern computer similar to **.SVG** files? What graphics design tool is common to both?

Sample Final Exam

<1>   One point questions.

	True or False: A 3½-inch diskette is a "hard disk".
	True or False: A USB flash drive is a "hard disk".
	How many bits will be in each packet when converting binary to octal?
	What is the base 2 logarithm of 13?
	How many bits are there in four Kilobytes?
	True or False: 3D adds information to a chart or graph produced in Excel.
	Which chart type is best for showing trends over time?
	Which chart type is best for showing proportions of a whole?
	Which chart type shows a total for corresponding points from several series?
	True or False: A legend is needed when a chart shows multiple series.
	True or False: Linear Search is faster than Binary Search.
	True or False: In order to perform a Binary Search, the list must be sorted.
	In Excel, May 5, 2016 has value 42495. What then is June 15, 2016?
	What is the internal time fraction returned by `=TIME(18,0,0)` ?
	Yes or No: Can the value returned by the Excel formula `=1/10` be represented *perfectly* as a double-precision float, with no round-off error?

<2>   5 Points – One quantity represents the number of centimeters per inch {cm/in}, and another contains the number of centimeters per meter {cm/m}. Which of the following expressions gives me the number of meters per inch {m/in}? Circle the correct answer.

        {cm/in} × {cm/m}   {cm/in} ÷ {cm/m}   {cm/m} ÷ {cm/in}

<3>   5 Points – Short Answer – Why are *comma-and-quote-delimited* text files important to both spreadsheets and databases?

<4>   10 Points – Trace the following flowchart and show the final printed result.

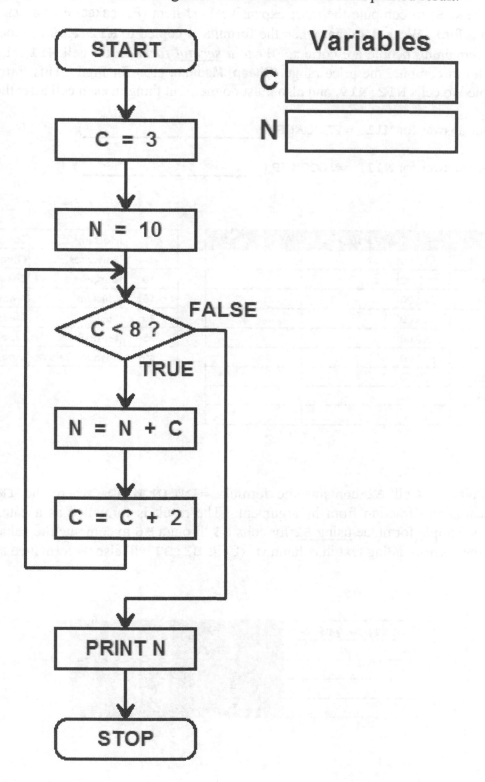

Variables

C

N

<5>   12 Points – *Write a formula* with the **VLOOKUP** function for cell **M11** (using the table in **P10:R16**) to compute the most expensive food item (**Pancakes**, **Burger**, etc.) that Fred can afford. Write it so that when the formula is copied to **M12:M19** the food items for all remaining people are correct. *Write a __second__ formula* for cell **N11** (also using the table) to compute the price range (**Cheap**, **Medium**, etc.) for Fred. This formula will be copied to cells **N12:N19**, and also must do the right thing in each cell after the copy.

Your answer for **M11**: =VLOOKUP (_____)

Your answer for **N11**: =VLOOKUP (_____)

	J	K	L	M	N	O	P	Q	R	S
9										
10		NAME	BUDGET	FOOD ITEM	PRICE RANGE		0	Nothing	Sorry!	
11		Fred	$17.00				5	Pancakes	Cheap	
12		Sam	$8.00				10	Burger	Cheap	
13		Mary	$23.00				15	Chicken	Medium	
14		Carol	$16.00				20	Sushi	Medium	
15		Joe	$7.00				25	Prime Rib	Expensive	
16		Bob	$27.00				30	Sashimi Deluxe	Expensive	
17		Tom	$9.00							
18		Bill	$3.00							
19		Sue	$15.00							
20										

<6>   8 Points – Cell **B2** contains the formula **=INT(NOW())**, where the **INT** function discards any fraction from its argument. The result is formatted as a date, as shown. Write simple formulae __using B2__ for cells **B3** through **B6** to compute the values indicated by the corresponding text in column **C**. (Cells **B3:B7** will also be formatted as dates.)

	A	B	C	D
1				
2		Thursday, May 05, 2016	RIGHT NOW	
3			TOMORROW	
4			THE DAY AFTER TOMORROW	
5			EXACTLY ONE WEEK FROM TODAY	
6			THE DATE 60 DAYS AGO	
7				

<7>   5 Points – Cell **S10** contains: `=Q8+V15*12-$T$9+R$12-X7`, which is then copied to cell **V15**. What is the resulting formula in cell **V15** after the copy has been completed?

<8>   5 Points – Write a formula to compute the average of four items: cell **C5**, cell **C6**, cell **C7**, and the result of adding cells **F1**, **F2**, and **F3**.

<9>   10 Points – Here is a spreadsheet that describes a file containing a video file. In each **empty** outlined cell in column **B** *write a formula* to compute the desired quantity listed in column **C**. Do not compute or use actual numbers! We want formulae that refer only to cells!

	A	B	C	D
1				
2				
3		320	Image Width (Pixels)	
4		240	Image Height (Pixels)	
5		3	Bytes per Pixel (Color)	
6		30	Frames per Second	
7		15	Length of Video (Minutes)	
8		60	Seconds per Minute	
9			Pixels per Frame	
10			Bytes per Frame	
11			Bytes per Seconds	
12			Length of Video (Seconds)	
13			Bytes (Total)	
14				

For **all** database problems **on this and the following page** use the tables shown here: **Day Names** and **Solar**. Table **Solar** represents the performance of my new roof-top photovoltaic power system, installed in late March, 2016, where the **Daily KWH** field shows the number of kilowatt-hours produced by the system on each day. **Solar** is <u>indexed</u> on the **Calendar Day** field.

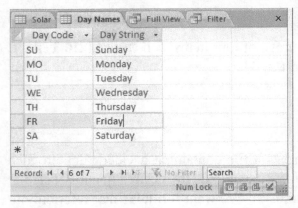

<10> 10 Points – Examine the tables closely.

A. Does table **Day Names** have an *index*?

B. What is the most appropriate *numeric subtype* of the Daily KWH field?

C. What is the minimum possible *field width* of the Day of Week field?

D. How many *records* are in the **Solar** table?

E. What is the number of the *<u>current record</u>* in the **Solar** table?

F. What is the number of the *<u>current record</u>* in the **Day Names** table?

G. (2 points) If <u>neither</u> table had an index, how many *comparisons* would be performed in a join where the Day of Week field is joined with the Day Code field?

H. (2 points) What kind of *relationship* (1:1, 1:many, many:many) actually now exists between **Solar** and **Day Names** when the Day of Week field is joined with the Day Code field?

<11> 10 Points – In the form below, set up a complete *inner join* query between the tables. The result must show the Day String, Calendar Day, and Daily KWH fields (in that order), but only where the Day of Week field matches the Day Code field. The result must be sorted in ascending order on the Calendar Day field. Include everything necessary in the query.

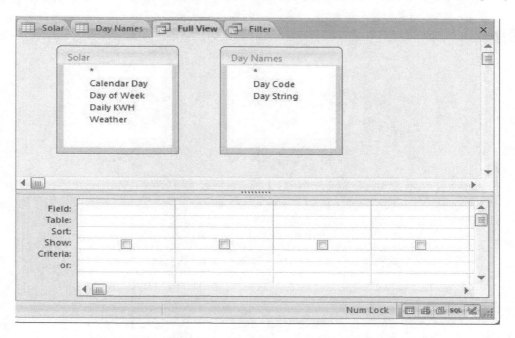

<12> 5 Points – Set up a *simple query* in the form below to list the Calendar Day and Daily KWH fields for all Wednesdays where the daily kilowatt hours is at least 75 and the weather is exactly the string "Sunny". Include everything necessary in the query.

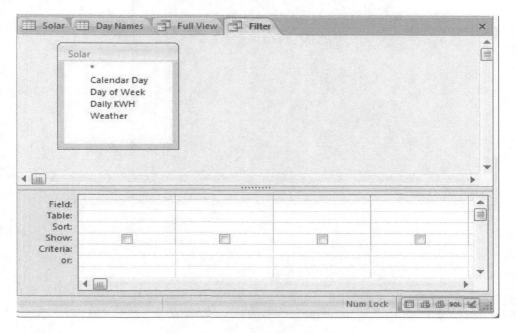

<13> 5 Points – How many records result from the query in the previous problem?

Notes

Notes

Notes

Notes

Notes

Notes

Notes

Notes

Notes

Notes

Notes

Notes

Notes

Notes

Notes

Notes

Notes

Notes

Notes